A Network for Instructional Improvement

A Network for Instructional Improvement

How Teachers and Leaders Made It Work

Sara DeMartino
Anthony Petrosky
Glenn Nolly

BLOOMSBURY ACADEMIC
NEW YORK · LONDON · OXFORD · NEW DELHI · SYDNEY

BLOOMSBURY ACADEMIC

Bloomsbury Publishing Inc, 1359 Broadway, New York, NY 10018, USA
Bloomsbury Publishing Plc, 50 Bedford Square, London, WC1B 3DP, UK
Bloomsbury Publishing Ireland, 29 Earlsfort Terrace, Dublin 2, D02 AY28, Ireland

BLOOMSBURY, BLOOMSBURY ACADEMIC and the Diana logo are
trademarks of Bloomsbury Publishing Plc

First published in the United States of America 2026

Copyright © Anthony Petrosky, Glenn Nolly, and Sara DeMartino, 2026

Cover design by Kathi Ha
Cover image © iStock.com/Sylisia

All rights reserved. No part of this publication may be: i) reproduced or transmitted in any form, electronic or mechanical, including photocopying, recording or by means of any information storage or retrieval system without prior permission in writing from the publishers; or ii) used or reproduced in any way for the training, development or operation of artificial intelligence (AI) technologies, including generative AI technologies. The rights holders expressly reserve this publication from the text and data mining exception as per Article 4(3) of the Digital Single Market Directive (EU) 2019/790.

Bloomsbury Publishing Inc does not have any control over, or responsibility for, any third-party websites referred to or in this book. All internet addresses given in this book were correct at the time of going to press. The author and publisher regret any inconvenience caused if addresses have changed or sites have ceased to exist, but can accept no responsibility for any such changes.

Library of Congress Cataloging-in-Publication Data is available

ISBN: HB: 978-1-5381-9516-1
PB: 978-1-5381-9517-8
ePDF: 979-8-7651-5412-0
eBook: 978-1-5381-9518-5

Typeset by Integra Software Services Pvt. Ltd.
Printed and bound in the United States of America

For product safety related questions contact productsafety@bloomsbury.com.

To find out more about our authors and books visit www.bloomsbury.com
and sign up for our newsletters.

Contents

Preface vii
List of Abbreviations xv
Acknowledgments xvi
Introduction xix

1 How Did the Big City SD/IFL NSI Project Work? 1
2 An Overview of the Qualitative and Quantitative Outcomes 53
3 How the Network of Teachers Became an Improvement Community of Practice 91
4 PLCs that Support Instructional Inquiry: Building In-school Improvement Capacity at Arlington High School 113
5 Leadership for Instructional Change: Rose-Wood High School and Zora Neale Hurston Middle School 141
6 Supporting *Every* Student's Engagement in Cognitively Demanding Studies: Miles Middle School 169
7 Two Teachers Adapt the Student-centered Practices to Their Instructional Contexts: Richard Wright Middle School 199
8 How We Assessed the NSI Instructional Changes and Their Implementation 219

9 A Theory of Improvement for Instructionally Focused Change 235

Appendix A 253
Appendix B 254
Bibliography 256
Index 263
About the Authors 269

Preface

With funding from the Gates Foundation, the Institute for Learning (IFL) partnered with a large urban school district (here referred to as the Big City School District or BCSD) to improve literacy outcomes for students in fourteen middle and high schools. With our district colleagues and others from the Learning Research and Development Center (LRDC) and the Center for Urban Education (CUE), both at the University of Pittsburgh, we created a Network for School Improvement (NSI). The project was originally funded from the fall of 2018 through June of 2023, but it was extended for a sixth year through June of 2024.

The goal was to improve students' literacy so they would be college and career ready by 9th grade. The mechanisms or tools for this endeavor came from the field of improvement science. Using its language, our "tests of change" were a small set of student-centered practices that made space in classrooms for students' deep engagement with the ideas in texts and the ideas of their classmates. (See Figure P.1 for a graphic representation of the practices.)

Improvement Science in Education

Improvement science, with roots in manufacturing industries and agriculture, has recently been popularized in education and health care. Still, some readers may be unfamiliar with how it works in an educational context. We describe it briefly here.

Improvement science—or "continuous improvement"—is basically the iterative practice of understanding a problem, implementing change to solve it, studying the results of the change, making evidence-based adjustments, studying the results, and if necessary, making further adjustments.

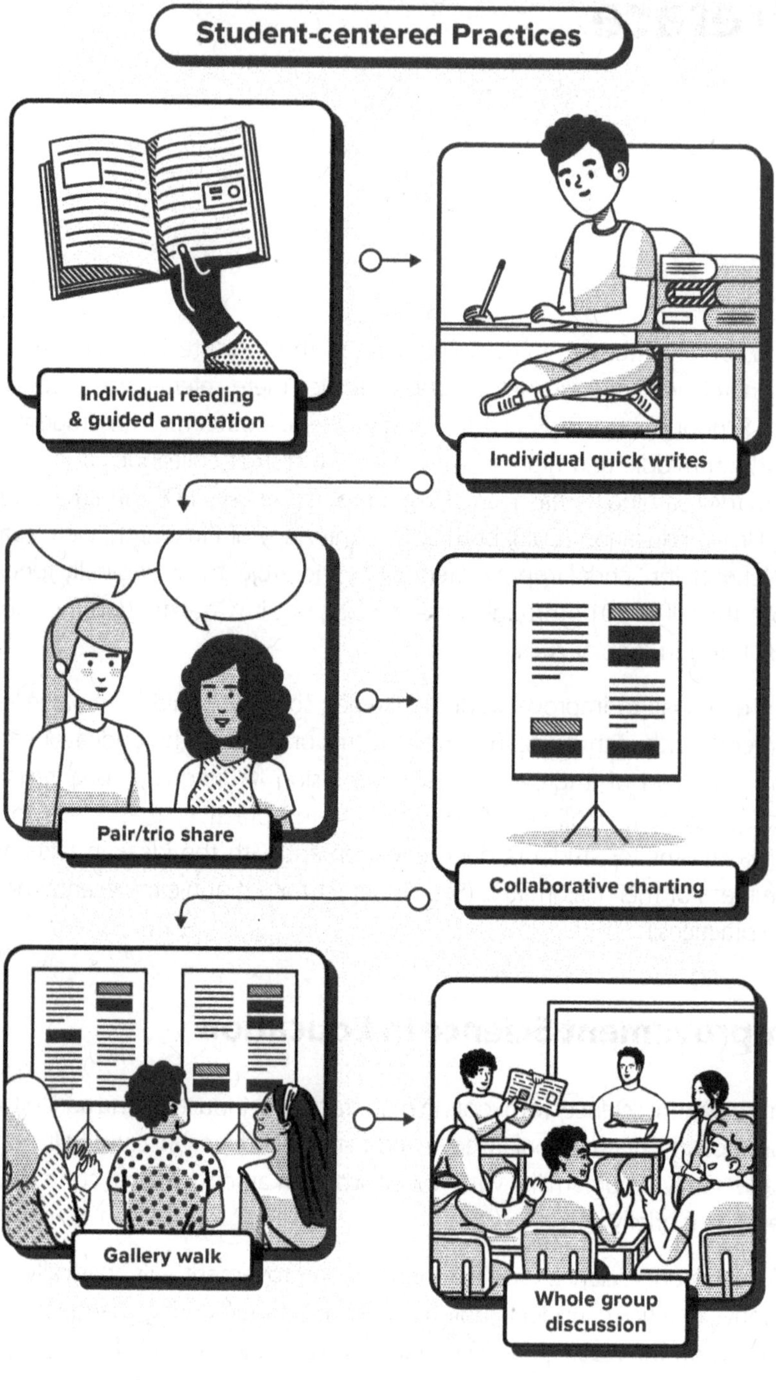

Figure P.1 The student-centered practices.

Improvement science in education takes its conceptual and operational framework from a book by Tony Bryk and his colleagues published in 2015 titled *Learning to Improve: How America's Schools Can Get Better at Getting Better*.[1] The framework is represented by six core principles.

The first principle is understanding the problem of practice that needs to be solved by collaborating with those affected by the problem. Identifying and agreeing on a common problem of practice is critical. The second principle has to do with understanding the variation in performance related to the problem to identify its root causes. Identifying inconsistencies in outcomes (e.g., why some literacy classrooms succeed and others struggle) can point to problematic systemic designs or flaws. The third principle involves understanding the system that is responsible for the problem. Improvement science asserts that problems are the results of systems and not just individual actions.

Knowing whether the changes being implemented actually work is the fourth principle, which suggests the use of various practical measures to collect data on the implemented changes. Without measures of the results of changes, we don't have data to support our understandings of the effects. The fifth principle, at the heart of implementing change, is the use of disciplined inquiry to test hypotheses about what drives change. This takes the form of iterative cycles of planning change, implementing it, studying the results, and acting on what's learned from the results (known as a Plan, Do, Study, Act cycle, or PDSA). The sixth principle is the use of networked improvement communities (NICs) of practitioners, content field experts, and researchers to collaboratively engage in the improvement process.

The NSI project presented in this book followed these six principles, making adaptations and changes to some of them as they were warranted. Bryk and colleagues, for instance, emphasize rapid, repeating cycles of testing and learning, but our changes to literacy instruction were seldom rapid and generally developed over multiple lessons that spanned days or weeks. Consequently, planning, implementing, and studying change happened over a longer arc. We relied heavily on the NSI's cross-school networks of teachers and principals in regularly scheduled monthly Network meetings to develop more extended cadences for their inquiry cycles. We certainly could not have done the work of the NSI just through professional learning and coaching. The Network meetings, supported by our school-based coaching, created a regularly occurring space for our collaborations that included relationship building, sharing of lessons and artifacts, and reflections on changes and their results. Our Network collaborations echoed one of cognitive science's most important understandings about learning—that it is social. We learn with and from each other.

As we wrote this book after the project ended, we continued to meet with our district colleagues to make sense of the wealth of information and data collected over six years. They provided clarifications and insights into their instructional changes and leadership, offering us interviews and meetings during their busy days. We also were having difficulty disengaging. Many of our relationships with teachers, principals, and key district leaders developed over years. We missed them, their energy, and their commitments to their students and each other. We took every opportunity to bring them and their thinking into this book even though, finally, it was in everyone's best interest for us to de-identify* them, the district, and their schools. Nevertheless, they did give us permission to use their ideas and language and their stories as we wrote the case studies.

We also used archived files of NSI documents and meetings that included interviews with our district colleagues, activity logs filed monthly for years by IFL NSI coaches, colleagues' notes and minutes from NSI meetings, transcripts of videotapes of instruction, empathy interviews with NSI teachers, records from the monthly three-hour Network meetings with teachers and the two-hour meetings with principals of the fourteen schools, lessons developed and taught by NSI teachers, and monthly reports written for our Senior Program Officer at the foundation, as well as her questions to us and her responses to the work as it evolved. The NSI analytics team, chaired by Chris Schunn at LRDC, produced regular evaluation reports beginning in the third year that were shared with district colleagues at all levels in the district. You'll be able to dig into the data from those reports in Chapter 2, and you'll see them referenced throughout the cases as well.

Like all books, this one has multiple agendas. We want to present the project to you in all its complexity and through the rapidly changing societal contexts of those six years. We want you to see and feel the commitments

---

* All names of teachers, school and district leaders, students, and schools used in the book are pseudonyms. Some names of tests, programs, curricula, and other materials have also been changed. Unattributed teacher quotations come from interviews with teachers that were excerpted in internal bright spots reports and from anonymous teacher comments in a network health survey.

of the teachers and leaders to their students and to each other. We were in their schools almost every day when they were open and with them virtually during the pandemic, listening and learning as they solved problems to enable successful online teaching and learning. Our district partners and the university colleagues that made up the NSI had a vision for success and a belief in the possibilities of improvement for all of us, but especially for the thousands of students the NSI teachers taught.

The Book Structure

We organized the book to take you first to the heart of the project—the change ideas built on the student-centered practices. The introduction explains the practices and offers examples of how they were adapted by the NSI teachers. They are important to your understanding of the project and to the case studies, so we've intentionally led with them.

Chapter 1: How Did the Big City SD/IFL NSI Project Work? describes the nuts-and-bolts of the NSI. You'll learn how we organized the NSI and when and why our ways of working changed. This is a lengthy chapter that offers year-by-year explanations of key initiatives, adaptations to improvement science tools, and challenges both resolved and unresolved.

Chapter 2: An Overview of the Qualitative and Quantitative Outcomes presents data from the internal evaluation reports that we began sharing with district colleagues in the third year. We include yearly reports on teachers' implementation of the student-centered practices, the relationship of the degree of implementation to students' performances on the Northwest Evaluation Association's Measures of Academic Progress (MAP) reading comprehension and state assessments, descriptions of the Network gleaned from third-party surveys of participants, 8th and 9th grade on-track reports, and samples of teachers' and leaders' comments on aspects of the project from empathy interviews with them. Overall, this chapter provides strong, detailed evidence that student-centered English Language Arts (ELA) instruction improved student outcomes.

> *"We argue that networks like this one can be one of the most important professional learning tools for educators, including for those supporting the implementation of high-quality curriculum."*

Chapter 3: How the Network of Teachers Became an Improvement Community of Practice digs into the cross-school networks of teachers and principals. We discuss what the monthly teacher meetings looked like before and after they became a community, the ways things changed during the pandemic, and how teachers benefited from the community when they had to teach a new curriculum with little preparation. We argue that networks like this one can be one of the most important professional learning tools for educators, including for those supporting the implementation of high-quality curriculum.

Chapter 4: PLCs that Support Instructional Inquiry: Building In-School Improvement Capacity at Arlington High School is a case study on the ways in which one high school ELA team used its Professional Learning Community (PLC) meetings, with the support of the principal, to engage in inquiry cycles to develop and test lessons with the student-centered practices. We also describe ways in which the principal made system changes to support teachers in their work.

Chapter 5: Leadership for Instructional Change: Rose-Wood High School and Zora Neale Hurston Middle School tells the stories of two principals and the different ways that they supported their ELA teams' engagement with the student-centered practices by developing common understandings of the instructional changes, creating time for the planning required to enact those changes, and using the non-evaluative Learning Walk®[2] to give teachers feedback on their lessons.

Chapter 6: Supporting Every Student's Engagement in Cognitively Demanding Studies: Miles Middle School is a case study of a 7th grade ELA teacher who shifted her instructional practices to honor the language assets emergent multilingual students brought to her classroom and to help them develop the English skills they needed to be successful on the state assessment and beyond.

Chapter 7: Two Teachers Adapt the Student-centered Practices to Their Instructional Contexts: Richard Wright Middle School tells the stories of how a middle school principal guided change and removed barriers to improvement, how one afternoon's classroom visits turned around a skeptical district leader, and how two teachers adapted the practices for changing instructional situations.

Chapter 8: How We Assessed the NSI Instructional Changes and Their Implementation, by Anna E. Premo and Chris Schunn of the NSI analytics team, explains how they developed a measurement system to assess the impact of instructional changes on individual student growth and school growth. The measures helped the NSI correct course, gain district leadership support, and provide convincing evidence of teachers' and students' successes.

Chapter 9: A Theory of Improvement for Instructionally Focused Change is a reflective chapter that organizes the NSI's findings in a discussion of our theory of improvement, the structures that supported alignment and coherence, the shared problem of practice, the focused set of change ideas, the structured support for implementation and the integration of adaptations, and the NSI's networked collaboration. We also take up the implications of the NSI's work for literacy improvement in districts committed to instructional and system change.

Who Is This Book For?

Readers interested in instructional change and secondary literacy will find much here to think about and likely to argue with, particularly in the chapters that present case studies of change driven by the student-centered practices (Chapters 4 to 7). In these chapters, we also describe how teachers adapted the student-centered practices for various reasons and integrated them into their instruction. We suggest that adaptive integration encouraged teacher uptake and ownership of the practices while allowing teachers to maintain instructional coherence around a common vision of student-centered teaching and learning.

Those interested in improvement science will also find much to dive into to understand how a long-term instructional improvement project used and adapted improvement science practices and tools. We think that Chapters 2 and 8 on the evaluations of the implementation of the student-centered practices will interest those colleagues in districts and professional learning organizations who want to understand how we used practical measures to gauge teacher implementation and how and why we related implementation to students' performances on MAP and state assessments. We suggest throughout the book that the cross-school networks of NSI teachers and principals, described in detail in Chapter 3, drove the professional learning, collaboration, and change that were critical to the NSI. District colleagues and professional learning providers are the readers we have in mind when we argue that when teachers took ownership of those Network meetings important changes occurred, including those that involved the middle school teachers' implementation of a new high-quality curriculum.

Professional learning providers may also be interested in the ways that we used teacher surveys, class observations, and student surveys to gauge teachers' implementation of the student-centered practices. In Chapter 3, we discuss the need for simple and efficient ways to measure the effectiveness of professional learning other than participant surveys, however useful those might be. We think providers such as IFL should be asking questions about the degree of teacher uptake and implementation of the content of their professional learning, but that's not enough. We also need ways to understand the effects of implementation on student outcomes.

We want all of our readers, but especially teachers and education students, to see what we learned from the use of simple, focused change ideas such as the student-centered practices to jump start and carry intellectual discourse among students when they have high-quality texts and tasks and the time to collaboratively engage with them. We would like to show readers that when students, teachers, and leaders see students succeeding, expectations and beliefs about students' capabilities can change.

Finally, funders, like the senior program officers and deputy directors from the Gates Foundation who worked with us, as well as those who came to conferences and meetings to learn about the NSI, have considerable influence with the decisions they make to support projects. We want our funder readers to see what we learned about change over time in schools, especially how Network meetings developed into networked improvement communities that became true communities of practice. We hope funders will also be interested in the measurement approach we took to understanding teachers' adaptations to and implementations of the student-centered practices.

Notes

1. Anthony S. Bryk, Louis M. Gomez, Alicia Grunow, and Paul G. LeMahieu, *Learning to Improve: How American's Schools Can Get Better at Getting Better* (Cambridge, MA: Harvard Education Press, 2015).
2. The Learning Walk is a registered trademark of the University of Pittsburgh.

List of Abbreviations

AVID	Advancement Via Individual Determination
BCSD	Big City School District*
BOY	Beginning of Year
CoP	Community of Practice
DCA	District Course Assessment*
ELA	English Language Arts
EML	Emergent Multilingual
EOY	End of Year
HQIM	High-Quality Instructional Materials
IDC	Instructional District Coach*
IFL	Institute for Learning
IPC	Instructional Planning Calendar
ISC	Instructional School Coach*
MAP	Northwest Evaluation Association's Measures of Academic Progress
MOY	Middle of Year
NIC	Networked Improvement Community
NSI	Network for School Improvement
PDSA	Plan, Do, Study, Act
PL	Professional Learning
PLC	Professional Learning Community
RNH	Reaching New Heights*
SA	State Assessment
SES	Socioeconomic Status
SwSN	Students with Special Needs
SY	School Year
ToC	Tests of Change
ToI	Theory of Improvement

* pseudonym

Acknowledgments

This book would not have been possible without the students, teachers, and school and district leaders in the district we have called Big City in this book. We owe them a debt of gratitude for the work and collegiality they shared with us during our six years with them. We are forever grateful for their commitments to teaching and learning.

Teresa Rivero, a senior program officer at the Gates Foundation, supported us as our program officer, colleague, and critical friend over the six years of the NSI. She helped us up when we fell and celebrated our accomplishments. We were so fortunate, Teresa, to have you with us on this journey.

Vivian Mihalakis, deputy director, K-12 education at the Gates Foundation, showed us how important it was to regularly report on our work and share our successes and challenges with other grantees at the NSI Community of Practice. There was no one better to be a sounding board for our approaches to coaching, practical measures, and assessing the effectiveness of the NSI's tests of change.

Special thanks go to Faith Schantz, who supported us as an editor and colleague, expert in all that is print, and to Ryan Thompson from Placeholder Design, whose professionalism was second only to his patience with us as he developed the book's figures, tables, and graphics.

Nathan Davidson, our editor at Bloomsbury Publishing, made this book possible, collected reviews, helped us imagine changes prompted by them, and saw us through major revisions. Hollis Peterson and Jasmine Holman helped us understand the technical requirements for everything from tables to styles and responded to our endless stream of emails with grace.

We would like to thank the following members of the NSI and acknowledge their contributions to our work. It was a team effort in every way. NSI members often served on multiple teams and as the project progressed, people left, others joined, and teams combined. Here, listed alphabetically, are the members of the final NSI internal teams that were based primarily at the University of Pittsburgh.

Analytics Team

Aaron Anthony
Hannah Goldstein
Jennifer Elise Iriti
Adrian Larbi-Cherif
Anna E. Premo
Jesse Rubio
Jennifer Lin Russell
Christian D. Schunn
Yunmin Zou

Equity Team

Tequila Butler
Peter Compitello
Kenny Donaldson
Dana Thompson Dorsey
Courtney Lynn Francis
T. Faith Milazzo
JoeAnn Nguyen
Glenn N. Nolly
Anna E. Premo

Practical Measures Team

Tony Bryk, Carnegie Foundation for the Advancement of Teaching
Hannah Goldstein
Paul LeMahieu, Carnegie Foundation for the Advancement of Teaching
Angel Li, Carnegie Foundation for the Advancement of Teaching
Jon Norman, Carnegie Foundation for the Advancement of Teaching
Anthony Petrosky
Anna E. Premo
Christian D. Schunn
Yunmin Zou

Steering Committee

Rosita Elodia Apodaca
Denise Collier
Peter Compitello
Sara DeMartino
Dana Thompson Dorsey
Jennifer Elise Iriti
Glenn N. Nolly
Anthony Petrosky
Kim Rugh
Jennifer Lin Russell
Christian D. Schunn

IFL NSI Coaches

Rosita Elodia Apodaca
Tequila Butler
Denise Collier
Peter Compitello
Sara DeMartino
Glenn N. Nolly
Anthony Petrosky

Management and Communications

Peter Compitello
Aaron Lang
Carmela Rizzo

Introduction: The Student-centered Practices

This chapter introduces you to the instructional heart of the NSI project—the student-centered practices. It begins by orienting you to the tumultuous contexts of the project that began a year before the COVID-19 pandemic and continued through it and past it. From there, the chapter offers a big-picture framework of what we learned in the form of a short list of big ideas that we'll refine and elaborate on throughout the book. The next section explains the student-centered practices and their centrality to the NSI. They were the NSI's tests of change. We introduced the student-centered practices to NSI colleagues in the Big City School District (BCSD) through task sheets. Task sheets are written, student-facing explanations of the work students are asked to do: its purposes, the tasks, the order in which students would do them, and help in the form of scaffolded suggestions or tips. The section on task sheets includes an example and a few representative samples of teachers' reactions to them.

Tumultuous Contexts

From 2018 to 2024, the IFL team of approximately twenty research practitioners and support staff worked with school teams of English Language Arts (ELA) teachers and coaches from fourteen of the BCSD's lower ranked secondary schools (by the state) to form the BCSD/IFL Network for School Improvement (NSI). Our goal was to work together in a cross-school network to apply improvement science methods to increase the numbers of Black, Hispanic, Emergent Multilingual (EML) learners, and students from low-income homes who were proficient in ELA, on track to graduate, and ready for college and careers. We brought together teachers, coaches, and school and district leaders to collaborate on the development of equitable literacy instruction for students who did not have the same academic opportunities as their peers in highly rated schools.

As we said in the preface, we wrote this book because we have stories to tell about the successes and struggles of the BCSD/IFL NSI participants. Who wouldn't, after six years of collaborations with dedicated and diverse groups of teachers and students who supported each other through a shifting political climate, the rise of COVID-19, the trauma of watching the murder of George Floyd, and then having to learn how to be together again after two years of seeing each other only online?

During this journey, we have been thought partners, cheerleaders, and shoulders to cry on. We've watched first-year teachers grow into experienced educators, we've seen experienced educators leave the profession out of frustration, and we've mourned when Network students, teachers, and leaders passed away.

Throughout these years, we've learned that building trusting relationships must be woven into the fabric of collaborations. Building these relationships takes intention, and as a 9th grade teacher told us, "It just takes time to talk to someone who is outside of the bubble, and just being able to speak with people … people who actually really listen and try and work with you." We all had to put aside our fears of criticizing the system, speak openly as critical friends, and really listen, as this teacher said, to collaborate with mutual respect and patience over those six years.

Given the significance of the events that took place during the years we worked with BCSD, collaborating with teachers to develop equitable literacy instruction became even more important. Students wanted to discuss the events they were watching unfold on television and in their communities. They wanted to study and talk about who they were as individuals and as communities of peers navigating an educational system that didn't always invite them in. In many cases, the system kept them at arm's length in favor of instruction that prepared them to take standardized tests rather than to think in depth about challenging texts and ideas.

During the nationwide protests over the murder of George Floyd, a 9th grade NSI teacher whom you'll meet in Chapter 5 invited his students to read *Between the World and Me* by Ta-Nehisi Coates[1]—a powerful book written as a letter to his son about his experiences being a Black man always under threat in a White world. He told us that Coates's book "gave them the platform to get some feelings off their chests, get some thoughts out ... that I hadn't seen before...." His students identified with Coates's experiences and took the opportunity to tell their stories and share their takes on his. To extend his students' opportunities to think more deeply and personally about the issues Coates's book raised, he invited them to write cultural autobiographies that they shared with their peers in discussions. Books like Coates's ask us to share their messages along with our experiences. They offer windows into big things such as culture, race, and personal relationships. Students need them. We all need them.

Experiences play an important role in our book as well. In the chapters that follow, we tell stories about the Network through a series of cases that represent what we've learned when improvement is focused on instruction. The cases share the experiences of teachers and leaders as they did the hard work of improving instruction, work that honored the assets students brought into the classroom, while adapting the NSI's goals to their contexts.[2] The stories tell how NSI participants built on those assets to create school and classroom communities where students saw value in instruction beyond a means to pass tests.

Every year also brought changes within the Network. At times we felt as though each year reset the NSI because between 20 percent to 35 percent of the NSI teachers turned over. Leaders in key positions with whom we had established relationships also shifted roles or left the district. Every year began with a series of meetings with new teachers and new key leaders to reintroduce ourselves, the NSI, and what the Network was learning about instructional change.

These were not the only changes that mattered. We also experienced the slow evolution of coherence. Our Network became a community of practice that gelled around a vision of teaching and learning. Student-centered practices that were once new grew to be familiar. Practices that were exceptions grew to be regular. We learned about each other's ways of using language and thinking about teaching and learning. Teachers' cross-school collaborations strengthened, becoming the rule rather than the exception. Teachers became critical friends who felt comfortable sharing lessons and students' work.

A high school literacy coach put it this way:

> I'm seeing teachers [new to the project] learn to think about old things in very new ways.... At first I was walking them through how we start ... and as we went through and time went on, I began seeing those teachers automatically thinking that way whenever we sat down on a new project, a new lesson that we wanted to teach, or a new piece of reading.... And then [the teachers are] texting me and saying, "Okay, this is working, you need to come and see this."

We think of this evolution of coherence as the socialization of our learning as a community.

Big-Picture Framework

The cases describe how instructional changes took root and grew in different contexts, under different circumstances, and with different kinds of building and district support. They point to the commitments of teachers and leaders to their students, and to students' desires to be engaged in imaginative, meaningful studies. We think that they offer hope in schooling and hope in students and educators. Hope doesn't come easy in public education, a field regularly beaten up by politicians and pundits. These stories—shaped by struggles through the turmoil of these years—push hard against notions of silver bullets, teaching a curriculum with standardized fidelity, one-size-fits-all solutions to problems of practice, and the rush to solutions before understanding the problems and the systems that enable them.

"If there is one lesson threaded through all of the cases, it is that learning, no matter where or at what level in an organization, is always social, and that intelligence grows in and from this socialization."

Our experiences highlight the power of communities of practice across and within schools in network with one another to adopt and adapt instructional changes. If there is one lesson threaded through all of the cases, it is that learning, no matter where or at what level in an organization, is always social, and that intelligence grows in and from this socialization.

The big ideas that follow come from our experience with the NSI. We present them here to frame the work before you delve into the stories.

1. It was important for everyone—students, teachers, and leaders—to understand and work together from a shared vision of teaching and learning. This vision focused on encouraging students to engage with challenging texts and tasks, think critically, and write about the big ideas they encountered in texts. Peer discussions about these ideas were also key. We used what we call student-centered practices, which we'll explain in more detail a few pages on.

2. Everyone in the system—teachers, coaches, and leaders—benefited from engaging as learners in the student-centered practices with demanding, relevant texts. This echoes what we know about the importance of learning by doing and experiencing the practices as insiders.

3. When participants worked from a common vision of teaching and learning, they could build instructional coherence and adapt instructional changes[3] for different contexts (rather than trying to enforce standardization and fidelity).

4. As the Network became improvement communities, regularly bringing together teachers and principals from different schools to collaborate as critical friends and test solutions to common challenges, the meetings provided participants with opportunities to learn from one another.

5. The power of witnessing students' successes with challenging texts and tasks shifted expectations and provided evidence for arguing against deficit views of students' abilities.

6. It was crucial that the NSI, as a change-driven project, had the support of various district role groups that support teachers. This support helped teachers work together, learn from one another, and make changes to their teaching methods, lessons, and curriculum.

7. Teachers needed safe spaces for school planning and monthly Network meetings where they could collaborate. Since learning and this type of work are social, these meetings gave teachers the chance to plan lessons using student-centered practices and offer each other honest feedback as supportive colleagues, all without fear of judgment.

8 It was important for the NSI to track how instructional changes affected both teachers' instruction and students' outcomes. Practical measures such as quick, five-to-ten question surveys for teachers and students, along with classroom observations, provided immediate feedback. Quantitative data, that show the extent to which changes are being implemented and how they relate to student growth and achievement, helped build a strong case for the impact of these instructional changes over time.

"The student-centered practices involve starting with a question that encourages students to think about a text, writing informally to capture their thoughts about the text, engaging in conversations in small groups, charting the group's thinking, sharing the charted ideas, and engaging in whole class discussions about the learning."

The Student-centered Practices

The student-centered practices were the instructional heart of the project. Briefly, they involve starting with a question that encourages students to think about a text, writing informally to capture their thoughts about the text, engaging in conversations in small groups, charting the group's thinking, sharing the charted ideas, and engaging in whole class discussions about the learning.

These practices are not new. They are embedded in some curricula. They are inherent to writers' workshops where writers talk with each other about what they've written. They are frequently used in classrooms when students are introduced to new ideas and asked to turn and talk, for instance, about the ways that they understand them. There's a body of research[4] on their effectiveness when they're used to support rigorous intellectual work that involves peers using their writing and discussions to make their thinking and reasoning visible in the spirit of being critical friends to each other.

When we first started working with the schools in BCSD, we heard that some teachers thought they were engaging students in student-centered practices. And during our first visits to Network teachers' classrooms, we saw some evidence of students being asked to turn and talk. However, they often didn't have much to talk about, mostly because the texts were weak. Teachers were quick to point out their frustration that students just didn't have a lot to say. In other classrooms, we saw teachers using smartboards or slides to present texts or information to students, often followed by questions—some literal and some analytic—in formats that mirrored the exercises on the state test. We heard teachers doing almost all of the talking. Students were either being called on or raising their hands. The downside of that kind of instruction was that few students got to talk in response to teachers' questions. There were few opportunities for them to engage in peer-to-peer discussions to dig deeply into a text's ideas or each other's thinking.

> *"The practices opened spaces in classrooms for students' engagements with all sorts of texts, their classmates' ideas, and each other."*

After we introduced them, the student-centered practices became the engines for instructional change in the BCSD/IFL NSI. In the language of improvement science,[5] they were the NSI's change ideas. Teachers tried them out in an intentional sequence designed to gradually give them and their students a coherent instructional model that developed with different kinds of tasks—comprehension first, analysis, and interpretation—to put students' thinking in various types of discussions at the center of instruction. The practices opened spaces in classrooms for students' engagements with all sorts of texts, their classmates' ideas, and each other. As a middle school teacher said, the practices encouraged students "to take risks and to bounce ideas off of each other because they're constructing the learning together instead of me telling it to them." Their use changed expectations and beliefs about what students could do. They helped construct classrooms as communities, as social scenes where students talk seriously with and write for each other.

To support students in engaging in complex texts and demanding tasks, a teacher might use the following sequence of student-centered practices. This is the sequence that we initially used in a gradual roll-out to introduce the practices as change ideas. In the classroom, teachers combined and adapted the practices once they understood the sequence and began to use student-facing task sheets for their lessons. (We will have more to say about the task sheets later in this chapter.)

1. Begin with a high-level, open-ended, text-based question that prompts students to think about what they understand from the text, focusing on conceptual comprehension (meaning making) first. Once they've understood the text's big ideas, for instance, they move into analytic and interpretive tasks.
2. Provide opportunities for students to write informally about the text, using annotations and quick writes (brief, unstructured writings) to jot down their initial thoughts.
3. Encourage students to discuss their ideas and reasoning with peers in groups of two or three.
4. Offer opportunities for student groups to represent their thinking visually by charting it, making it visible for classmates.
5. Guide students in reflecting on their thinking through activities such as gallery walks, during which they read and respond to their peers' posted charts, take notes, and raise questions.
6. Hold a whole class discussion once students have prepared for it in their small groups by sharing notes and deciding what ideas and questions they'll raise.

This sequence isn't static or fixed—except for the need to always begin with conceptual comprehension first—and it can vary depending on the text and task at hand. For instance, texts might be read independently by students who then complete a quick write before engaging in a whole class discussion. Other texts might require students to pause during independent reading to answer text-based questions about what's happening or the unfolding meaning before collaborating with a partner to synthesize their responses into a quick write that addresses a broader question about the text's meaning. Yet other texts might lend themselves to students discussing an open-ended question about the text's meaning in small groups before jumping into a whole group share-out where everyone gets to talk. The heart of the student-centered work is always the opportunities for students to flesh out their thinking and to share it with others—in small groups, on charts, and with the whole class.

We also learned there were critical components necessary for students to find the practices meaningful.

- The first is a relevant and engaging text that has content worth talking about. If the text has nothing to work with, students quickly see that there really isn't much to write or talk about.
- The second is an open-ended, text-based conceptual question that invites students to do the heavy lifting of making meaning. These types of questions invite students to wrestle with the ideas in a text, whether it's to say how they comprehended the ideas, how they analyzed aspects of the text such as an author's use of dialogue to learn about who gets to talk and why, or how they interpreted ambiguous but important passages or ideas.
- The third is the use of pair and trio discussions—rather than larger small groups—and a classroom set-up that allows students to face each other at desks or tables. This type of configuration, rather than larger groups of four to six at rows of desks, offers a safer small space where students can feel at ease while being accountable to each other and the work at hand.

Our first round of work with teachers and leaders in the Network was to engage *them* in reading and writing experiences with the student-centered practices. We chose rich texts that could be used with 8th and 9th grade students, such as the Coates's text mentioned earlier, an NPR broadcast titled "Scientists Start To Tease Out The Subtler Ways Racism Hurts Health,"[6] and "Ain't I A Woman?"[7] by Sojourner Truth.

Teachers noted a difference between the practices and what they were doing in their classrooms. They often had expected students to share their thoughts and reasoning with each other on the spot. By engaging in the practices themselves, they learned that students could benefit by taking more time to think and to gather their thoughts in a quick write before sharing with others. They could further refine their thinking by sharing it in pair/trio discussions with others working on the same task.

As teachers began to use the practices to frame student talk and make students' thinking visible, they also found that the practices allowed students to collaborate more when they edited and revised their writing. Students had been taught to use specific criteria to give each other feedback on writing, such as identifying passages that seemed unclear or confusing or that would benefit from more explanation. NSI teachers also coached students to reference the text when they explained their ideas about it. A steady diet of this kind of collaboration among students, based on the practices, helped shape classes into communities rather than groups of individuals working on their own, and helped everyone to internalize writing practices as well as peer-to-peer talk.

A middle school teacher described using the student-centered practices to create a learning community. She began by:

> incorporating many opportunities for kids to [share ideas] in a smaller group before coming back and sharing out whole group ... to create a culture in a classroom that's respectful of different viewpoints, respectful of different cultures, different backgrounds.... You kind of have to coach them into the student-centered [practices] because ... you're taking away the concept [that] the teacher is going to dump the information into your brain.

Task Sheets

For many teachers, the use of task sheets was the first test of change. When we say task sheet, we don't mean a worksheet that asks students to fill in correct answers. A task sheet speaks to students as critical partners in their own learning. It provides them with clear, simply written information that they need to complete the task successfully—a description of the task itself, its purpose, steps to complete it using the practices that the teacher decides are appropriate, and helpful suggestions. It's also a great tool for preventing the inevitable, "What are we doing again?" from students.

Figure I.1 provides an example of a comprehension task sheet for "Ain't I A Woman?" by Sojourner Truth. In keeping with the NSI focus on high-level literacy instruction, the task sheet begins with a comprehension question, but not the kind you'd see on a test. The questions NSI teachers created asked students to begin by thinking about the ideas, arguments, or meaning in a text, which we referred to as "comprehension first."[8] "I feel like the routine is so, so important," a 9th grade teacher said, "because they knew we're coming to class, we're going to do a warm-up, we're going to read a story, and we're going to do the task sheet. And the task sheet is going to require you to comprehend the story."

Two things are worth noting. The first is that NSI teachers initially struggled with the idea of beginning text-based lessons with comprehension work. We learned quickly that they were accustomed to thinking of comprehension as multiple-choice recall questions. For them and their students, comprehension was a version of strip-mining a text to find the details asked for on the test.

It took considerable experience with comprehension as the understanding of a text's big ideas or meanings to change this. As one 9th grade teacher said, "Comprehension used to be asking them who the characters are and what's the plot. And the IFL comprehension questions are much more holistic and more geared toward collaboration.... I thought, well, that made sense. But it took me a while to get that.... We were all so conditioned to think about that word comprehension in a different way."

Second, in many districts, including BCSD, standards-aligned instruction doesn't always or even usually begin by asking students how they understand a text. In BCSD, based on the pacing guide and the "focus standards," students could begin by analyzing the structure of the sentences, or analyzing the text for its use of metaphor or organization before considering what they understood it to be about.

After working to develop new questions, a high school teacher told us they were "a really cool way to get them talking, to get them motivated to read, and to do the learning ... I get to see the kids thinking in ways that they haven't thought before." While comprehension-first questions focus students on understanding the ideas or arguments in texts before being asked to do anything else with them, they also give students opportunities to understand their peers' thinking and reasoning. A body of research[9] supports this approach.

The task sheet we show here could take one to two days of instruction, depending on class time, how deeply the students get into the speech, and the questions they raise. It focuses on one comprehension task with the steps inviting students to do the lifting in various ways to share and extend their understandings. Other task sheets could move, for instance, from comprehension to interpretive questions that ask students to engage with ambiguous, complex, or confusing passages, and relate those passages to their sense of the whole text. Task sheets can be paper tools. They can be created in slide decks, and they can be digital tools developed in platforms

TASK SHEET
Comprehension

Purpose: Today you will read the speech, "Ain't I A Woman?" delivered by Sojourner Truth. The purpose of this first task is for you to understand Truth's argument.

Step 1: Please read "Ain't I A Woman?"

Read like this:
- First read the whole speech to get your head into it.
- Then reread the speech.
- While you reread, please annotate the speech.

To annotate it, mark or underline or circle sentences that seem important to Truth's argument. Write brief comments next to those sentences or summaries of the ideas that seem important to her argument. You can decide which ones really matter after you read and go back to review your annotations.

After you have finished rereading and annotating the speech, please compose a quick write in response to the following questions.

- **What's the speech about? What's Truth's argument?**

Keep your annotated speech next to you when you write so that you can refer to your annotations and comments when you compose your quick write.

Tips: Quick writes are times for you to use writing to think on the page. Most people write them quickly in 3–5 minutes. They don't need to have correct sentences or even complete sentences. They don't need to have correct spellings. They are your thinking on the page with writing to get your ideas down as quick as you can.

Before you do your quick write, glance back at the speech and the passages you marked and wrote comments on. Refer to this as you think your quick writing into writing.

Step 2: Take 5 minutes to share the ideas in your quick write with a partner. Share your ideas. Don't just read your quick writes. As you share, take notes on the ideas that you have that are similar and different about Truth's argument in the speech.

Create a T-chart of you and your partner's ideas on a sheet of chart paper. Put your ideas in one column and their source in the speech in another. Be sure to write about which ideas were similar and which were different. And write down questions you may still have about the speech. Post your chart paper.

Step 3: When asked, please engage in a gallery walk. As you read each chart take notes on ideas that seem important to you, maybe ideas that are new to you. Write down any questions that you wonder about with the ideas on the charts.

We will discuss what you noticed and wondered about in a whole group discussion.

Step 4: To prepare for our whole group discussion please meet with your partner. Review the speech, your annotations, and the notes you took on the charts. Decide what ideas you want to talk about and what questions you want to ask.

Figure out who will say what in the discussion. You both should talk and respond to what others have to say.

Step 5: After our whole group discussion, please write another quick write to reflect on your thinking. Use the following questions:

- How has your thinking about what Truth is arguing in this speech changed or been confirmed after the gallery walk and whole group discussion?
- What did you hear from your peers that confirmed or changed your thinking?

Figure I.1 Example of a task sheet.

such as Google Classroom or Pear Deck. The NSI has collected hundreds of different versions of them as teachers adapted the basic idea.

Here's what a 9th grade teacher said about task sheets:

> In more traditional lessons, you might start with the purpose, you go over it, but then you kind of forget what the purpose is because you start doing these activities. And then it starts to feel disconnected, or you're moving from activity to activity, but with the task sheet ... the purpose is always there. It's really easy to just always connect back to that purpose, for me, and for students.... So, with the quick writes, with the collaboration, with the charting, all that kind of stuff, you're really thinking about what activities can I use in order to accomplish this purpose.

We devoted these early pages to an explanation of the student-centered practices because the social and academic engagements among students they encourage and their overall purpose are important to your understanding of the book, and especially of the cases. We'll continue to refer to them as the student-centered practices, but as we mentioned earlier, in improvement science language, they were our tests of change. We also at times refer to them as instructional interventions or instructional changes. They occupied a specific space in the project that people recognized at times with different language.

Questions for Reflection

1. How would you explain the reasoning for beginning text-based instruction with rigorous texts with comprehension first tasks or questions to someone who is accustomed to comprehension as those recall and detail questions on tests?
2. How would you imagine the student-centered practices playing out in disciplines other than ELA—in social studies, math, or science, for example?

Notes

1. Ta-Nehisi Coates, *Between the World and Me* (New York: Spiegel & Grau, 2015).
2. For a smart, concise discussion of improvement teams making adaptations to tests of change (e.g., the NSI's student-centered practices), see Alicia Grunow, Sandra Park,

and Brandon Bennett, *Journey to Improvement: A Team Guide to Systems Change in Education, Health Care, and Social Welfare* (Lanham, MD: Rowman & Littlefield, 2024), 191–93.

3   Grunow, Park, and Bennett, *Journey to Improvement*, 191–93.

4   Research and scholarship on student-centered practices (often referred to as learner-centered) reaches back decades into situated cognition and has been done in the disciplines and with well-documented practices such as Questioning the Author. See Linda Davis, "Toward a Lifetime of Literacy: The Effects of Student-Centered and Skills-Based Reading Instruction on the Experiences of Children," *Literacy Teaching and Learning* 15 (2020): 53–79; Gholdy Muhammad, *Cultivating Genius: An Equity Framework for Culturally and Historically Responsive Literacy* (New York: Scholastic, 2020); Jeffrey Cornelius-White, "Learner-Centered Teacher-Student Relationships are Effective: A Meta-Analysis," *Review of Educational Research* 77, no. 1 (2007): 113–43; John Seely Brown, Alan Collins, and Paul Duguid, "Situated Cognition and the Culture of Learning," in *Subject Learning in the Primary Curriculum: Issues in English, Science, and Mathematics*, ed. Jeni Riley and Roy Prentice (London: Routledge, 1995), 301–19; Margaret G. McKeown, Isabel L. Beck, and M. Jo Worthy, "Grappling with Text Ideas: Questioning the Author," *The Reading Teacher* 46, no. 7 (1993): 560–66; Lindsay C. Matsumura, Cheryl Sandora, Sara DeMartino, and Diana Zook-Howell, "Student-Centered Routines for Analytic Writing Online and In Person," *The Reading Teacher* 75, no. 4 (2022): 513–19; Steve Graham and Michael Hebert, "Writing to Read: A Meta-Analysis of the Impact of Writing and Writing Instruction on Reading," *Harvard Educational Review* 81, no. 4 (2011): 7107–144; and Steve Graham, Xinghua Liu, Brendan Bartlett, Clarence Ng, Karen R. Harris, Angelique Aitken, Ashley Barkel, Courtney Kavanaugh, and Javed Talukdar, "Reading for Writing: A Meta-Analysis of the Impact of Reading Interventions on Writing," *Review of Educational Research* 88, no. 2 (2018): 243–84.

5   Grunow, Park, and Bennett, *Journey to Improvement*, 113–19.

6   Rae Ellen Bichell, "Scientists Start To Tease Out The Subtler Ways Racism Hurts Health," NPR, broadcast audio, November 11, 2017.

7   Sojourner Truth, "Ain't I A Woman?" (Speech, Women's Rights Convention, Akron, Ohio, 1851).

8   Philip Capin, Kristen Dahl-Leonard, Caitlin Hall, Nayoung Yoon, Eunsoo Cho, Eleni Chatzoglou, Sarah Reiley, Michelle Walker, Emily Shanahan, Tara Andress, and Sharon Vaughn, "Reading Comprehension Instruction: Evaluating Our Progress since Durkin's Seminal Study," *Scientific Studies of Reading* 29, no. 1 (2025): 85–114, https://doi.org/10.1080/10888438.2024.2418582.

9   There are hundreds of studies on teaching reading comprehension. These are relatively new and far reaching: Philip Capin et al., "Reading Comprehension

Instruction," 85–114; Michael J. Filderman, Christina R. Austin, Alexis N. Boucher, Kelly O'Donnell, and Elizabeth A. Swanson, "A Meta-Analysis of the Effects of Reading Comprehension Interventions on the Reading Comprehension Outcomes of Struggling Readers in Third Through 12th Grades," *Exceptional Children* 88, no. 2 (2022): 163–84; National Institute of Child Health and Human Development, NIH, DHHS, "Report of the National Reading Panel: Teaching Children to Read: Reports of the Subgroups" (Washington, DC: U.S. Government Printing Office, 2000); and Ernest Zindel Rothkopf, "Reflections on the Field: Aspirations of Learning Science and the Practical Logic of Instructional Enterprises," *Educational Psychology Review* 20, no. 3 (2008): 351–68. For a summary of teaching reading comprehension first, see Kathryn Grace Rowe Novotny, "Reading Comprehension in the Secondary Classroom" (masters paper, Minnesota State University, Mankato, 2011), Cornerstone: A Collection of Scholarly and Creative Works for Minnesota State University, Mankato, https://cornerstone.lib.mnsu.edu/etds/102/.

1 How Did the Big City SD/IFL NSI Project Work?

This chapter describes the NSI through its six-year evolution with a focus first on how it was organized into district teams and IFL NSI Hub teams. After that we give a quick year-by-year overview, so that you can see a big picture for each year and for the scope of the project over its six years. We then provide a more detailed discussion of each year's key initiatives, so that you get a sense of the depth of the project as well as an understanding of its main successes, challenges, and failures.

As you read, keep in mind that midway through the project, COVID-19 disrupted school districts across the country. Big City School District (BCSD) went to complete online instruction from April to June of 2020. The following year, the district put instruction in place for classes that were both in person and online at the same time. During this time, teacher shortages swept through the district. Some middle schools had only one or two certified English Language Arts (ELA) teachers when they needed four or six. The Network provided teachers with a community, a space where they taught each other how to teach online, shared their successes and struggles, and supported one another under unbelievably difficult conditions. As one teacher wrote, "I firmly believe in the influence and power of the Network.... I would not be the teacher I am today without the things I learned from the NSI."

Such a complex project involving teams of educators from outside and inside of the district takes time to understand. In addition to the approximately twenty professionals in the IFL NSI Hub Team, the BCSD side of the project included ninety to one hundred teachers in the fourteen schools, instructional school coaches (ISCs), principals and assistant principals from each school, executive directors responsible for schools, and instructional district coaches (IDCs) who worked closely with executive directors to support their sets of schools. It took us two years to establish the basic organization of the project and to begin establishing connections with teachers and others. Many of the people we came to value and rely upon changed yearly and others did so over time. By the second year, the IFL NSI coaches were communicating with district colleagues not only in meetings but through emails, text messages, and phone calls. The IFL NSI coaches gave their personal phone numbers and emails to whoever asked for them, and so did many of our district colleagues. This fostered an as-needed availability that often led to collegial, trusted friendships.

The District Teams

Table 1.1 describes which role groups participated in the NSI work, how often we met, and what we did in our time together. As you'll see in the table and the accompanying narrative that follows, we met with some groups consistently over the five years while other groups—for example, 6th and 7th grade teachers—participated only in later years. The shifts in participation were due to what we learned along the way.

As you read the table, notice that the work with each role group was different based on their role in supporting high-quality teaching. Teachers, for example, engaged in lessons as learners and designed task sheets for students to engage them in discussions of challenging texts. Our work with school leaders centered on supporting them to understand what student-centered instruction looked and felt like so they could support teachers' implementation.

A Brief Year-by-Year Overview

During the initial two years (2018–20), we collaborated with a team of 8th and 9th grade NSI coordinators from the seven middle and seven high schools, who were ISCs or ELA assistant principals. Their principals assigned them to attend the monthly NSI meetings so they could learn about the project and relay the content of our NSI meetings to their respective teachers back in their buildings. However, by the end of the second year, we realized this cascading model—often referred to as train-the-trainers—wasn't effectively disseminating information or engaging the schools' ELA teachers.

Table 1.1 The district teams

Teams	Who	Meeting Schedule	What They Did
School Teachers	• All 8th & 9th grade teachers Years 1 & 2 • All 6th–9th grade NSI teachers in Years 3–5	• Bi-weekly PLC meetings with IFL Network coaches in their regularly scheduled ELA PLC time • Monthly in 3-hour Network meetings & as requested during their school's ELA PLCs	• Participated as learners with IFL NSI coaches in PL that mirrored students' instruction with NSI texts, tasks, & student-centered practices • Developed student-facing task sheets with IFL NSI coaches, studied features of complex texts, tested complex texts & tasks, adopted & adapted student-centered practices for their instruction
School NSI Coordinators	Principal appointed teams that included: • 2 NSI coordinators • 1 instructional school coach • 1 ELA assistant principal per school • 1–2 representative grade-level teachers	Monthly in 3-hour NSI meetings either during district scheduled PL time or after school during Years 1 & 2	• Participated as learners in PL with IFL NSI coaches on tests of change & student-centered practices • Carried the PL to their school ELA & special needs teachers in a cascading PL process • Supported teachers in their buildings with the NSI tests of change • Conducted *learning walks* in NSI teachers' classrooms with BCSD/IFL NSI coaches, school principals, & executive directors
School Leadership	Principals for the 14 NSI schools	Every other month for 2 hours with the IFL NSI coaches	• Participated as learners with the NSI/teacher texts, tasks, & student-centered practices • Read & discussed pertinent research reports • Watched & discussed teaching video exemplars • Advised on school-based implementations
District Leadership	7 executive directors responsible for the NSI schools	Every other month with the principals when possible during Years 1 & 2, every month with IFL NSI coaches Years 3–5	• Same participation as principals • Advised on district communication, meetings with leaders, & NSI evaluation

Three early-adopter schools, however, began to integrate the student-centered practices into their existing curricula and provided other school teams with their task sheets, lessons, and student work during Network meetings. This turned out to be the jump start we all needed.

In response to the issues with effectively disseminating NSI work, we proposed a new approach to involve all NSI teachers directly in our monthly meetings going forward from the third year, emphasizing the benefits of direct engagement and sharing of instructional change practices. This suggestion was well received and proved to be valuable to the teachers, as they indicated by their yearly positive feedback on surveys conducted by outside evaluators.

During these first two years, IFL NSI coaches also participated in selected bi-weekly Professional Learning Community (PLC) meetings with the ELA teachers, at times to introduce them to the project by engaging them as learners in lessons that featured the use of the student-centered practices, and at times supporting their uptake of the work relayed to them by their school's NSI coordinator. The IFL NSI coaches took advantage of these meetings and their times in the buildings to introduce themselves to building leaders and to plan observations, what we refer to as *The Learning Walk*, of NSI teachers' lessons. At other times, the IFL NSI coaches met with the ELA teachers to support their development and use of challenging texts and student-facing task sheets for lessons that featured the student-centered practices.

Starting with the third year (2020–21), when instruction in classes was simultaneously online and in person to accommodate parental preferences in response to COVID-19, we expanded the NSI to include ELA 6th and 7th grade teachers, following suggestions from principals and executive directors who observed successes in 8th grade classrooms (the NSI began with the ELA 8th and 9th grades). While three middle schools participated in this expansion, the other four opted out partially or entirely until the fourth or fifth years of the project for various reasons. As the IFL NSI coaches developed their understandings of the types of support that 6th and 7th grade students would need, they worked with teachers at those grade levels to develop approaches to lessons that incorporated strategies known to benefit students transitioning to middle school and Emergent Multilingual (EML) students. In BCSD, EML students entered 6th grade after having bilingual teaching and supports in Spanish through to 5th grade, with the understanding that their lessons and testing would from 6th grade on be in English.

The third year was also the first year that we formally evaluated the program, assessing the impact of the student-centered practices on the district's Northwest Evaluation Association's Measures of Academic Progress (MAP) reading comprehension data for 8th and 9th grade students. The evaluation revealed significant relationships between the level of implementation of the student-centered practices (as determined by teacher surveys and class observations) and student performance. High implementation benefited all students, with especially strong effects for Black students and those with special needs. The teachers in those classes used the student-centered practices at least three to four times per nine-week period.

More specifically, from fall 2020 to winter 2021, we saw 4 percent or greater MAP growth (4 percent is the national norm) for these student groups in high-implementation classes:

- 35 percent of Black students (compared to 23 percent in low-implementation classes)
- 38 percent of students with special needs (SwSN) (compared to 24 percent in low-implementation classes)
- 35 percent of male students (compared to 24 percent in low-implementation classes)
- 38 percent of EML students (compared to 34 percent in low-implementation classes)

Overall, 37 percent of all students in high-implementation classes saw 4 percent or greater growth in MAP scores compared to 31 percent in low-implementation classes. We shared these data, collected from the year in which classes were being simultaneously taught online and in person, with district leadership, principals, and teachers in our regularly scheduled meetings with them. We believe it reinforced the decision to extend the NSI to 6th and 7th grades.

In the fourth year (2021–22), the district opened completely, and everyone returned to their buildings for the first time since April 2020. ELA teachers continued to meet monthly in the three-hour NSI online meetings as did the principals in their two-hour online meetings. IFL NSI coaches continued to support teachers in weekly online and in-person PLC meetings, especially in those schools with significant teacher turnover. IFL NSI coaches returned to in-person *learning walks* along with school and district leaders.

During *learning walks* in the beginning of the year, IFL NSI coaches and district leaders noticed that teachers still taught primarily through online instruction, in a phenomenon one executive director termed "teaching online in person." The IFL NSI coaches supported teachers to balance the use of online tools with in-person instruction, so that students could benefit from the academic and social effects of peer-to-peer discussions.

During the fourth year, we also conducted a more thorough evaluation of the effects of the level of implementation of the student-centered practices on 6th to 9th grade students' performances on the MAP reading comprehension exam; the 9th grade ELA State Assessment (SA); and the District Course Assessment (the DCA), which was designed to predict students' performances on the SA. The data on the effects of implementation make a strong case for students in high-implementation classes continuing to outperform their peers in low-implementation classes on all district measures.

To share these findings, we produced a comprehensive report that we made available to district colleagues in October 2022. The report—discussed in detail in Chapter 2, on the quantitative and qualitative outcomes—included the quantitative analyses of those measures and teacher implementation along with data from a third-party survey, teacher empathy interviews (also published internally in a bright spots report), and 8th and 9th grade on-track measures of college and career readiness.

In the fifth, and what was to be the final year of the project (2022–23), we saw the normalization of in-person instruction; the voluntary piloting of what we're calling the New Curriculum, an ELA curriculum, in the NSI middle schools (more on that later in this chapter); and a district reorganization of leadership mid-year. The NSI continued to evaluate students' performances on district assessments in relation to teachers' levels of implementation of the student-centered practices. As in earlier years, high-implementation classes saw students' performances on growth and achievement assessments significantly outpace those of students in low-implementation classes. This was also the year in which the NSI analytics team developed an algorithm for finding appropriate comparison schools to the NSI schools in BCSD and in the state. When they tracked changes in ELA SA performance (the percentages of students who scored proficient and above) into Years 4 and 5, they found across the analyses that students in the NSI schools outperformed their peers in the matched schools, with especially significant differences at the high school level. These findings and others were published in a fifth year evaluation report that was shared with district colleagues.

The meeting structures of the monthly NSI meetings changed, so that the IFL NSI coaches could support the middle school teachers who piloted the new ELA curriculum while also supporting the high school teachers who continued to teach from the same curriculum they had been using throughout the project. This meant that the middle school teachers met together once monthly for three hours while the high school teachers also continued to meet monthly in their own meetings. In effect, the number of NSI monthly meetings doubled when we split the grade levels into their own dedicated meetings. IFL NSI coaches continued to support school PLC meetings on an as-needed basis, especially when school teams took on a significant number of new teachers. *Learning walks* continued in person.

The sixth year, made possible by funding from BCSD, focused on capacity building. We had numerous capacity-building threads running through the project year after year, but in our final year, we took deliberate actions to turn the project over to the district. The monthly Network meetings shifted membership again to include the IDCs (instructional district coaches) who supported vertical networks of schools that were assigned to executive directors. Both district leadership and the IFL NSI coaches decided to give the NSI middle school teachers the option of not attending and relying on the school demonstration teachers, working as coaches, to bring the work back to their school teams. The middle school teachers told us that they were overwhelmed with the district-wide roll-out of the New Curriculum. They asked if the IFL NSI coaches could work with them in school PLC meetings and through their demonstration teachers. The high school meetings continued with the 9th grade teachers and coaches.

The IFL NSI Hub Teams

The IFL Hub operated through seven working teams: Data and Analytics, Equity, School Team Support, School and District Leadership Support, Research, Management and Communications, and the Steering Committee. Most team members served across multiple teams. These teams evolved in goals and responsibilities each year, with the Management and Communications team, for instance, merging with the Steering Committee that met every other week. Despite occasional challenges in decision-making, our experiment in distributed leadership proved largely successful.

Key Initiatives Year by Year

This section reports in more detail on the project's key initiatives year by year, so that you can develop an overview of the NSI's actions with BCSD colleagues as they unfolded over the six years. You should expect some redundancies in the year-by-year reports since the core actions of the NSI continued through monthly (1) three-hour Network meetings with teachers and NSI school coordinators, (2) two-hour Network meetings with principals, and (3) meetings with district executive directors. IFL NSI coaches participated in school ELA PLC meetings and in *learning walks* in NSI teachers' classrooms with school and district leaders. While the core actions continued throughout the six years, we adapted them to changes brought about by the pandemic, significant teacher turnover in schools, the district mid-year reorganization in the fifth year, and NSI teachers' growing use and internalization of the student-centered practices, especially for those teachers who logged three to five years in the project. The IFL NSI coaches grew in their understandings of the district as a system and the importance of establishing relationships with colleagues in key roles in the system. The IFL NSI coaches also grew in their understandings of how to adapt to changing district policies and the constant shifts in district colleagues in leadership positions, while the teachers grew in their adaptations of the student-centered practices to their instruction. We continue to refer to this as the adaptive integration of the NSI's goals and actions to district and school contexts.

Looking back, we see things we would have done differently as well. For example, being assigned participating schools by the Chief Academic Officer rather than recruiting volunteer schools affected the project in many ways. If we could begin again, we'd take a year to meet with school representatives and ask for volunteers from a wider range of types of schools that met key enabling conditions such as willingness to participate, and both building- and district-level support from leadership to do so.

Had leaders and teachers volunteered because they understood the project and could commit to its goals, the NSI could have had a faster start. The participants also would have had knowledge about the project from the get-go rather than having to build all of it over the first year. A more varied range of types of schools in the project would have given all participants clearer examples of how school contexts affect instruction. As it shook out, most of the fourteen schools' teachers and leaders were willing and enthusiastic participants. Only two schools infrequently participated.

Year 1 (2018–19) Key Initiatives: Root Cause Analysis and Prioritizing Actions for Change

At the project's outset, we drew on improvement science methods[1] in collaboration with NSI coordinators and principals. Our main focus during the first year involved conducting a root cause analysis of students' literacy underperformance, incorporating both quantitative data from state and district assessments, and qualitative data such as analyses of teacher-developed assignments, classroom observations, student work samples, and teacher-conducted empathy interviews with students and other teachers. Through this process,[2] we learned that classes were predominantly teacher-centered, with low-level tasks that lacked intellectual challenges. While we observed some instances of student-centered collaboration, we didn't see student-centered classes.

We engaged in this process of studying and mapping root causes from data with the school teams in monthly meetings for almost six months. Using tools such as fishbone diagrams, we categorized and visualized our inferences from the data. That led to the identification of key goals and actions.

The school teams' coordinators took the diagrams representing the root cause analyses back to their building teams to adapt and adjust for each building. We collected those representations, and from those, our data and analytics team produced a master root cause analysis that led to the development of multiple iterations of the NSI driver diagram (see Figure 1.1). We identified the primary drivers to change as (1) the improvement of instructional quality in ELA and (2) the improvement of equity in instruction.

The final version of the driver diagram visually maps the flow of ideas from overarching goals to primary and secondary drivers and change actions for those goals.

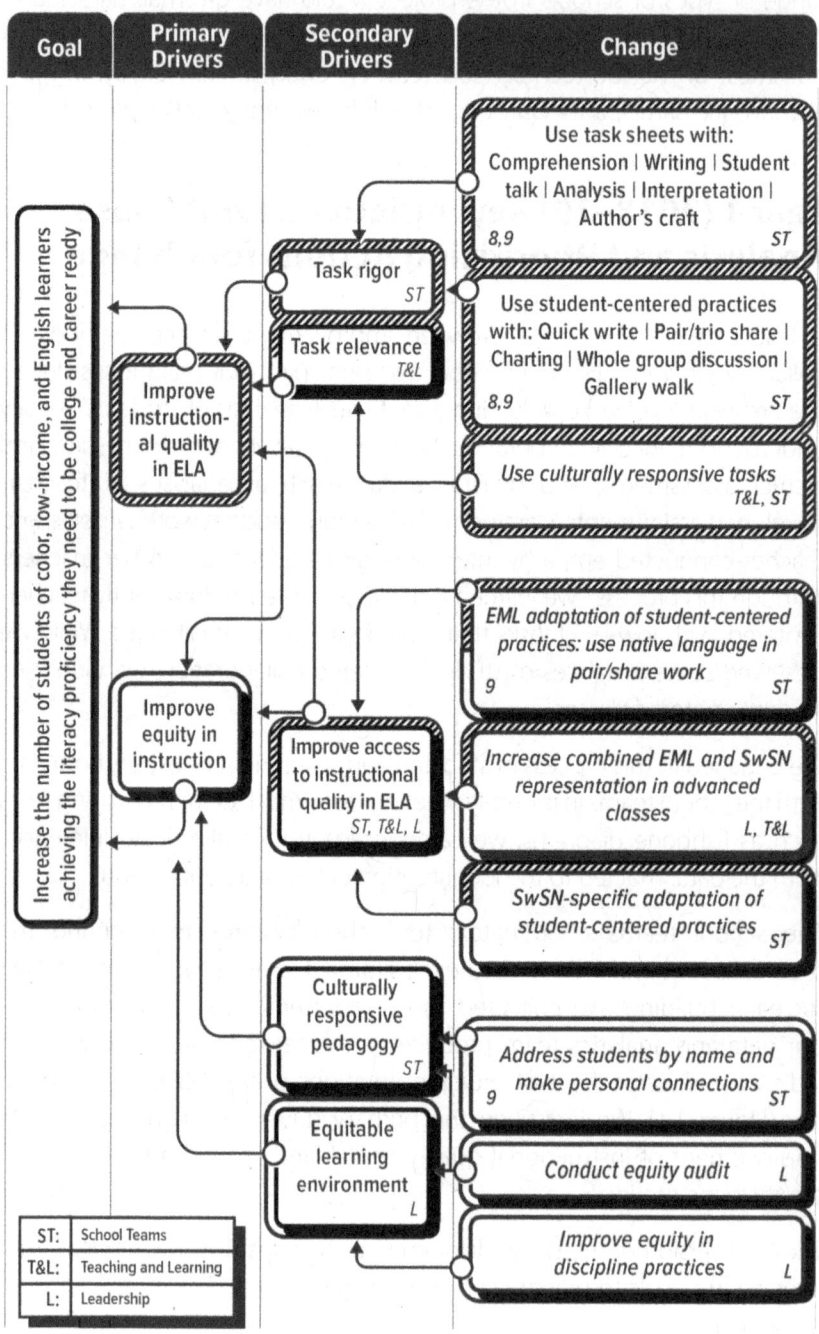

Figure 1.1 Driver diagram.

Prioritizing Actions for Change

Using the driver diagram, we collaborated with the school teams to prioritize changes. As you can see by the right column, we identified changes supported by research to achieve the goals associated with each secondary driver. For the initial year, our priorities included supporting teachers in:

- Selecting challenging and relevant texts for students.
- Using culturally responsive tasks.
- Using student-facing task sheets to develop coherent sequences of text-based tasks, starting with comprehension of big ideas, and progressing to analysis and interpretive tasks.
- Adapting the student-centered practices to support EML students.
- Addressing students by name and making personal connections.
- Implementing a small set of student-centered practices—drafting quick writes and engaging in pair and trio discussions of responses to text-based questions. While some teachers encouraged these small groups to chart their ideas and participate in gallery walks with the whole class, these activities weren't introduced as tests of change until the second and third years.

To facilitate implementation, we used an improvement science tool called PDSA[3] (Plan, Do, Study, Act) tracking sheets for teachers to record the PDSA for every lesson. However, we discontinued these forms in the second year due to feedback from teachers, who felt they were burdensome compliance tools rather than aids to their understanding of the lessons they taught. Instead, we retained the spirit of the PDSA in NSI monthly meetings with the school NSI coordinators because they were focused on developing, implementing, and reflecting on lessons presented to students in task sheets.

> *"From PLC sessions, we learned the importance of engaging the teachers as learners in the lessons with the student-centered practices presented in the learner-facing task sheets, so they could understand them from the inside, so to speak, and have a concrete feel for student-centered instruction."*

After completing the root cause analysis mid-year, we had difficulty gauging the building-level ELA teachers' engagement with the NSI team coordinators, so we surveyed the coordinators about their building-level work. The survey data painted a variable picture of the school teams' engagement from minimal to all-in. Feedback from the NSI coordinators led us to believe that the schools' teacher teams would benefit from coaching and professional learning with the IFL NSI coaches, so we began to schedule regular meetings with them during their weekly PLCs. From these PLC sessions, we learned the importance of engaging the teachers as learners in the lessons with the student-centered practices presented in the learner-facing task sheets, so they could understand them from the inside, so to speak, and have a concrete feel for student-centered instruction.

We also learned, from examining variation across schools, that school ELA teams were much more likely to use the student-centered practices presented in task sheets when they were directly supported to do so by their principals. This support made it possible for the ELA teachers to blend the NSI work with existing curricula. For schools in which the principals were not already involved, visits and professional learning by the IFL NSI coaches helped to engage them. These sessions with school leadership led us to customize professional learning for leaders, including for the executive directors.

We also went into the first year assuming that BCSD would have a strong foundational curriculum in place where we could embed the NSI work. As it turned out, the district leadership had decided during the summer before our launch that it would develop its own curriculum with texts and material provided through a popular textbook series for ELA. In practice over the year, this meant that the curriculum was being rolled out electronically to teachers week by week. Implementation was somewhat mysterious and uneven across schools. Teachers had some support from district coaches on using the curriculum but key electronic tools for that support hadn't been developed. Consequently, we offered PLC and email support to the NSI coordinators, thinking that they could pass it on to building teachers, for using task sheets and high-level tasks with the student-centered practices in planning daily instruction from the curriculum. By the end of the first year, as we mentioned earlier, we had serious reservations about the effectiveness of the cascading train-the-trainers model of supporting teachers through coordinators. In the second year, we transitioned away from it to monthly meetings with all the ELA teachers instead of just the school coordinators.

A Sidebar: Transitioning from a driver diagram to a more district-friendly representation of goals and actions to achieve them

Although the driver diagram outlined our theory of action, we realized that only the IFL Hub teams found it useful. By the end of Year 3, we recognized the need for a more user-friendly representation of our Network's actions. We developed the "BCSD + IFL Vision for Collaborative Work" in 2021–22, the fourth year of the NSI.

Over many iterations, this chart evolved into a valuable tool. It provided specific information on roles and responsibilities for district participants and the IFL Hub teams in supporting NSI classroom instruction. The chart, presented in Table 1.2, became instrumental in articulating goals and actions to project stakeholders. By mapping our sequences of activities for each role group, it facilitated a deeper understanding of actions across the system, surpassing the driver diagram's capabilities.

Compared to the driver diagram, the vision chart is much more specific about who does what to enable teachers' instructional changes, and it uses categories of district role groups familiar to everyone in the district to divvy up responsibilities.

Year 2 (2019–20) Key Initiatives: Adapting to Test Preparation, Network Meetings, Exit Tickets, and Shifting to Online Instruction

Adapting to Test Preparation as Instruction

During the second year, we developed an understanding of how much test preparation for the SA influenced BCSD's curriculum and teachers' instruction. All but one NSI school—a high school—had been labeled close to underperforming or underperforming based on state criteria strongly tied to students' performances on the state test. Due to their low performance ratings, these schools—like so many schools across the country—had limited autonomy in their use of the curriculum and in their professional learning choices.

Table 1.2 BCSD + IFL NSI Vision of Collaborative Work 2022–23

Continuous Improvement for Equity Process	NSI Hub [IFL in collaboration with BCSD IDCs] aligns to district goals and adapts NSI TOC to district ELA curriculum and projects	NSI School Teams work collaboratively to identify, plan, & reflect on TOC that make teaching more student centered & support spread with schools	Teachers in collaboration with their students test, refine, and review NSI initiated TOC to create student-centered ELA classrooms
Planning + Doing Strategic identification of Instructional TOC and related supports	Design and lead opportunities for teachers to learn the NSI Instructional Model in Network Events Curate instructional resources (e.g., task sheets) to be used in Instructional Tests of Change (TOC)	Collaboratively plan sequenced student-centered ELA instructional tasks & slides Develop adaptations to NSI Instructional Model and Instructional Tests of Change (TOC)	Test adaptations to NSI Instructional Model and Instructional Tests of Change (TOC) in their classes Enact Foundations of Equitable Literacy Instruction
Reflecting + Adapting Systematic, data-based reflection on Instructional TOC	Introduce data tools & routines teachers can use in Instructional Tests of Change (TOC)	Make sense of teacher-collected student data for adopt-adapt-abandon decisions (e.g., Quick Write Tool, Exit Tickets, Student Work Protocol, etc.)	Document instructional adaptations & collect data on enactment using data tools and routines (e.g., Quick Write Tool, Exit Tickets, Student Work Protocol, etc.)
Learning/Sharing Identification & distribution of learning about student-centered literacy TOC	Consolidate and spread Network learning generated through Instructional Tests of Change (TOC) Track relationship between uptake of NSI Instructional Model & student achievement Provide webinars on Foundations of Equitable Literacy Instruction	Actively participate in Network Events / complete and share bridges-to-practice Engage in webinars on Foundations of Equitable Literacy Instruction	Complete pre-event learning work / bridges-to-practice Engage in webinars on Foundations of Equitable Literacy Instruction Communicate NSI progress and successes in Network Events

APs + NSI Coordinators monitor progress toward student-centered ELA TOC & identify school level barriers	Principals create school level conditions for NSI TOC to thrive	EDs + IDCs create paths for the NSI work to progress & create coherence with other district initiatives	Superintendent, Assoc. Superintendent, T & L Chief & Dep. Chiefs, + School Leadership Chief & Dep. Chiefs create & refine system structures to support student-centered ELA instruction
Collaborate on 9-week Instructional Plan Calendars that incorporate NSI work Organize *Learning Walks* (e.g., scheduling, communications) focused on the enactment of *Equitable Literacy Instruction*	Create conditions for NSI work in the schools (foundational school culture; create school teams; schedule collaborative planning time; orchestrate *Learning Walks*) Communicate focus on *Equitable Literacy Instruction*	Align NSI work to other initiatives and district priorities Communicate focus on *Equitable Literacy Instruction*	Create coherent ELA curriculum, assessment, and evaluation systems that support the *NSI Instructional Model* Support & participate in the adult learning approach (*Network Events + Learning Walks*) Communicate focus on *Equitable Literacy Instruction*
Identify school and district barriers and communicate to principals	Help resolve within school barriers; communicate district policy barriers; and identify & follow up on next steps from *Learning Walks*	Create paths for the NSI work to progress and expand including creating opportunities for partnerships between the NSI and other district programs Respond to barriers that get identified by school teams & the Hub	
Actively participate in *Network Events* / complete & share bridges-to-practice Communicate NSI progress & success in *Network Events* Initiate opportunities for professional learning	Initiate opportunities for professional learning Actively participate in *Network Events* and *Learning Walks* Communicate NSI progress and successes in district forums	Integrate best practices into district policy and artifacts	

Through class observations and participation in school ELA PLC meetings, we learned that many, though not all, teachers and leaders involved in the NSI viewed instruction primarily through a lens of test preparation. Students regularly engaged in writing and answering questions in formats mirroring those of the SA. For instance, students were directed during instruction to adhere strictly to essay formulas and multiple-choice formats dictated by state exam formats. When they wrote essays, they were regularly limited to the exact word count allowed in the exam essays. This narrow focus led us to categorize this type of writing as a distinct genre of its own: test preparation writing.

The detrimental effects of exclusively adhering to this formulaic approach to writing[4] accrete over time. If students mostly write using these test formats from middle through high school, they miss out on the benefits of diverse writing experiences, such as crafting stories, poems, personal essays, and analytic essays structured to handle complex issues. They also miss imaginative and playful experiences with writing.

To mitigate this as much as we could, we introduced quick writes as a student-centered practice to broaden students' writing experiences, offering them opportunities to engage in writing to learn and express their thoughts freely. Though we hesitated at first, we adapted to suggestions from school coordinators to frame quick writes as drafts for test preparation essays, recognizing the potential value to students in aligning these practices.

We hoped to use our alignment to this goal to demonstrate to teachers and students the interconnectedness of spoken and written expression. For instance, explaining one's reasoning in discussions mirrors the process of doing so in writing. While not identical, these processes are similar enough for students to recognize the parallels. To support this understanding, we encouraged NSI teachers to utilize tools such as Venn diagrams to make these connections between talk and writing explicit, framing it as an opportunity to enhance students' ability to write explanations for the SA essays.

Throughout the year, we observed various test preparation activities shaping daily instruction. During PLC meetings, for instance, teachers analyzed past state exams to anticipate likely test standards and questions for the upcoming year. Standards were typically assessed by one or two questions consistently formatted with specific language. Students practiced these questions with passages of text that resembled those from past exams.

Despite efforts to incorporate more interactive methods, such as the pair/trio discussions, the emphasis, particularly during the months preceding SA administration in April, remained on preparing students for specific question types. Schools also were encouraged to hold test preparation camps for weeks before state testing. Some schools' camps included Saturday classes for students who volunteered to attend.

The district reinforced these practices by identifying "power standards" students typically struggled with and requiring teachers to focus on them. Assistant principals and school coaches were supposed to closely monitor scripted instruction on these questions to ensure that they were being taught. The district provided schools with reports on the district exams (i.e., the DCAs) that predicted likely SA performance, so that teachers could post student performance data in classrooms, further fostering a culture centered on test preparation.

> *"Witnessing students' enthusiastic engagement in discussions and visible reasoning, despite the backdrop of test preparation, led many of the NSI teachers to gradually shift their beliefs about teaching, and fostered collaborative classroom cultures."*

Given these challenges, adapting to the prevalent culture became a significant focus of the NSI. We reasoned that if we wanted to gain traction and eventually integrate student-centered practices into instruction, we had to adapt. Despite the influence of test preparation, NSI teachers did integrate student-centered practices into their lessons for about seven of the ten months of the school year, supported by school leaders who recognized the value of these approaches. Witnessing students' enthusiastic engagement in discussions and visible reasoning, despite the backdrop of test preparation, led many of the NSI teachers to gradually shift their beliefs about teaching, and fostered collaborative classroom cultures.

Although the IFL NSI coaches understood and were sympathetic to arguments about the district's responsibility to prepare students for high-stakes tests, we argued that a body of research pretty clearly pointed to regular, ongoing, rigorous instruction as the pathway to that goal.[5] BCSD's concerns over test preparation aren't unique. Districts all over the country have taken similar approaches to preparing students for high-stakes exams. This reaction to these exams—the shaping of instruction into exam preparation—isn't surprising, even though high-stakes advocates have argued and continue to argue that better tests will drive better instruction.

As a result of our understanding of the key role played by the state accountability system in schools, we concluded that the SA played an outsized role as an instructional lever in the system within which the fourteen schools functioned. Principals were responsible for supporting this influence and holding their teachers accountable. Teachers internalized the accountability, telling the IFL NSI coaches that they felt a weighty responsibility for supporting their students to do well on the SA since so much hinged on their performance and ranking. Students often engaged enthusiastically in the achievement-oriented instruction, and it wasn't unusual to see building-level prep rallies before SA administration.

Network Meetings

Although we'll have more specific things to say about the Network meetings in Chapter 3, we thought we should step out here for a handful of paragraphs to mention the purpose and results of those meetings and to let you see what teachers had to say about them in an external evaluation.

To improve the quality of ELA instruction, IFL NSI teacher and principal networks focused on our two primary drivers for change: (1) providing all students with challenging, relevant texts and tasks, and (2) giving all students opportunities to engage and elevate their voices in their learning through a set of student-centered practices designed to encourage student-to-student academic talk and writing.

By focusing narrowly on those two specific issues, rather than attempting to address broader challenges such as the impact of poverty on literacy, the meetings brought instructional coherence to a vision of student-centered teaching across schools and teachers. It made it possible for the project to adjust to district policies, and to shift its focus when needed, for example, to accommodate the roughly 30 percent annual teacher turnover by offering onboarding support for new participants.

Throughout the evolution of the NSI, the networks emerged as powerful tools for professional development, fostering shared understandings among participants over time. Participants forged personal connections, leading to the development of critical friendships and the bridging of professional, logistical, and geographic barriers that often hinder coherence within and especially across schools. Survey data from external evaluators showed that teachers really wanted to learn from each other. Teachers pointed to the Network meetings as offering them consistent opportunities for sharing knowledge.

Teachers overwhelmingly said that they "valued collaborating with and having deep discussions with peers from other campuses about articles, texts, and tests of change." They valued "the feedback and the work ethic we have toward getting the most out of our students." They saw it as "a growing process in which teachers were allowed to interject with their own ideas ... outside the box." As one teacher put it:

> I have valued the authenticity of members participating in the Network. Through the partnership, we have developed trust, especially for those of us who have been together for a while. We know that when someone shares authentically, they are doing it from a solutions-oriented place. This bond shows incoming members they are in a safe space to be respectfully candid.

Exit Tickets

Improvement science relies on real-time classroom data[6] for educators to understand the effects of instructional changes and to make decisions about the content and teaching approaches that make up those changes. Unlike standardized tests that serve as lagging indicators of students' performances, improvement science's focus on practical measures of classroom performances aims to assess students' perceptions of instruction to give prompt feedback to teachers. At their best, practical measures—usually administered to students as brief surveys—give teachers snapshots into the effects of their teaching on students' learning. They typically present students with five to ten focused questions about the lesson. Students' responses are aggregated by question into class reports, which are given to teachers to help them reflect on potential changes to their teaching or the lesson. Class sets can also be aggregated, tracked over time, and shared among teachers and coaches in PLCs and in Network meetings, so that groups of teachers using the same or similar lessons can reflect on students' responses. The data from such practical measures also can reveal the need for follow-up professional learning and coaching.

The IFL NSI analytics team and coaches developed iterations of exit tickets—surveys for students to complete before they exit a class. The exit tickets gauged students' perceptions of the relevance and difficulty of the texts they read, and the types of activities teachers presented them with (e.g., annotating texts, using task sheets, composing quick writes, engaging in pair/trio discussions, and so on).

The NSI began experimenting with exit tickets in 2019 and developed them as paper and pencil surveys. These original versions required considerable effort to process, were in English only, didn't gather students' written comments, and the reports had to be manually generated. It often took a week or longer to return the summary reports to teachers and by then they had moved on to other lessons, making it difficult to reflect on them in PLCs and in Network meetings. Figure 1.2 shows an example of the paper and pencil version, and Figure 1.3 shows a report generated from it.

The lesson today... (check all that apply):
- ☐ only repeated what I already knew.
- ☐ built on what I know.
- ☑ helped me learn new ideas.
- ☐ was too long.
- ☑ helped me stay focused.
- ☐ had me working by myself the whole time.
- ☑ allowed me to talk with other students.
- ☐ none of these!

Comments: I loved it ♡

The task sheet today... (check all that apply):
- ☑ helped me to understand the text.
- ☑ was easy to follow.
- ☑ made sense.
- ☐ was sometimes confusing.
- ☑ had enough information.
- ☑ included all the steps to complete the tasks
- ☐ none of these!

Comments:

Figure 1.2 Student-facing paper & pencil exit ticket survey.

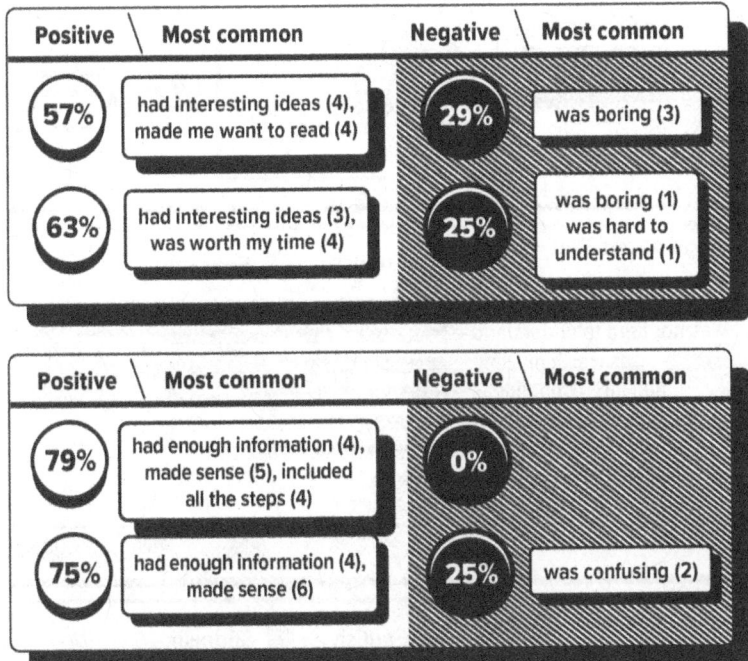

Figure 1.3 Paper & pencil exit ticket summary report.

In spring 2020, when the district went to online teaching because of the COVID-19 pandemic, we focused on revising the exit tickets by embedding them in the instructional routines, producing data that identified instructional issues, and providing timely feedback to teachers. We also shifted to producing bilingual English/Spanish tickets.

Figure 1.4 shows an example of the online version of an exit ticket report that includes the questions students responded to in Google Forms (see "Feelings about Text" and "Feelings about Task Sheet"). These reports were automatically generated and sent to teachers with a 24-hour turnaround from administration. The online forms could be administered in person and remotely.

Teacher uptake of the exit tickets varied considerably by teacher and school. In late 2020, we convened a Design Team of teachers and principals to collaborate with the IFL NSI coaches on the content of Network meetings. In 2021, we asked the Design Team to review the exit tickets and the uptake

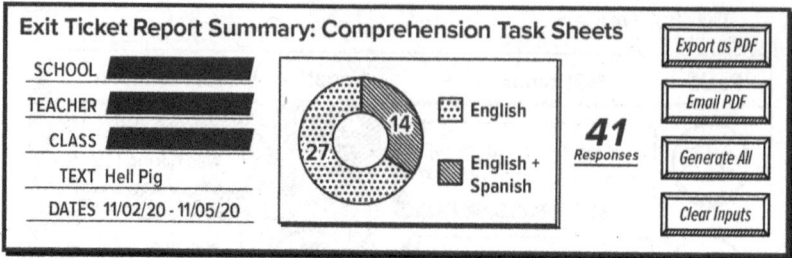
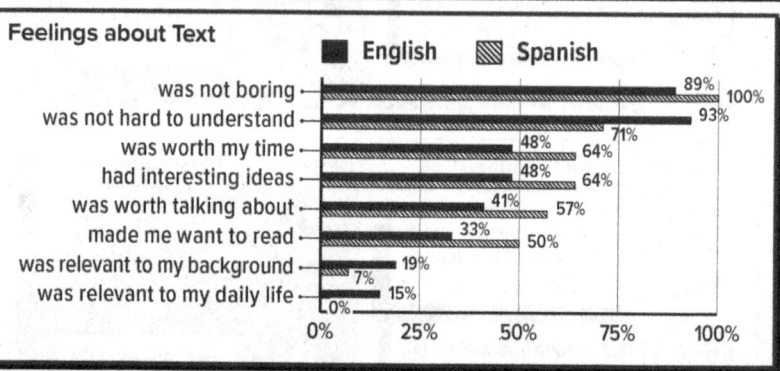
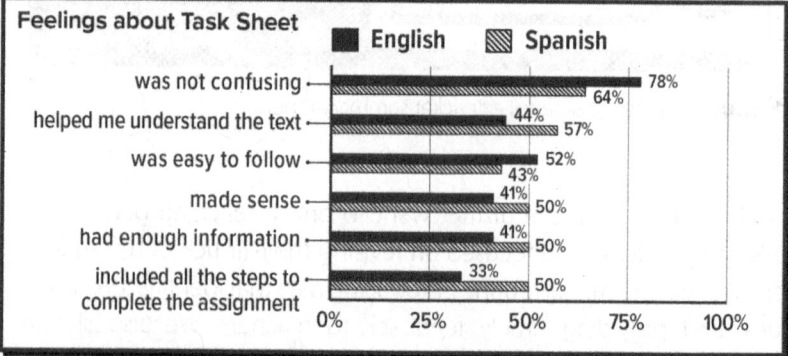
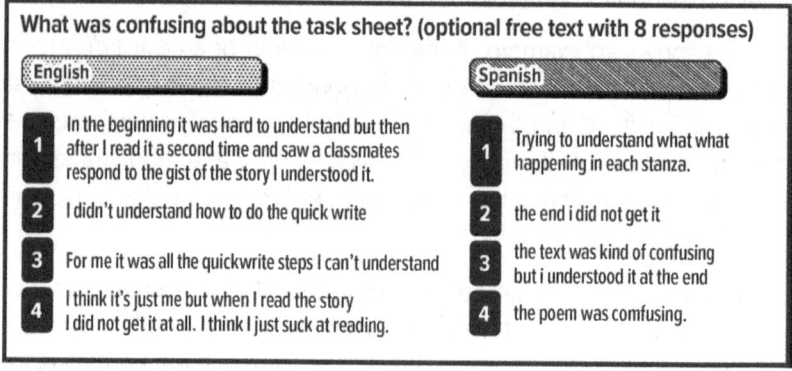

Figure 1.4 Online version of the exit ticket report.

of their use by teachers. Design Team members conducted focus groups of teachers by grade level and met with teachers individually to better understand the barriers to their uses of the exit tickets.

In the third year of the project (2020–21), motivated by the Design Team's findings and suggestions as well as by the move to online instruction, we refined the exit tickets' content and process. That year we collected over 1,100 responses to the exit tickets and generated thirty teacher-facing reports.

From the work of the Design Team and the IFL NSI coaches, we learned that we likely asked students the wrong questions. When we asked the set of questions about the text they read, for instance, we thought that students' responses would prompt teachers to reconsider the texts if students found them not relevant to their backgrounds or the texts didn't make them want to read. In fact, few teachers thought about changing texts when they saw those responses on the exit ticket summaries, for several reasons. Teachers had moved on. They didn't have the time to go back to reconfigure the text or search for others because they were on to new texts in new lessons. Moreover, few middle school teachers enjoyed the autonomy to choose texts. Because of their low state ratings, the NSI schools were required to teach from scripted lessons that focused heavily on preparing students for the state test. A few middle schools did have the freedom to use alternative texts and teacher-developed lessons, but that required the support of the principal and the executive director responsible for the school. Those stars didn't always align.

The high schools were a slightly different story. The 9th grade teachers had wider access to a more robust curriculum and could as a team choose texts and sequence them, again, with the support of the principal and the school's executive director. Like the middle schools, the high schools also received scripted lessons, but teachers were not as aggressively monitored as they were in the middle schools. Still, the 9th grade teachers' use and uptake of the exit tickets was as weak as the middle school teachers' uptake.

The exit tickets were not solely focused on the text and its comprehension. We posed questions about all the tests of change. When we shared the summaries with teachers, we assumed they would find them useful and study them to see what changes in instruction they might point to. In reality, teachers had little time to gather to review them even when they participated in regular weekly PLC meetings. We also didn't do a very good job of preparing teachers to reflect on the results of the exit tickets, so they used them primarily to verify that students were generally okay with the texts and instruction. We eventually heard from improvement projects in other districts that they prepared the district coaches to review the results with teacher teams, which encouraged more teachers to reflect on students' feedback and make adaptations and adjustments.

Shifting to Online Instruction

March 2020 in the Big City was cold but sunny. Late in the month, we held a Network meeting for school NSI coordinators and teachers. News about the COVID-19 virus and a possible pandemic surfaced regularly in mainstream media, and at the meeting, participants talked about it. BCSD was scheduled for its spring break beginning the following week. One of the NSI coordinators mentioned that the district leadership had provided his school with laptops for all teachers, and students were supposed to pick up their laptops by the end of the week. Some teachers asked if others had heard anything about coming back after break. Were the laptops going home with students because the district was planning to shut down? By the time the meeting concluded, we had all convinced ourselves that the district would likely close for a week or two, if at all, after spring break. In reality, the district went to complete online instruction from April to mid-June.

So much happened between April and June during the second year of the NSI. The district pushed out advice on licensed platforms for online instruction. Few teachers or administrators knew their way around the platforms, so the learning curve was steep for everyone. The district settled on Google Meets for instruction and encouraged teachers to use Google Classroom for assignments and students' work. Other platforms that played well with Google Classroom provided more specific services for interactive online learning. Tech tools such as Padlet, Nearpod, and Pear Deck made their way into teachers' repertoires. However, there were other problems to solve. BCSD is a geographically large urban district. Tens of thousands of students initially lacked internet service. The superintendent formed a coalition of educators and business leaders to solve the problem, and many households benefited from his initiative, but service was still unreliable when a family, for example, had more than one student. Even when they could get online, many students were uncomfortable making their faces visible, so screens often showed names without faces.

The IFL NSI coaches worked with the NSI teachers and coordinators to learn the platforms and tools and to figure out how to support teachers' continued use of the student-centered practices. During these three months, teachers continued to meet weekly online in their PLCs and planning meetings.

It's difficult to capture the intensity of their work during these months. We were all living in a real-time experiment. Teachers learned to use digital tools and tried them out with students as they were learning them. They experimented with platforms to present lessons and to engage students in discussions and writing. They planned and met each week to evaluate their successes and struggles with online instruction. They were relieved, as we were, when the state announced that it would not administer the SA that year. NSI teachers took advantage of the test cancellation to forgo test preparation in favor of instruction developed to engage students with compelling texts.

The IFL NSI coaches regularly attended the weekly online PLCs and many of the teachers' planning meetings. We continued the monthly Network meetings online and used them to support the teachers as they experimented with digital tools. A good part of this support involved giving them opportunities to share what they were using and learning alongside them.

We held office hours online and telephone conversations to think with the teachers about the instructional issues they wanted to deal with, especially the ways that students were reacting to online instruction and their reluctance to show themselves on screen. We tried the digital tools with them, thought through how they might support students to talk with each other, and learned along with them that students preferred to write to one another, rather than talk, in response to discussion tasks. That pushed us all back into the catalogue of district digital tools to find those that might best support students' writing to each other or to the class in response to tasks.

By the end of the school year, almost everyone we worked with said they were exhausted from the online environment and wondered how it could be sustainable for the coming year.

Year 3 (2020–21) Key Initiatives: Hybrid Online Teaching and Relating Implementation of Student-Centered Practices to Students' Test Performance

Hybrid Online Teaching and Its Effect on Teachers, Students, and Network Meetings

August of 2020 stepped into BCSD teachers' and leaders' lives (and ours) like a wild rave that wanted more than anything to be a line dance. Dissonance, anxieties, and disagreements, it seemed, marked every decision about online schooling. The COVID-19 pandemic raged, killing hundreds of thousands every month, and children no longer appeared to be insulated from its spread. Parents, concerned about their children's schooling or lack of it, voiced strong opinions on whether the district should return to in-person attendance. Thousands of homes still did not have reliable internet service. The superintendent continued to work with service providers, but it was a difficult problem to solve. Some teachers with health issues refused to return in person, and others decided to leave the profession. District leaders were of different minds on these issues, but the decision was made—without really being able to understand its consequences—to open schools with a hybrid instructional model. Instruction would proceed in person for those students whose parents agreed to send them to school and simultaneously online for those parents who did not. For both options, attendance dived.

Teaching in person and online at the same time makes sense as an idea. In reality, it handed teachers a difficult situation at best and impossible at worst. The thinking was that teachers could use their smart boards to stream instruction while it was happening in person in a class. A teacher could speak to both those present and those online. The online participants could participate in class work and complete assignments while those in the classroom did the same.

In reality, every class in every building online at the same time was more than district and internet servers could handle. Google Meets and other online tools regularly crashed. It was difficult for online participants to hear and follow the in-person class. Online students kept their cameras off, making it impossible for teachers to know if they were there. Students quickly learned how to game the system by showing up for attendance and then disappearing.

The NSI teachers tried to follow the district plan, developing their lessons to be taught online and using the online tools during in-person instruction. It was difficult for online students to participate in peer-to-peer discussions or follow along with those that occurred in person. The solution was to ask the online students to use a tool such as Flipgrid or Pear Deck to participate in groups by writing responses and reading each other's writing. That approach had worked fairly well when everyone was online from April to June, but this time it was different. Teachers who took this approach found it difficult to monitor both the in-person and the online groups. For students, writing to each other was better than not communicating at all, but it didn't have the same socializing benefits that talking with each other provided.

The IFL NSI coaches continued the monthly Network meetings online. During the first half of the year, they collaborated with teachers to adapt their use of student-centered practices to different online tools. By mid-year, we learned the importance of consistency and coherence. Instruction in person and online made sense to students when they could anticipate the tools and approaches teachers used. While the district continued to make new online tools available, NSI teachers began to use those few that worked well enough, were accessible to both in-person and online students, and could carry adaptations of the student-centered practices. Google Classroom emerged as a reliable platform for presenting students with tasks and for collecting students' written work. It could be used with interactive tools such as Padlet and Pear Deck that made it possible for all students to see each other's written work whether it was in the form of digital sticky notes (Padlet) or written responses (Pear Deck).

IFL NSI coaches regularly attended NSI teachers' weekly PLCs. We collaborated in those meetings with the teachers as they developed their lessons using online tools. At times we made suggestions as to which tools might work best and, at other times, we responded to the teachers' lessons before they taught them. It was a grueling online schedule for everyone but especially for the teachers whose hybrid instruction required substantial additional planning outside of designated planning time.

Key Takeaways from Hybrid Online Teaching

In our Network meetings, teachers reached a consensus: students were more engaged when tasks involved writing, sharing their writing, and providing feedback to peers, rather than when teachers tried to engage them in verbal discussions. As a result, written responses to tasks became the norm. Initially, teachers expressed frustration over students' reluctance to engage in verbal discussions online. However, they observed increased participation when students had the freedom to write, whether through chat features or by using Google Documents for longer explanations and peer feedback.

By the midpoint of the school year, NSI teachers had established digital routines that supported students to interact with texts, tasks, and discussions through writing. Teachers were organizing learning opportunities for students in new and effective ways. We saw teachers using single slides designed to resemble a classroom that had embedded hyperlinks to the tools and resources students needed to be successful with the day's or week's instruction. We saw evidence of clusters of schools using simple webpages that laid out the work of instructional units and linked that work to specific digital tools that supported students engaging in student-centered practices with writing. We saw teachers building community with students they had not met in person by organizing ten minutes at the end of every class on Fridays to play an online game together.

"We knew that teachers needed space and time to talk through what was happening in their classrooms, so we invited teachers who were finding pockets of success to lead the Network meetings. Hearing about similar struggles made what our teachers dubbed 'teaching to the void' easier."

The sharing aspect of our Network meetings became critical spaces to keep teachers engaged in the NSI community. Early in the 2020–21 school year, though, we sensed uncertainty, tension, and frustration in Network teachers. While they had the support of the IFL NSI coaches, teachers had ended the 2019–20 school year largely on their own when it came to figuring out how to engage students online. In August 2020, one veteran teacher wrote to us saying, "As for how it's going, I'm learning as much about the limitations of my own skills as much as I am about my students. I'm not a middle school teacher, and many of these [9th graders] are still in middle school intellectually and emotionally. All that to say that I hope I'm having some kind of positive impact on them."

We knew that teachers needed space and time to talk through what was happening in their classrooms, so we invited teachers who were finding pockets of success to lead the Network meetings. Hearing about similar struggles made what our teachers dubbed "teaching to the void" easier. In this way, we provided space for teachers to engage in self-work related to their experiences, something they felt they hadn't been asked to do by anyone since the beginning of the pandemic.

Relating Implementation of Student-Centered Practices to Students' Test Performance

Students' performances on high-stakes tests matter in the Big City (and all public school districts). We were often asked how the NSI work would affect students' scores. From the beginning of the project, we knew that we needed to develop a reasonable method to relate teachers' implementations of the student-centered practices to students' performances on tests that mattered to the district.

To assess the impact of the NSI tests of change on students' growth, as we discussed briefly earlier in this chapter, we asked teachers to complete an annual survey on how often they implemented each of the student-centered practices. We also coded observations of lessons for their uses of the practices. Using those two data sources, we divided the teachers into two groups—those implementing many NSI practices / more often and those implementing few practices / rarely. We then calculated students' growth scores on the MAP Reading assessment from baseline at the beginning of the year to mid-year, and matched teachers' survey results to their students' growth on the test. The MAP assessment has strong psychometric properties. It was also useful as the only available data source in BCSD that offered a measure of student growth during this school year (i.e., had a pre- and a post- on a common scale). Additionally, it was the closest match to the NSI focus on comprehension tests of change, with one caveat. NSI teachers approached comprehension through writing and student-to-student talk. However, we didn't use MAP to assess students' comprehension growth through writing. MAP does not directly assess writing, although it has a proxy writing assessment through multiple choice. We decided that such a representation of writing was not appropriate for our purposes.

The evaluation showed substantial gains for all student groups in classrooms of NSI teachers who were high implementers of the student-centered practices, with especially high gains for Black boys. In these data, we see a strong case for high implementation of the NSI's instructional practices, confirming our theory of action. We discuss this evaluation and others that our analytics team conducted and reported on in more detail in Chapter 2, which considers the project outcomes.

Year 4 (2021–22) Key Initiatives: Mitigating Online In-School Instruction, Dealing with Teacher Turnover, Focusing on Equitable Instruction, Delivering and Using Data, and the Role of the BCSD + IFL Vision of Collaborative Work

In the fourth year, schools re-opened. Students returned to meet classmates in person for the first time in a year and a half. Many middle school students who were in 6th grade when the pandemic began entered high school without having seen their classmates in school during that time. About 60 percent of the NSI teachers had taught in the district's hybrid simultaneous online and in-person initiative. The other 40 percent were mostly new to the district.

When we conducted our first *Learning Walk* at a high school with the school leadership and its executive director, we hoped to see students engaging in discussions with each other, charting their ideas and sharing them in gallery walks, and participating in teacher-led whole group discussions. Instead, in many classes, we saw students sitting at desks, sometimes in rows and sometimes facing each other, on their computers while the teacher sat at a desk also on a computer. Students received their readings and tasks online, completed their quick writes online, and responded to each other's ideas in writing online while the teacher either observed their work unfold on the computer or walked around the class and read over students' shoulders. As we mentioned before, the executive director referred to this type of teaching as "online in person." He was concerned that although students did the work individually, they didn't seem engaged and there was little to no social interaction. The students, he said, seemed compliant and still learning as if they were at home on their computers.

Not all classes we observed that fall were like this. We saw NSI teachers, for example, using computers to share slides of task sheets with students while asking the students to turn and talk with a partner after they composed quick writes. We saw teachers asking student groups to complete charts of their ideas to share with the class using either paper or online charts that could be displayed one-at-a-time on the large white boards in front of the class. In some of those classes, teachers invited students to write in notebooks and share their ideas and responses to the charts in whole group discussions by gathering in a circle to talk.

"We learned from talk with teachers that both the habits teachers and students had developed during the year and a half of online instruction, and the habits that students hadn't developed, were underlying issues."

There were enough of the "online in person" classes, though, that the IFL NSI coaches decided to open a discussion with teachers about it during the monthly meetings. We hoped to encourage teachers to return to in-person instruction more fully, taking advantage of students being together for discussions. We learned from talk with teachers that both the habits teachers and students had developed during the year and a half of online instruction, and the habits that students hadn't developed, were underlying issues. Students weren't accustomed to talking with each other in pairs and trios, many didn't know their classmates, and the reluctance to engage seemed to be a version of appearing online without showing their faces.

The newly appointed superintendent declared that this would be the year of student engagement, the year of elevating students' voices, underscoring that disengagement was a district-wide problem. During our Network meetings, teachers shared their thinking. They took various approaches to reteaching students how to engage. For example, some returned to using discussion stems. We saw lists of phrases reappear in classes, such as, "I'd like to build on that," "I understand what you're saying but I think …," and "I agree with X but also think that…." (We had seen teachers using discussion stems before the pandemic, but many had released students from using them by the middle of the second year. By that point, students had internalized the goals of the discussion stems and developed a larger repertoire of academic language from the discussions.) Other teachers modeled ways to engage in discussions by thinking aloud as they demonstrated composing quick writes or responded to students' quick writes or charts. Some teachers asked students to model for their classmates, especially those students who were familiar with discussion routines.

The problem of how to balance the use of students' computers during in-person instruction also needed to be solved. During Network and PLC meetings, NSI teachers shared the various ways that they tried to balance their use. At the same time, they acknowledged that computers were now integrated into school life, and new routines needed to be established. In that vein, we began to observe interesting adaptations.

In one school, we saw middle school teachers asking students to compose their quick writes using their computers, so the quick writes could be displayed on the white board for discussion. Others asked students to chart online or to use Padlet with sticky notes that could be displayed either on everyone's screens or on the white board at the front of the room. Teachers in other schools asked students to collaborate in pairs or trios on producing quick writes or charts they would then share with the class via the white board. We saw one classroom where charts were displayed one student group at a time with the group members coming to the front of the class to explain their thinking and standing afterwards for questions from their classmates. Virtual charting with in-person discussions followed by questions from the class and teacher began to trend in NSI middle schools after this format was presented in a Network meeting.

We were excited by the district's focus on student engagement in learning, and by the NSI teachers' imaginative problem-solving to balance the use of computers with in-person student-centered practices. Computers made it possible for students to read one another's writing and to respond to it either online or in person, and teachers could use the white boards now networked to all the students' computers to display their work. We and district leadership continued to make the case that in-person talk mattered, and that its socializing benefits far outweighed students' initial reluctance or unease. We also made the case that cognitively challenging instruction depended on it because all students in a class need opportunities to learn from peer-to-peer discussions, from explanations and arguments made orally in real time, and from making their thinking visible so others can understand it and comment on it.

Teacher Turnover

In the second year of the project (2019–20), 26 percent of teachers returned to their buildings from the previous year. In the third year, it was 43 percent, and in the fourth year, it was 39 percent. Table 1.3 conveys the significance

Table 1.3 Percentage of ELA teachers returning to buildings from the previous year for grades 6–9

	2019–20 (2nd Year)	2020–21 (3rd Year)	2021–22 (4th Year)
Overall	26%	43%	39%
Middle Schools Overall	22%	46%	45%
High Schools Overall	32%	40%	33%
High School 1	29%	47%	43%
High School 2	32%	47%	43%
High School 3	50%	21%	78%
High School 4	31%	34%	32%
High School 5	33%	56%	41%
High School 6	26%	35%	13%
High School 7	19%	40%	29%
Middle School 1	15%	53%	53%
Middle School 2	18%	27%	47%
Middle School 3	28%	38%	27%
Middle School 4	26%	48%	50%
Middle School 5	30%	60%	48%
Middle School 6	30%	61%	48%
Middle School 7	11%	43%	36%

of the turnover in the percentages of returning teachers and the variance by building.

The variability by building is striking. The overall consistency of turnover is also striking. Teacher turnover in the NSI schools (as in the district overall) posed challenging problems. By January of 2022 when turnover finally stopped and assignments were stable, our regular monthly meetings needed to be broken into two groups. One group was composed of continuing NSI teachers who had learned about and implemented the NSI tests of change. The other group was composed of teachers new to NSI buildings who needed to learn a lot about the project to participate. Many of those teachers were also new to the profession. They required considerable coaching from the IFL NSI coaches, the district coaches, and NSI building coordinators to move from teacher-centered to student-centered instruction.

Coaching alone wasn't enough, though, because we didn't have the capacity to meet regularly in buildings with the new teachers. The IFL NSI coaches collaborated with members of the Design Team to develop onboarding sessions for the monthly meetings with the new teachers. The sessions ranged in topics from planning bell-to-bell lessons, to experiencing the student-centered practices as learners, to trying them out and bringing stories and artifacts to the meetings. We also gradually phased in information on the improvement science methods we used for the root cause analysis, the results of that analysis, and the NSI workings over the years. And we devoted meeting time with the continuing teachers to discussions of their suggestions for mentoring and coaching new teachers and for their help in doing so.

Focus on Equitable Instruction

The scholarship on equitable instruction[7] argues for (1) creating instruction that engages all students in intellectually challenging tasks and texts that take up culturally relevant issues, (2) developing classroom cultures that feature students' voices as integral to their academic studies, (3) positioning students with dignity and respect in classrooms that acknowledge and honor the assets they bring to learning, (4) supporting teachers to identify implicit biases and assumptions that can manifest in classrooms through their interactions with students, text selection, and pedagogical practices, and (5) encouraging educators in various roles to study the ways that stereotyping, deficit thinking, trauma triggers, and microaggressions can manifest in their interactions with students, and strategies for addressing them.

During the fourth year, the IFL NSI coaches continued to focus on equity work in our monthly meetings with teachers. In the first online convening of the year, teachers read about and discussed equitable literacy instruction. They engaged in conversations with one another about what they noticed in definitions of equitable instruction, how they viewed their instruction at the time, and how it related to the definitions that were developed by the NSI Hub Equity Team. The teachers also revisited the tests of change for the past three years and discussed in breakout groups (1) which tests of change they would begin with to focus on literacy instruction, (2) how those choices would help them work toward equitable instruction, and (3) the support they would like from the IFL NSI coaches to plan and enact their next NSI test of change.

In the next four monthly convenings, teachers focused on these related activities and topics in this order:

- Discussions about what equitable instruction looked like in their schools.
- Discussions of sequences of text-based tasks to see how they could contribute to equitable literacy instruction.
- Analysis and discussion of a video lesson on "Ain't I A Woman?" by Sojourner Truth[8] in which the teacher conducts a student-centered inquiry discussion using a response protocol for follow-up questions with a diverse group of students. After their analysis and discussion of the video, the teachers engaged with the follow-up response protocol to complete a mid-year reflection on the ways literacy instruction can support all students.

Also, during the fourth year, the NSI Hub Equity Team completed its first draft of the NSI Equity-Focused Webinar Series. The six 30- to 45-minute webinar modules were designed to operationalize for educators what the NSI team meant by equitable literacy instruction by addressing topics on implicit bias, stereotyping, deficit thinking, microaggressions, trauma-informed practices in schools, and the ways that instruction can support all students in classrooms. Taken together, the webinars were designed to build foundational knowledge that could help educators better understand and connect with students to develop strong, respectful relationships.

They provide educators with a balance of research-based knowledge and instructional design strategies and tools.

Data and More Data

In the spring and summer of 2022, the NSI Data and Analytics Team produced a report evaluating the impact of the project on students from Year 1 to Year 4. The report is discussed in detail in Chapter 2. It was available to district colleagues in October 2022.

The quantitative data told a compelling story about the positive effects of students' engagements with student-centered practices and NSI teachers' views of the Network. Chapter 2 includes a detailed discussion of the types of assessments we used and how we evaluated the impact of the work. For now, we want to point out these key results.

- For every specific group of students—economically disadvantaged, Black, Hispanic, EML, and SwSN—performance on the 2022 state ELA/Reading assessment for grades 6–8 was higher in NSI middle schools than in other comparable district schools.
- In every grade, NSI middle schools outperformed comparable middle schools on MAP reading comprehension and ELA district formative assessments meant to predict students' performance on the state test.
- NSI students outperformed students in comparable district high schools on the 9th grade English SA. For every specific group of students, performance was higher. The students of NSI high school teachers who implemented many NSI practices saw significant and overall large impacts for every student group, with larger benefits in this order for girls, Hispanic students, Black students, and SwSN.
- On surveys that included other networks, administered by a third party, the NSI received the highest rating from Network participants for (1) perceived benefits from participation, (2) continuous improvement confidence, (3) school team collaborative inquiry, and (4) cross-team learning and collaboration.
- On average, 98 percent of NSI teachers surveyed for the implementation study said they would like to continue to implement the student-centered practices if supported by leadership.

- Despite the challenges of hybrid teaching, most teachers who participated in the implementation study used each of the student-centered practices on a regular basis and adapted each approach to meet the needs of specific student groups (i.e., EML students and SwSN).

The IFL NSI coaches shared this evaluation of impact report with teachers for their discussions in Network meetings after we shared it with the executive directors and then with the principals. BCSD's protocols for such data sharing—focusing on sharing first with district leadership, then school leadership, and then teachers—worked in favor of the NSI using the data to continue making the case for the usefulness of the Network and its instructional changes. This was particularly true for the positive effects of the practices on students' engagement and on students' growth and achievement with measures that mattered to our district colleagues.

After students returned to schools and the NSI analytics team produced the evaluation report that we just briefly discussed, we began to receive requests from the executive directors to report on the implementation of the student-centered practices and students' assessment performances by school and by teachers. From an administration point of view, this made sense. They wanted to know which schools and teachers were performing well and which ones weren't. We resisted these questions, arguing that when we began the NSI, we promised teachers that we wouldn't provide building- or teacher-level data. We did this to protect the Network meetings as safe spaces for open discussions about teaching and learning. We also did it because we felt strongly that the NSI wasn't an evaluative project.

> "Principals and teachers needed to see that they had leadership support, especially from the executive directors, to continue with their commitments to the NSI. They also needed to see that the changes in instruction were making differences for students both in their engagement during class and in their test performances."

It's worth mentioning that the IFL NSI coaches felt it was important to continually make the case for the teachers' participation in the Network using the measures and data that mattered to district leaders. Their support was vital. Principals and teachers needed to see that they had leadership support, especially from the executive directors, to continue with their commitments to the NSI. They also needed to see that the changes in instruction were making differences for students both in their engagement during class and in their test performances.

The Role of the District + IFL Vision of Collaborative Work

Although we discussed the substantial revision of the NSI's original driver diagram that became the BCSD + IFL Vision of Collaborative Work early on in this chapter, we want to situate it here in our discussion of the other key initiatives during the fourth year as an artifact of our evolving understanding of BCSD as a system.

You might recall that this vision of collaborative work lives in a chart that presents the roles and responsibilities of key BCSD colleagues, as well as those of the IFL NSI participants, in implementing and supporting the implementation of the teachers' use of the student-centered practices. The original driver diagram (see page 10) identified the goals of the NSI, the problems of practice it chose to work on, and the categories of actions it could take to address those problems and through them, the goals. We felt that the vision of collaborative work took Network responsibilities and actions to a finer grain size with language that helped our district colleagues, NSI Hub members, and others outside of both organizations to visualize the types of work we were doing with each role group and the ways that each supported the teachers.

It took us three years to understand the system that's portrayed in the vision document. It's not that we were blind to it, but when we began to discuss a revision of the driver diagram in the third year, we realized it didn't specifically represent the system and the ways we interacted with it through its key role groups. The vision document gave us a way to be clear about what NSI Hub members were doing as well as what each district role group was doing and the ways we were supporting them. Our new understandings grew out of the opportunity to step back from the work and reflect on how it was actually happening, as opposed to how we had imagined it would happen in 2018–19. The reflection also occurred in the context of the fourth year's work that included a better understanding of the interrelated goals and actions of BCSD's role groups. The protocols we were using to share the wealth of data that we delivered in the fourth year, differentiation in the types of meetings we were having with key BCSD colleagues, and shifting NSI priorities from implementation to capacity building, all contributed to our deeper understanding of the NSI and the system within which we worked.

Year 5 (2022–23), the Final Year that Wasn't the Final Year, Key Initiatives: Middle School New Curriculum Pilot Test, BCSD Reorganization, Exceptionally High Implementation of Student-Centered Practices, Significant Student Outcomes on MAP Reading Comprehension and the ELA SA, Data on NSI Schools Versus Similar Schools Within BCSD and Within Other Urban Districts in the State

The fifth year of the NSI ushered in another round of project-changing adaptations. The NSI middle schools participated in the district pilot testing of the New ELA Curriculum. Mid-year, BCSD reorganized. All the executive directors that had been working with us changed and a new layer of administrators—associate superintendents—was put in place. A large part of their responsibilities included overseeing the work of the executive directors. At the same time, executive directors became responsible for K-12 schools in feeder patterns, whereas they had been largely responsible for schools more in line with their grade-level expertise. Data from the year was exceptionally strong, with almost all of the NSI teachers reporting high implementation of the student-centered practices. Students' growth and achievement rose with rising implementation with a few exceptions.

The Middle School New Curriculum Pilot Test

Up until this year, the district had been providing the NSI middle schools with scripted curriculum in the form of slides that could be used for instruction, usually with some modifications to make them more classroom ready. The NSI middle school teachers had been adapting the curriculum to include the student-centered practices and, at times, to teach challenging, relevant texts that engaged students. A few of the schools had added culturally relevant novels to the curriculum in a bold move that principals and executive directors supported because their students were doing well on local and state high-stakes assessments. Others planned to integrate novels into the curriculum once they had seen how well students responded to them in their colleagues' schools. Since the scripted lessons being pushed out to the schools remained basically the same from year to year, NSI teachers had developed a library of lessons into which they had integrated the student-centered practices. School teams had shared lessons and novel units, and teachers had become comfortable with the changes to the curriculum they'd been working on for two to three years.

All of that changed in the fifth year when the NSI schools took up the challenge of pilot testing the New Curriculum (6–8). When the decisions were made, very few NSI teachers knew much about the New Curriculum, except for positive anecdotal reports from a few middle schools that had experimented with it the year before. The IFL NSI coaches were given access to the New Curriculum in the fall of 2022. The teachers received access in the spring of 2023. We scheduled a June retreat with ELA central staff and executive directors around our own three days of studying the New Curriculum so that we could support the NSI teachers who would be using it in the fall.

We learned from the ELA director and staff that teachers would receive a version of just-in-time professional learning around the curriculum during the summer of 2023 and again in August during their return-to-school meetings. The executive directors we met with after we had studied the curriculum agreed that we would support the NSI teachers, as we had in the past, to integrate the student-centered practices into the New Curriculum when it was appropriate for the texts and tasks. We also talked with them about encouraging the NSI teachers to backwards plan from the unit assessments in the curriculum to determine what they would teach in each unit. Everyone we met with seemed to agree that there was too much in the curriculum for teachers to be able to teach it all, and backwards planning would at least give students what they needed to successfully complete the assessments.

The pilot testing didn't go as we had planned and hoped it would. The district rolled out sessions on the New Curriculum over the summer with a focus on logistics—how to set up student accounts and use the online tools that accompanied it, and how the curriculum itself was organized—but teachers needed more. It's a complex, multilayered curriculum with work for students to do together and individually. Those pieces needed to be coordinated. The pacing needed to be adjusted as well, given what teachers decided they would teach, and given the different schedules of individual schools. Some schools had double-block 90-minute ELA classes while others had 45-minute classes. The teachers' manual didn't cover these sorts of issues. Looking back, it seems as though we all underestimated the amount of planning involved in using the New Curriculum. We especially didn't understand that without deep work during the summer in the curriculum itself—work that would have involved the teachers in reading its texts and completing at least some of its tasks themselves—teachers would have to do that deep work week-by-week as they planned for teaching in their PLCs. The teachers' manual referred to this deep work as "internalizing" the lessons and the curriculum. We recognized "internalizing" as similar to our strategy of engaging teachers as learners in the work that they would ask of students.

Teachers had difficulty backwards mapping to decide what to teach; they struggled with the pacing since it was all new to them and the students, and they were mostly left on their own to figure out what and how to teach.

To support the NSI teachers, we split the monthly meetings into separate middle and high school sessions, so that each group could focus on the work in its curriculum. We continued to support the high schools with the integration of the student-centered practices into their lessons, but we decided not to focus on this with the middle school teachers until well into the year, after they had opportunities with the IFL NSI coaches and their colleagues to share their experiences with the curriculum. It seemed like too heavy a lift to ask them to think about embedding the student-centered practices into the curriculum as they were working to understand it, its pacing, and how to backwards map—all during their 45-minute PLC meetings. We then decided to use the first three monthly NSI meetings with the middle school teachers to ask them to tell us and their colleagues what they were doing that was successful and where they struggled. We also decided to hold the first of these meetings in September in person at one of the middle schools, so that we could all reconnect with each other socially as well while the teachers shared their experiences.

After studying the New Curriculum, we wondered if it had ever been taught and revised based on the experiences of teachers and students in classrooms. It didn't seem likely, given that it was so layered and so intensely paced to cover all the state standards. It seemed to us to be a curriculum begging to be adapted by teachers to their students and their schools and to their teaching approaches, rather than to be taught with fidelity, as some administrators were telling principals. In our experience, ELA textbooks have more content than any teacher could reasonably teach. Instead, teachers determine what they'll use based on their goals, their students, and their teaching approaches.

To draw this story to a close, we want you to picture this. Teachers were so engaged in solving the problems of how to teach the New Curriculum that our first NSI meeting on the New Curriculum with them ran over its usual three hours by an hour. They spent their time taking turns running the meeting, sorting out the curriculum layers, and passionately explaining in detail what they taught and how they reached common ground as school ELA teams on how best to adapt for students' success. The next three NSI meetings were virtual but no less engaging. Teachers brought examples of lessons they used, many that they had adapted, and some that integrated the student-centered practices. They mostly agreed that the curriculum focused on students working individually, with some turn-and-talk tasks. They saw a need for adapting it to be more student-centered with what they referred to as "reasonable pacing."

By January, the NSI teachers spoke positively about their work with the curriculum. District leaders had responded to their concerns about teaching it with fidelity, and they were now officially encouraged to adapt it. All but one NSI school continued to use it through the end of the year. The one school that dropped out of the pilot did so because of an administrative decision, not because of teacher resistance. Many other non-NSI middle schools also dropped out of the pilot. The principals of the NSI schools told us that those who dropped out would have benefited from the types of regular Network support that the NSI offered the teachers as they worked to understand the curriculum and internalize its texts and tasks. We should call this the demonstration of an old saw in education—that the written curriculum and the implemented curriculum will always be and should be different, so that teachers can adapt it to their students, their pacing, and their teaching approaches. In the best of worlds, underlying the difference is a vision of student-centered teaching that guides adaptations rather than admonishments to teach with fidelity.

BCSD's Reorganization

BCSD's organization resembled those of many districts. We refer to it as two sides of the house. One is Teaching and Learning. The other is Leadership. Each has its own chief and deputy chiefs. From there, the administrative differences surf on the division. Teaching and Learning has directors of subject areas while Leadership has executive directors of schools. All the district's coaches—school- and district-level—live under the Leadership umbrella.

When we began the NSI in 2018, the organization was in place. We developed working relationships with people in role groups on the vertical ladder of each side of the house. Over the years, a few people in those positions changed annually, but it was relatively easy to establish relationships with new people. In 2023, though, the district changed its Leadership organization. Until then, executive directors oversaw schools in their grade-level areas of expertise. If they had deep experience, for example, in secondary schools, they would most likely supervise secondary schools but not elementary. Executive directors with secondary experience, to continue this example, would often supervise middle and high schools in a feeder pattern but not the elementary schools. In 2023, the executive directors changed. The NSI schools now all had new executive directors. Their appointments changed to give them responsibility for all schools in a vertical feeder pattern—elementary to high school—regardless of their personal grade-level expertise. The majority of newly appointed NSI school executive directors had personal elementary expertise.

The other major change in Leadership was the addition of associate superintendents to whom the executive directors reported. They were all newly appointed to these new positions. We knew only one of the associate superintendents and one of the newly appointed executive directors, but he was no longer supervising NSI schools. In one day, in other words, all the NSI's relationships with key leaders changed. Some of those relationships with executive directors grew from years of working together. They understood the project, we had walked many classrooms with them, and they largely supported the NSI and its focus on changing instruction to include the use of student-centered practices.

The changes and the turnover associated with them produced considerable uncertainty for the NSI and for the schools. Principals and teachers wanted to know if the newly appointed leaders would support the NSI, as did the IFL NSI coaches. The NSI's lines of communications went down quickly after the reorganization. It took the remainder of the year for the IFL NSI coaches to re-establish communication with the newly appointed leaders.

We navigated these changes as strategically as we could, given that it was mid-year and that the NSI was scheduled to conclude its work with BCSD at the end of June 2023, even though we were in negotiations to extend the NSI into a sixth year. We briefed the new executive directors on the NSI as a group, and we planned with them to walk teachers' classrooms in the NSI schools, so we could develop a common understanding of the teachers' use of the student-centered practices and how they changed students' participation and engagement with texts and each other. We met once with the newly appointed associate superintendents to brief them on the NSI and, looking forward to a sixth year, agreed to meet again in the summer of 2023 to dive deeper into the NSI and the work of its teachers and students.

We had intended the fifth year to focus heavily on building district capacity to continue the Network meetings in the NSI schools, to spread the integration of the student-centered practices into the New Curriculum and high school curricula, and to initiate district-level capacity building with the IDCs who worked closely with executive directors to support specific schools. Once it was certain in November 2022 that the district would reorganize in the coming January, the executive directors and their ICs had other issues to focus on than building NSI capacity. Both groups assumed correctly that their appointments and roles would change, so the level of capacity building that we had planned for didn't materialize. The district did fund a sixth year of the NSI with the understanding that the sixth year would focus on capacity building.

In July 2023, the IFL NSI coaches met with the newly appointed executive directors of the NSI schools along with the principals to develop a capacity building plan. Table 1.4 shows the actions each group of leaders agreed to take. Notice the differences in how each role group developed its plan to reflect its level of influence or engagement.

There are a few key things to notice about these actions. One is that the executive directors agreed to include the student-centered practices in the Instructional Planning Calendar (IPC). The IPC for a school functions as

Table 1.4 Capacity-building actions

IFL NSI Coaches	Executive Directors	Middle School Principals	High School Principals
• Focus the NSI monthly meetings on capacity building by engaging participants to collaborate on best ways to do it. • Streamline the use of the NSI landing page that houses the NSI materials from all the monthly meetings. • Work directly with the Instructional District Coaches, with the executive directors' support, to build the student-centered practices into exemplary lessons and the Instructional Planning Calendar for the curriculum. • Support the Demonstration Teachers to build capacity and create capacity-building protocols with new teachers. • Meet with all new teachers in NSI schools in a four-hour session during June 2023 to onboard them; engage them in the student-centered practices as learners with engaging texts.	• Include the student-centered practices in the coaching cycle. • Collaborate with other non-NSI executive directors and their principals to support and deepen the work of the NSI. • Create a plan to purposefully pair schools to create smaller planning networks. • Make sure that the Demonstration Teachers receive NSI training. • Make sure that the Instructional District Coaches receive NSI training.	• Do some of the sense making for teachers to help them understand the ways the NSI work supports other initiatives such as the International Baccalaureate, AVID, the New Curriculum, etc., rather than being something separate. • Use the veteran NSI teachers on campus to build capacity for the NSI practices with new teachers.	• Provide time for the NSI 9th grade teachers to plan/make space in schedules for planning. • Leverage other campuses to learn from each other. • Help teachers support students to engage in the student-centered practices in class but also when they're working independently. • Ask teachers "How can I support you?" (what do you need?).

a day-by-day overview of what's being taught, and, in some cases, how teaching occurs. It serves as a guide for administrators who walk classrooms, so they know what to expect. It also serves as a guide for building teachers who plan their instruction and enter those plans into the IPC. When an IPC includes references and links to the student-centered practices for specific lessons, it gives anyone who uses it the opportunity to dig into the practices to understand them and to use them.

Another thing to notice is that the practices would be included in the coaching cycle. This means that instructional school coaches and instructional district coaches would have access to the student-centered practices, would be trained in their uses, and would be encouraged to use them when they coached teachers with specific texts, tasks, and lessons. And when teaching approaches such as the practices appear in the coaching cycle, they take on an official standing.

The final thing to notice is the way that the principals agreed to normalize the practices and support teachers to make sense of them by providing time to plan and by making use of veteran NSI teachers to build capacity with new teachers.

Supports for Teachers' Successes

The teacher implementation survey results for the fourth and fifth years indicate noticeably high implementation of the student-centered practices. The fifth year shows exceptionally high implementation, with 100 percent of the reporting teachers indicating regular use of pair/trio discussions and over 90 percent indicating regular use of the comprehension pre-work, text annotation, and quick writes. The implementation percentages are even higher for the NSI high school teachers. There's a more detailed discussion of the survey results and their implications in Chapter 2.

> "In response to the third-party survey in both years, almost all NSI teachers indicated that they highly valued the monthly convenings and that they took advantage of supporting each other's instruction across schools during those convenings by sharing their lessons and uses of the student-centered practices."

In addition to teachers' high implementation of the student-centered practices this year and students' performance on district assessments, we believe that protected, regular collaborative time for the NSI teachers in the three-hour monthly convenings allowed them to collaborate with NSI support in their implementation of the New Curriculum and the 9th grade curriculum as well as with the integration of the student-centered practices into those curricula. In response to the third-party survey in both years, almost all NSI teachers indicated that they highly valued the monthly convenings and that they took advantage of supporting each other's instruction across schools during those convenings by sharing their lessons and uses of the student-centered practices.

Another factor that supported success in the NSI schools was the substantial support of the school and district leadership in those NSI schools with high implementation. Of particular importance was the support of the principals and the ELA coaches in these buildings.

Finally, we believe that the teachers' use of the student-centered practices drove their strong attendance at the monthly convenings and their growth in understanding the ways in which these practices give students opportunities to reason about the meaning of texts and to voice their views.

When success eluded teachers and students, as it did for some of the middle grades and some of the schools, it was often because the school leadership didn't support the teachers to integrate the student-centered practices into their curriculum-based instruction. The reasons also can be traced to particular teaching approaches (e.g., test preparation, or the use of scripted curriculum slides produced by the district) promoted by the school's executive director who then holds the school leadership responsible for their implementation. This was the case with three of four schools showing weaker results. The fourth, a high school, faced a combination of issues, including an unsupportive school coach, high turnover of teachers, and a principal unwilling to focus her coach's attention on support for the NSI teachers.

All NSI schools were affected by the district's emphasis on test preparation beginning in January/February and extending through to the end of testing in May. Test preparation largely consisted of students studying exam questions, deconstructing them, and then practicing answering those types of questions until they seemed to have mastered them. This practice was followed by mock exams. The lack of regular curriculum-based instruction during these test-preparation activities and the extent of the preparation (e.g., in some schools, students came to additional sessions on Saturdays) diminished students' opportunities to learn from the curriculum and from engaging with the student-centered practices. Considering the importance of this preparation to NSI teachers, we developed two monthly meeting sessions to focus on the use of student-centered practices in test preparation, reasoning that even this adaptation would benefit students. We only had anecdotal evidence on teachers' uptake of these test-preparation variations, so we don't know whether it had a positive effect.

Year 6 (2023–24) Key Initiatives: Capacity Building with Instructional District Coaches and Demonstration Teachers

This section will be brief since one of the major changes during 2023–24 is covered in Chapter 3 on the NSI Network. That change involved reconfiguring the participants in the monthly Network meetings to enable the IFL NSI coaches to work regularly with the IDCs and the school ELA demonstration teachers.

For this overview, it's useful for you to know that during this sixth year, the IFL NSI coaches worked closely with an executive director on the Leadership side of the house. He enabled two key changes to the NSI that allowed us to focus the year's work on building capacity, so that should schools decide to continue the NSI work, they would have resources and key people available to support them. From our perspective, the change that mattered the most for this work was the green light to collaborate with the IDCs who had responsibility for the NSI schools while continuing to work with the demonstration teachers in the NSI buildings. The other change—to the participants in the monthly NSI meetings—directly supported this by shifting the middle school meetings to include only the IDCs and the demonstration teachers. In this way, we could focus our work on capacity building while still supporting teachers through the IDCs and the demonstration teachers. The monthly high school meetings continued to include the 9th grade teachers, building ELA coaches/assistant principals, demonstration teachers, and IDCs.

The IDCs played key roles in supporting school teams. They regularly attended ELA school team meetings in their buildings and conducted observations to gauge the implementation of the professional learning they provided and to give teachers and building administrators feedback on the instruction. The IDCs supporting the middle schools also had the responsibility to coach teacher teams on the use of the New Curriculum.

The school demonstration teachers worked like literacy coaches. They taught one class and used the remainder of their time to coach teachers, meet with the ELA team to interpret test results, and teach demonstration lessons when they were called for. They also took on responsibility for building-level support for implementing the New Curriculum. This meant that they planned the curriculum units and lessons with the ELA school team and observed the teachers' classes to give feedback on the instruction.

We had hoped to work directly with the IDCs throughout the last three years of the NSI, but we only received permission to do so in the sixth year. Once we understood their roles in supporting teacher teams in schools, which happened during the third year when we turned to thinking about the district as a system of role groups, we asked to work directly with them. Our understanding is that there were many initiatives in their wheelhouses, and we didn't make the priority list until the last year of the NSI when our focus was on capacity building.

Once we began to interact with the IDCs and the demonstration teachers, we supported them in the middle schools to integrate the student-centered practices into model lessons that they shared with the ELA school teams. In the high schools, they continued to support the 9th grade ELA teams to develop additional lessons with culturally relevant texts centered on the practices.

Because of the changes in the Network meetings, we didn't administer a teacher implementation survey in the sixth year, although we did administer a student survey to understand how students perceived their engagements with the student-centered practices. We were interested in knowing which practices they experienced and how frequently they experienced them. Our analytics team related the number and frequency of the practices that students experienced to their performance on the middle of year (MOY) MAP reading comprehension. There was a significant linear relationship to the number and frequency of reported experiences with the practices to students' growth on the MOY MAP. We have more to say about this in Chapter 2.

We hope that this summary of the key initiatives and year-by-year changes will serve as a framework for the overall project in your mind as we dig into the details in future chapters.

Questions for Reflection

1. What did the NSI's organization allow it to do and not do? How, in other words, did its organization and way of operating allow it to do certain things and prevent it from doing other things?
2. Speculate beyond what's already been said on how the NSI would have been different if it were a collaboration of schools and teachers who volunteered rather than being assigned to it.
3. What might be an argument *against* relating teachers' implementation of the student-centered practices to students' performances on the district tests, the MAP, and the SA?
4. How would you explain the variability in the implementation of the student-centered practices?
5. How could the NSI have better supported the implementation of the New Curriculum in the sixth year?
6. What are your thoughts on and experiences with the use of high-stakes tests? Will they always replace instruction with test preparation?
7. How would you describe the NSI's capacity building from the third year on? What structures enabled capacity building and what got in the way of it?

Notes

1. Alicia Grunow, Sandra Park, and Brandon Bennett, *Journey to Improvement: A Team Guide to Systems Change.in Education, Health Care, and Social Welfare* (Lanham, MD: Rowman & Littlefield, 2024), 105–50.
2. Office of Elementary and Secondary Education, "Root Cause Analysis in Action," U.S. Department of Education, accessed February 27, 2025; https://www.ed.gov/teaching-and-administration/lead-and-manage-my-school/state-support-Network/ssn-resources/root-cause-analysis-in-action.
3. Grunow, Park, and Bennett, *Journey to Improvement*, 45–150.

4   Arthur N. Applebee and Judith A. Langer, "A Snapshot of Writing Instruction in Middle Schools and High Schools," *English Journal* 100, no. 6 (2011): 14–27.

5   Wayne Au, "High-Stakes Testing and Curricular Control: A Qualitative Metasynthesis," *Educational Researcher* 36, no. 5 (2007): 258; David Blazar and Cynthia Pollard, "Does Test Preparation Mean Low-Quality Instruction?," *Educational Researcher* 46, no. 8 (November 2017): 420–33, https://doi.org/10.3102/0013189X17725525.

6   Anthony S. Bryk, Louis M. Gomez, and Alica Grunow, "Getting Ideas into Action: Building Networked Improvement Communities in Education," in *Frontiers in Sociology of Education*, ed. Maureen Hallinan (New York: Springer Publishing, 2011).

7   Gholdy Muhammad, *Cultivating Genius: An Equity Framework for Culturally and Historically Responsive Literacy* (New York: Scholastic, 2020); CRLT at University of Michigan, "Equity-Focused Teaching Framework," Center for Research on Learning and Teaching, University of Michigan, accessed October 14, 2024, https://crlt.umich.edu/equity-focused-teaching; Gloria Ladson-Billings, *The Dreamkeepers: Successful Teachers of African American Children* (San Francisco: Jossey-Bass Publishers, 1994); Gloria Ladson-Billings, "Culturally Relevant Pedagogy 2.0: Aka the Remix," *Harvard Educational Review* 84, no. 1 (2014): 74–84; Zaretta L. Hammond, *Culturally Responsive Teaching and the Brain: Promoting Authentic Engagement and Rigor Among Culturally and Linguistically Diverse Students* (Thousand Oaks, CA: Corwin Press, 2015).

8   Sojourner Truth, "Ain't I A Woman?" (Speech, Women's Rights Convention, Akron, Ohio, 1851).

2 An Overview of the Qualitative and Quantitative Outcomes

In this chapter, we report on qualitative and quantitative outcomes of the NSI project. We do this year-by-year, as we did in Chapter 1 for the project's key initiatives. You should expect some overlap with our discussions of the initiatives, since it's difficult to pull apart interrelated initiatives and their outcomes, and although we briefly discuss the more prominent quantitative outcomes in Chapter 1, we dig more deeply into them in this chapter.

Over the course of the NSI's six years, we evaluated the project every year beginning in the third year. From the second year on, we used various types of measures and tools to understand teachers' engagements with the Network, their perceptions of it, and their implementations of the NSI's tests of change—the student-centered practices. We used student exit tickets as a practical measure of their responses to lessons designed with the student-centered practices, and in the final year, we surveyed students on their experiences with those practices.

During the NSI's six years, the various measures and tools we used included:

- a survey in the second year of school teams' uptake of professional learning brought to them by their team coordinators;
- annual surveys of teachers' levels of implementation of the practices;
- coded observational data from IFL NSI coaches on teachers' implementation;
- student exit tickets;
- measures of students' academic growth and achievement in relation to teachers' levels of implementation of the practices;

- comparisons of NSI students' growth and achievement to comparable classes and schools in the district and the state;
- teachers' and principals' engagement with the Network and improvement science methods reported in an annual third-party network health survey;
- empathy interviews with teachers and administrators;
- students' 8th and 9th grade on-track measures for college and career readiness; and
- a survey of middle school students in the sixth year on the depth of their experiences with the student-centered practices that we related to their performance on the Northwest Evaluation Association Measures of Academic Progress (MAP) reading comprehension assessment.

This chapter presents the key quantitative and qualitative de-identified data we systematically collected and reported internally to the NSI teams and the various district role groups that we reported to, including the NSI teachers. We've made some changes to the language in the excerpts from internal evaluation reports that we share in this chapter to de-identify the state, district, and schools. Since we also want this chapter to tell the stories of the Network's results and effects over its six years, in the detailed presentations of the data, especially for the fourth and fifth years, we also comment on and interpret them.

Summary of Data We Gathered and Reported by Year

In the first year (2018–19), we focused primarily on establishing strong relationships with teachers and leaders, co-constructing a driver diagram with the school teams, and spreading knowledge about the project and our use of improvement science methods across schools. We met regularly with district leaders who had responsibility for the NSI schools and central leadership to share the school teams' progress on identifying a problem of practice and the driver diagram that mapped a route to addressing it.

In our second year, altered by the onset of the COVID-19 pandemic in the spring of 2020, a number of early implementing schools began to use the student-centered practices and reported on that work in the Network meetings. From April to June of 2020, our work—like our teachers' and the district's—was all online. The state paused administration of the state assessment (SA) for 2020.

In the third year (August 2020–June 2021), instruction was hybrid (in person and online) simultaneously. During the hybrid year, the state administered the SA again in person, and the district administered the MAP exams in the fall, winter, and late spring. We reported on reading comprehension MAP outcomes for NSI schools from the beginning (BOY) to the middle (MOY) of the year by relating students' performance on them to the degree of their teachers' implementation of the student-centered practices. We seldom used end-of-year (EOY) MAP data, except for 2022–23, because our analyses of year-by-year administrations led us to believe there were statistical anomalies, perhaps due to how late it was administered (usually in June after the battery of SAs) and to students' very mixed engagements with it. We also conducted empathy interviews with teachers in the spring of 2020 after they moved to remote instruction because of the pandemic. Based on the interviews, in 2022 we issued our first internal bright spots report on using continuous improvement methods to improve instruction.

In the spring and summer of the fourth year, we completed an evaluation of impact report for the first four years. We reported on NSI school performance on the 2022 SA in ELA/Reading for grades 6–8 and the 9th grade English SA in a number of ways, including in comparison to similar schools and in relation to teachers' level of implementation of the student-centered practices. That same fall, our analytics team conducted a second round of empathy interviews with teachers and administrators. We issued our second bright spots report based on those interviews in 2023. We present the key findings from these reports later in this chapter.

As was our practice for all the internal NSI evaluation reports, we shared the fourth year evaluation of implementation report with the NSI teams and our district colleagues. We shared the bright spots reports widely with our district colleagues.

Our analytics team issued its outcomes report on the fifth year (August 2022–23) in October 2023. It included fifth year data on the teacher depth of implementation, SA performances, MAP reading comprehension, and the District Course Assessment (DCA) as well as comparisons of the NSI schools to matched district and state urban schools.

The sixth year report focused on an analysis of middle school students' responses to a survey on how often they experienced the student-centered practices and the relationship of the relative frequency of their experiences to the growth they showed on the 2023 BOY to MOY MAP reading comprehension.

Key First- and Second-Year Outcomes

When the NSI launched in 2018–19, we focused on conducting and managing the root cause analysis that we discussed in Chapter 1 and on developing relationships with the teachers, principals, and executive directors responsible for instruction in the fourteen NSI schools. We discuss how we developed these relationships in more detail in the overview of the NSI's key initiatives over the six years in Chapter 1 and in the discussion of the evolution of the monthly Network meetings in Chapter 3. In the Network meetings throughout the second year (2019–20), we identified three schools where teachers were early implementers of the student-centered practices. It was in those schools over the first two years that we developed trusting relationships with teachers, principals, and a few executive directors. Our collaborations with those schools during Professional Learning Community (PLC) meetings and *learning walks* gave our district colleagues opportunities to see the IFL NSI coaches as collaborators and consultants.

> *"Hearing the early implementers' stories, seeing the lesson artifacts, and being able to understand and internalize the PDSA cycle was a major outcome that rippled through all the Network meetings during the first two years."*

Those collaborations on instructional changes with the early implementers gave all the teachers in the Network opportunities to see their colleagues' task sheets, video clips of instruction, and artifacts of students' writing and charting. During Network meetings, all the teachers were able to hear their early implementer colleagues tell their stories about developing lessons, the kinds of decisions they made, the time it took, and the results of their implementation. They heard the stories of their colleagues' Planning, Doing, Studying, and Acting (i.e., the PDSA cycle of improvement). Hearing the early implementers' stories, seeing the lesson artifacts, and being able to understand and internalize the PDSA cycle was a major outcome that rippled through all the Network meetings during the first two years. We have more to say about the evolution of teachers' collaborations in the Network meetings in Chapter 3, but we want to be sure not to understate here the degree and extent of teachers' collaborations and their desire to learn from each other during the second year that began in those meetings with the early implementers.

In addition to these early outcomes, we collected data from surveys on PLC uptake of the professional learning that the NSI school coordinators brought back from the NSI meetings, teachers' use of paper-and-pencil exit tickets to gather lesson feedback from students, and Network meeting participation. In the second year, a team of researchers from a third-party evaluation project launched a network health survey. We report on network health later in this chapter when we discuss the outcomes for the fourth year, the first year that we included network health data in our evaluation reports.

Key Third-Year Outcomes

Teachers' Levels of Implementation

The NSI analytics team focused on collecting and reporting teacher implementation data from a survey they administered in late fall of 2020. They then used the data to divide teachers into those implementing many of the student-centered practices and those implementing few of the practices. For each group, they analyzed the percentage of growth for students on the MAP Reading scores from BOY to MOY. From this year on, we collected implementation data from teachers every year as we continued to relate it to students' performances on the SA, MAP, and the DCA. Of all the data we collected, those studies mattered most to our district colleagues who wanted to know that their uses of the student-centered practices benefited students on these valued assessments.

Table 2.1 shows the percentages of teachers who regularly implemented the student-centered practices and those who adapted their use for their students. Eighty-one percent of the sixty-four teachers who completed the survey were active participants in the NSI monthly Network meetings. These percentages represent 8th and 9th grade NSI teachers.

Table 2.1 Percentage of teachers who regularly implemented and who adapted student-centered practices in the 3rd year

Percentage of teachers who...	Have students annotate the text for meaning (i.e., more than vocab)	Have students do comprehension work before other text work	Have students work in pairs/ trios	Have students do quick writes about initial ideas about the text	Have students work from a task sheet	Average
...regularly implemented by mid-year of 20–21 school year	63%	61%	46%	84%	54%	**62%**
...adapted the approach for their students	98%	NA	100%	97%	97%	**98%**

Despite the challenges of hybrid instruction during this third year, most teachers, especially those participating regularly in the Network meetings, implemented each of the practices on a regular basis (more than three times in a nine-week period). Most teachers adapted each approach for the needs of their students, sometimes for online implementation and sometimes for specific student groups (e.g., students with special needs or multilingual students). This adaptive integration of the practices, as we discussed in Chapter 1, proved to be essential to teachers' integration of them into their lessons, whether they were teaching from the high school textbook, a middle school curriculum, district-provided scripted lessons, or supplemental texts.

Students' Academic Growth on MAP Reading Comprehension Relative to Teachers' Level of Implementation

In May of the third year, the NSI analytics team issued an interim quantitative evaluation of the impact of teachers' implementation of the student-

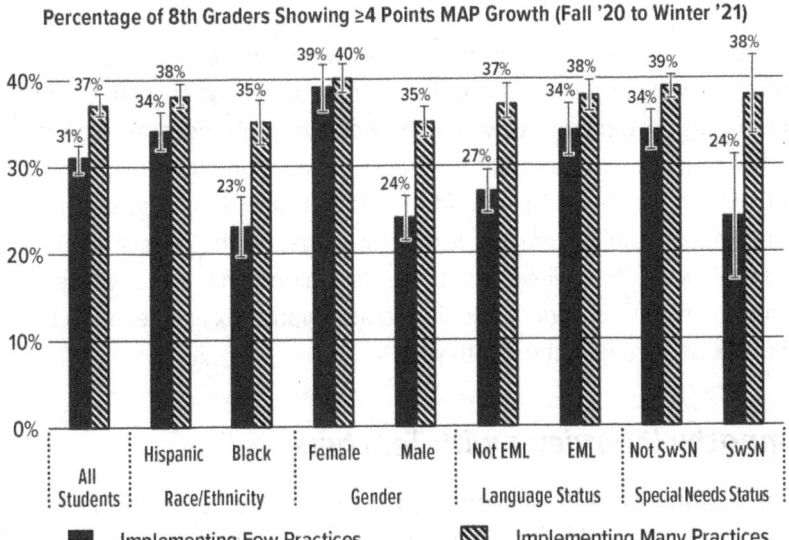

Figure 2.1 Percentage of 8th graders showing four points or greater MAP Reading Comprehension growth (with SE bars) for teachers implementing many or few student-centered practices.

centered practices on students in the NSI schools. The report focused on the percentages of students in each teacher's class who showed more than four points of growth on MAP reading comprehension scores. Four points of growth from BOY to MOY is the expected amount of growth from fall to winter in the national norms. It is also the amount of growth that is statistically significant and not attributable to measurement noise. Figure 2.1 shows the percentage of 8th graders with four points or greater in MAP reading comprehension growth from fall of 2020 to winter of 2021.

To understand this chart, it is important to know that there was very little variation across teachers in the amount of instructional time between the fall and winter test dates and not enough variation to influence outcomes. Although this chart represents the 8th grade findings, the 9th grade findings are similar. The findings also were similar whether the analysis controlled for attendance or not, likely because students with very low attendance tended to be missing BOY or MOY MAP data.

From the chart, we see consistently across all groups that 8th graders in high-implementing classrooms show significant MAP Reading growth, and high-implementing teachers show much smaller gaps by race/ethnicity, gender, language status, and special needs (SwSN) status. Most remarkably, perhaps, these are data from a time when instruction was hybrid—simultaneously in person and online. Before our analytics team conducted the analysis, we didn't know what to expect. Although anecdotal reports from IFL NSI coaches indicated that teachers were adapting the practices to their students and to both online and in-person instruction, class observations were primarily online, making it difficult to gauge the effects on students and their work. We believe that these data, along with principals' requests, contributed to the district's decision to add grades six and seven to the NSI Network beginning in the fourth year.

Empathy Interviews with Teachers

In the spring of 2021, a group that included NSI researchers from the analytics team and IFL NSI coaches began conducting empathy interviews with teachers to understand their perceptions of the Network, their engagements with it during the monthly Network meetings and in their PLCs, and their implementation of the student-centered practices. As we mentioned, these interviews became the basis for a bright spots report, which we issued in 2022. We present a brief thematic analysis of it here, with a discussion afterwards, so you can see what respondents regularly spoke about during the third year.

- Prioritizing comprehension during ELA instruction
  A 6th grade teacher who worked with students to comprehend and identify big ideas in a text said, "*We've seen students be able to see those big ideas much more clearly* ... I feel like it's encouraged conversation among students ... *they push each other to think, and not just think of the very first surface level idea....*"

- Using student-centered practices to focus on student engagement
  A 9th grade teacher commented on students' discussions of their comprehension quick writes in pair/trio sharing: "I feel *when it's a lot more student-centered, they're grasping it more.* So whenever I'm having them collaborate and work together, instead of me directly teaching, or teaching over and over again, then it helps them be able to grasp [the text's ideas]...."

- Adapting instruction for particular contexts
  An 8th grade teacher spoke about transitioning to online instruction:

  > I went to a Google slide deck, and I still keep it the same way that it's on the task sheet. And so once they get to their charting, *where in class they would usually use a piece of chart paper ... I put them in a breakout room ... I say, "Whatever is your breakout room, that is your number on your slide" ... [T]hey go and do all their big ideas there ...* and once I get to that slide, that student will unmute themselves, explain the slide....

- Students' productive struggle
  A 9th grade teacher said that:

  > *It was very apparent to me how students reacted differently to the questions we were giving them that actually made them think....* My students even said in the past all they had to do was read the question—read [what] that question was asking about.... [T]hey did complain about that part because they're like, *"Ohhh, your class got so hard all of a sudden."* ... But then they blossomed....

- Support for teachers from the Network
  Another 9th grade teacher said that the NSI IFL coaches

  > just start with asking us, "How is it in your classroom? What's going on? What have you guys been doing?" And we'll tell them, and we'll tell them our struggles, and then they'll be like, "Oh, why do you think that is?" And we'll talk about why, and then *we'll all come up collectively with solutions and things to think about and things that we could maybe implement in our classes....* So, to actually have a space and someone to ground you, to ask you to reflect, and then you actually have time to plan it and put it into motion, has been valuable.

Reading these comments now, years after they were included in the bright spots report, we see teachers and students (as reported on by the teachers) noticing differences in their classes when the instruction was student-centered. Prioritizing comprehension during instruction also surfaced as a major theme in the Network discussions. During the root cause analyses in the first year, teachers recognized that both the district curriculum and the teacher-created tasks they collected were missing what we called "comprehension first" support for students—tasks that helped them understand the big components of texts such as ideas, plots, and arguments before asking them to analyze aspects such as structure and the use of literary devices. Teachers noted repeatedly during the interviews that adding comprehension in first changed students' thinking and learning. We also see teachers adapting their instruction and task sheets to Google Slides and to their use of breakout rooms for students to work in small groups. We hear support for students collaborating more when the practices are being used as well as praise for the Network meetings as safe spaces for collective meaning making and collaborations among teachers.

Key Fourth-Year Outcomes

The fourth year was a year of strong teacher engagement in the Network meetings and in their adaptations of the student-centered practices to the curriculum and their instruction. As we mentioned earlier, the NSI analytics team produced an evaluation of impact on students for the first through the fourth years during the spring and summer of 2022. The report was available to district colleagues in October 2022.

Before we go into an in-depth review of the fourth-year data, here's a summary of the key findings in that report for teachers' level of implementation of the practices, students' academic performance, teachers' and leaders' engagement with the Network from the network health survey, and on-track 8th and 9th grade indicators.

On the fourth year implementation survey, 79 percent of the surveyed NSI teachers reported regularly implementing each practice in fall 2021. Ninety-eight percent of them expressed a desire to continue implementing the student-centered practices with leadership support.

In terms of academic performance and its relationship to levels of teachers' implementation, high school teachers implementing many of the practices saw significant and large impacts on the English SA for all student groups, particularly benefiting girls, Hispanic students, Black students, and students with special needs. Middle school teachers implementing many of the student-centered practices saw a small overall impact on the ELA SA, with larger benefits for Black students. NSI middle schools outperformed comparable schools on MAP Reading and the DCA across all grades, and all student groups in the NSI middle schools performed better on the 2022 SA in ELA/Reading (grades 6–8) compared to similar district schools. All student groups in the NSI high schools outperformed comparable district schools on the 9th grade English SA.

Teachers' and Leaders' Engagement with the Network as Measured by a Network Health Survey

Researchers from a third-party project launched a network health survey in 2021 to provide the NSI with relative strengths and weaknesses in the Network's development in six domains: Hub Leadership, Network Roles & Engagement, Network Connections, Network Culture, Continuous Improvement, and Contexts for Improvement. Here are key highlights from the fourth-year health survey that showed the BCSD/IFL NSI doing well in network value, benefits, and strengths in collaborations and team learning.

- The BCSD/IFL NSI ranked ninth overall out of thirty-four similar networks surveyed and fifth among networks aiming to improve classroom instruction, and received the highest ratings for perceived benefits, continuous improvement confidence, school team collaborative inquiry, and cross-team learning.
- Two-thirds or more of Network members reported high benefits from Network participation and indicated that the NSI fostered rich cross-school collaborations.

On-Track 8th and 9th Grade Indicators

We also looked at whether 8th and 9th graders were on track for completing high school, getting into college, and being successful in college and careers. The best available indicators are a combination of total completed credits, lack of failures, a GPA of at least 3.0, high attendance, and lack of suspensions. For the 2021–22 school year, attendance and suspensions were removed from the on-track evaluation due to large changes in reporting during COVID-19.

The on-track data were included as a part of the fourth-year evaluation of impact report.

NSI schools saw increased percentages from previous years of 8th and 9th graders meeting the on-track indicators, with dramatic gains on combined outcomes and better gains for all groups on the 2021–22 indicators. For 8th grade, 85 percent of all students met the combined measure, including 92 percent of Black students and 87 percent of Hispanic students. Ninety-nine percent of all students had sufficient course credits for promotion to the next grade and 89 percent of students failed no more than one semester course in a core subject.

For 9th grade, 59 percent of all students met the combined measure (compared to 45 percent in the prior year, 2020–21), with 56 percent of Black students and 62 percent of Hispanic students meeting it. Ninety-six percent of all students had sufficient course credits for promotion to the next grade and 71 percent of students failed no more than one semester course in a core subject.

We should note that although the NSI was required to use on-track indicators every year and contracted with a third-party vendor to provide the data, our analytics team felt strongly that these measures weren't good indicators of the NSI's effects. Our interventions were specific to ELA and would have had a relationship to the on-track indicators, but we didn't have a way to understand or report that relationship, although we did report our own analysis of the indicators in the fourth-year evaluation report.

A More In-Depth View of the Fourth-Year Data

Following this summary, we now describe in more depth (1) the teachers' levels of implementation of the practices, (2) students' growth on MAP Reading, and achievement on the DCA and the ELA SA compared to similar students in the district, (3) students' growth on MAP Reading and the ELA SA related to teachers' levels of implementation, (4) teachers' and leaders' engagement with the Network and improvement science from the network health survey, and (5) teachers' and leaders' empathy interviews 2.0.

Teachers' Levels of Implementation

To dig deeper into the implementation data, we'll begin by comparing the third and fourth year teacher survey results. You've already read the results from the third year (Table 2.1). So that you can see the change from that third year of hybrid instruction to the fourth year (Table 2.2) when in-person instruction returned, we summarize the differences in those years after Table 2.2.

Please note that our analytics team refined the survey in the fourth year, and cross-referenced teachers' responses to observations of their classes when possible, so although the comparisons aren't exact, they overlap in what they portray about teachers' levels of implementation for these two years.

In the third year, as you can see in Table 2.1 on page 58, 69 percent of teachers reported regularly implementing each student-centered practice. Only 46 percent had students work in pairs/trios in the third year, while 78 percent did so in the fourth year. Sixty-four percent asked students to annotate the text for meaning in the third year while 84 percent did so in the fourth. All in all, most teachers in the fourth year regularly implemented each practice (i.e., at least three to four times per nine-week period), indicated they could successfully implement each practice using their own or provided materials, and would have liked to continue implementing the practices if their use was supported by leadership.

The growth from the third to the fourth year in teachers' implementation and willingness to implement using their own materials or those provided for them was striking to us. For the most part, we felt confident in the teachers' uptake of at least some of the practices in the third year with 69 percent of the teachers regularly implementing them, but at the same time, only 46 percent asked students to work in pairs and trios. Pair/trio discussions were the primary opportunities for students to collaborate with their peers, to exchange ideas, and to reason about and from the texts with each other. Those collaborations seemed to us to be critical. Teachers' uptake of their use would matter to students. When we saw that in the fourth year, 78 percent said they regularly used the pair/trios for students, we began to feel confident that students' collaborations would support their growth in thinking and reasoning about and from texts.

Table 2.2 Percentage of teachers who regularly implemented student-centered practices in the 4th year

Percentage of teachers who…	Have students annotate the text for meaning (i.e., more than vocab)	Have students do comprehension work before other text work	Have students work in pairs/trios	Have students do quick writes about initial ideas about the text	Assign a rigorous text	Have students work from a task sheet	Average
…regularly implemented each practice in fall 2021	84%	78%	78%	80%	84%	73%	79%
…could successfully implement using provided materials	98%	98%	98%	93%	96%	89%	95%
…could successfully implement using own materials	93%	91%	87%	91%	78%	80%	87%
…would like to continue to implement (if supported by leadership)	100%	100%	100%	95%	98%	95%	98%

Students' Growth on MAP Reading Comprehension, the DCA, and Achievement on the ELA SA Compared to Similar Classes in the District

Reading Comprehension Growth and English Achievement for NSI Middle Schools

To read the middle school charts (Figure 2.2), you'll need to know that the NSI middle schools were part of a district project we're calling Reaching New Heights (RNH). The RNH initiative, which aimed to improve student performance through tutoring and other academic programs, began in 2019 with twenty-three middle schools.

In the fourth year of the NSI project, our analytics team generated data sets to compare the NSI middle schools with the other RNH schools, regardless of level of implementation.

From the chart, we see that NSI middle schools outperformed other RNH middle schools with similar BOY performance on MOY MAP reading comprehension and on the MOY ELA DCA in every grade, regardless of level of implementation. Although our working assumption was that all RNH schools received comparable support, we should note that most, but not all, of the NSI schools adapted the RNH protocol for PLCs to reflect their integration of the student-centered practices. They also adapted the monitoring protocols

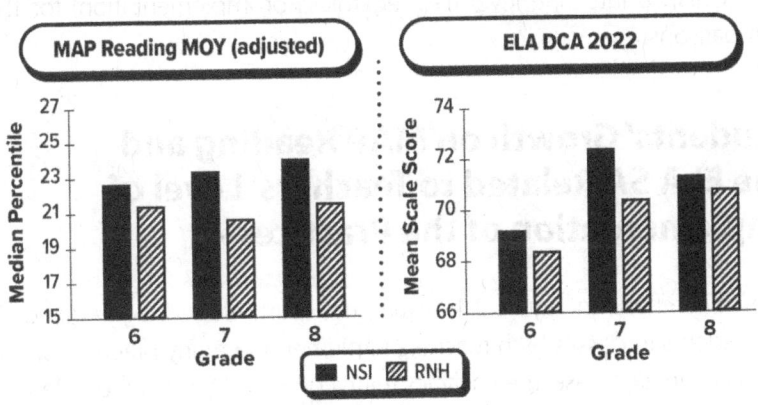

Figure 2.2 Comparison of NSI middle schools to non-NSI similar middle schools (RNH schools) on MAP Reading growth and the DCA in the 4th year.

that were used by school leaders to observe and coach teachers in their mostly scripted lessons, so that leaders could make use of the NSI's *Learning Walk* to focus on teachers' implementation of the student-centered practices.

The two charts in Figure 2.3 look at performance on the SA, disaggregated by subgroup. They compare the NSI middle schools with the other RNH middle schools and the NSI high schools with comparable district high schools, regardless of level of implementation.

From the charts in Figure 2.3, we see that when we compared NSI middle schools on the 2022 SA to the other district RNH middle schools for every specific group of students, performance was higher in NSI middle schools, with an especially large difference for Black students, regardless of level of implementation.

When we compared NSI high schools to comparable district high schools on 9th grade English SA 2022 scores, we saw that for every specific group, NSI students' performance was higher, with relatively higher performance for Hispanic, Black, and economically disadvantaged students, regardless of level of implementation.

Our analytics team did these comparisons regardless of level of implementation partly because during this fourth year implementation was strong, with 79 percent of the surveyed teachers reporting regular use of the practices, and partly because we wanted accurate school-by-school comparisons. The numbers of teachers in the NSI schools reporting low levels of implementation (i.e., 21 percent) was small enough to warrant their collapse into one level (i.e., regardless of implementation) for these comparisons.

Students' Growth on MAP Reading and the ELA SA Related to Teachers' Level of Implementation of the Practices

The three charts in Figure 2.4 display the fourth-year disaggregated data for students in classes with teachers implementing many practices and few practices. In each case, the analytics team controlled for minor differences in beginning of year reading levels.

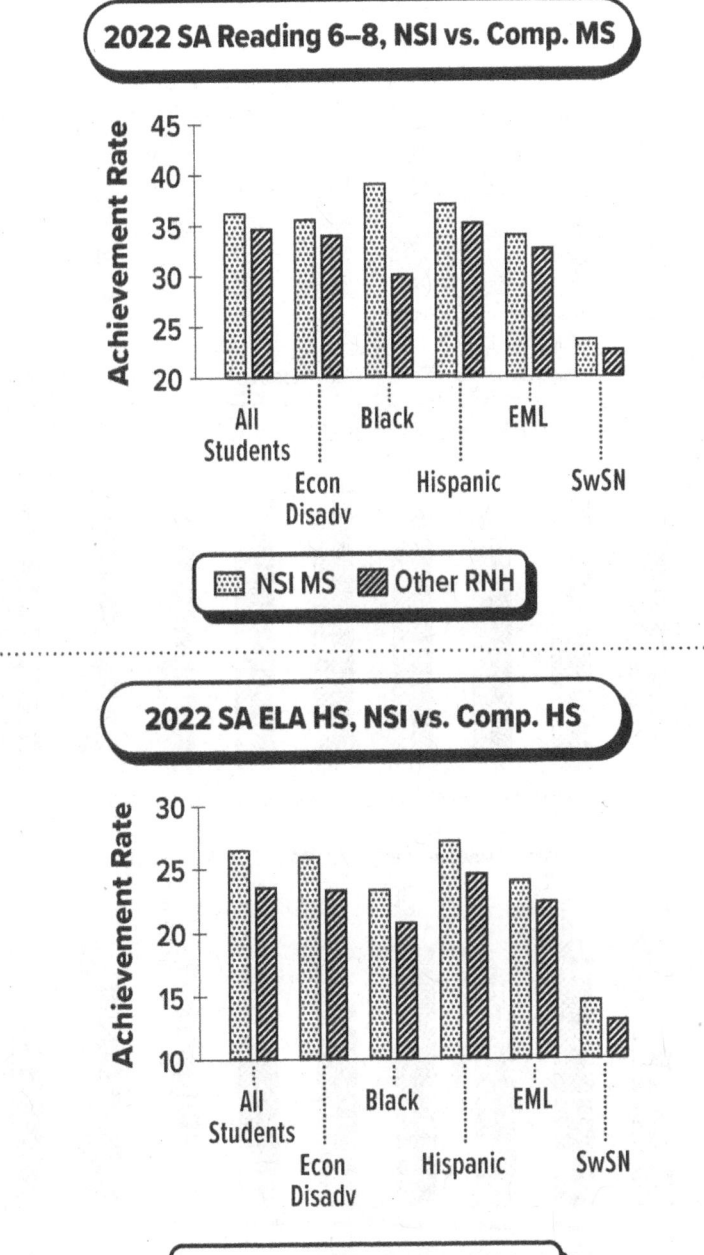

Figure 2.3 Comparison of NSI schools to non-NSI similar schools on the 2022 SA ELA (grades 6–8) and 9th grade English.

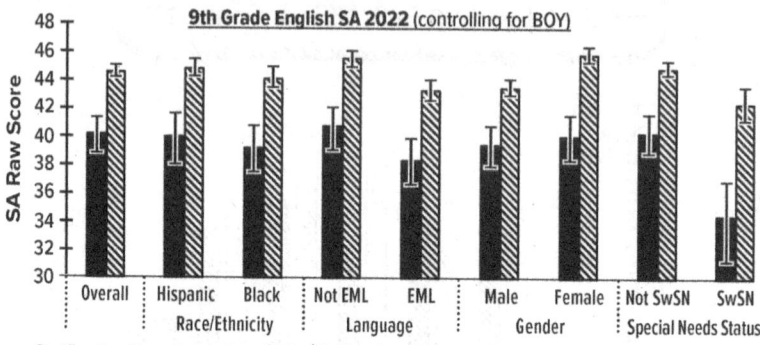
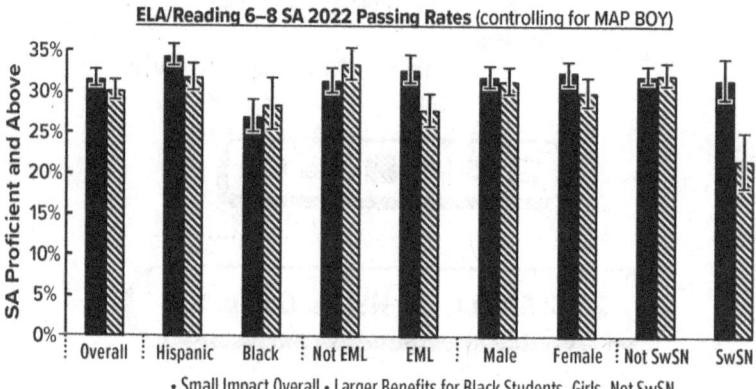
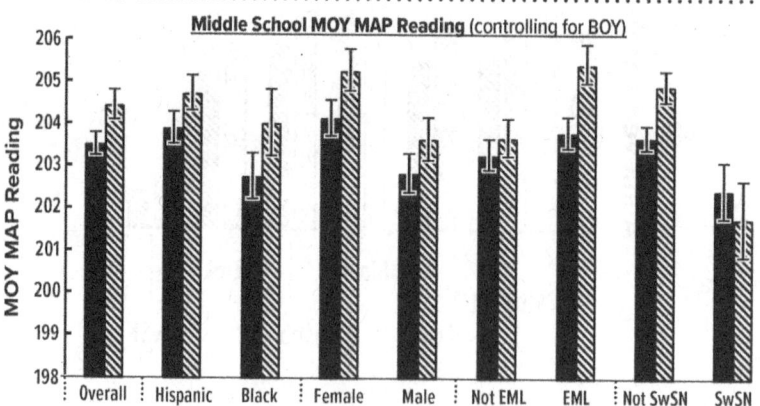

Figure 2.4 Year 4 SA ELA results for 6–8 th and 9th grades, and middle school MAP Reading, related to depth of implementation of the practices.

The first chart shows 9th grade English SA raw scores from the spring of 2022. The second chart shows passing rates (proficient and above) for 6th to 8th grades for the spring 2022 Reading SA. The third chart shows middle school students' scores on the MAP Reading test. ("SwSN" refers to Students with Special Needs. "EML" refers to Emergent Multilingual students.)

The analysis of student performance on the SA and MAP reading comprehension revealed a complex picture with varying impacts across different grade levels and student groups. From the first chart, we see that high school students in high-implementation 9th grade English classes demonstrated significant and substantial improvements on the SA. From the second chart, we see that middle school students showed only small differences in performance based on implementation levels. EML students, girls, and students with special needs did not show the same level of improvement.

Several factors may explain the relatively flat middle school performance. The SA underwent significant changes in 2022, including new item types and a shift to online administration. Middle school teachers reported that students struggled with the new online format, particularly with text annotation. The inability to annotate directly on the text as they had been taught, and having to move between the text on the computer and their annotations on notepaper, may have caused confusion and time management issues. And, of course, the degree of implementation may have had less of an effect in the fourth year compared to previous years.

Interestingly, from the third chart, we see middle school students in high-implementation classes significantly outperforming others on the MAP Reading test, for all student groups except students with special needs. We're not sure how to explain the differences for middle school students across the SA and MAP, although NSI middle school teachers were fairly certain that their students, particularly the 6th and 7th graders, were affected by the new SA online format and the array of different item types. It is also likely that MAP is both a more rigorous and consistent assessment of comprehension skills that the NSI focused on than the SA.

Teachers' and Leaders' Engagement with the Network as Measured by a Network Health Survey

The boxplots that you are about to see in Figure 2.5 show the BCSD/IFL NSI's performance in comparison to thirty-three other NSIs that were surveyed as a part of the third-party network health project over the third and fourth years of implementation, focusing on three key measures: benefits of network participation, school team collaboration, and cross-school team collaboration.

Key Features of the Visualization

The graph uses diamonds to represent the BCSD/IFL NSI's mean scores for each measure, while lighter boxplots with horizontal "whiskers" display the minimum and maximum values of the distribution of scores for the thirty-four NSIs. The visual arrangement provides the context for the NSI's performance relative to its peers.

Each boxplot contains several elements that offer insights into the data distribution, including:

- The box itself represents the middle 50 percent of the NSI scores, also known as the interquartile range.
- The horizontal line within the box indicates the median response.
- Vertical bars extending above and below the box show the full range of responses, including maximum and minimum values.

The positioning of the diamonds relative to the boxplots reveals areas where the BCSD/IFL NSI demonstrated sustained strength and improvement over the two-year period.

Interpreting the Boxplots

The boxplots reveal several key strengths of the BCSD/IFL NSI across three critical areas: network participation benefits, collaboration in school-based teams, and cross-school learning opportunities. The first boxplot indicates that a significant majority of the participants, at least two-thirds, strongly endorsed the benefits of participating in the Network. This high level of satisfaction, in comparison to the previous year, stems primarily from two key advantages: (1) access to fresh ideas and perspectives from colleagues,

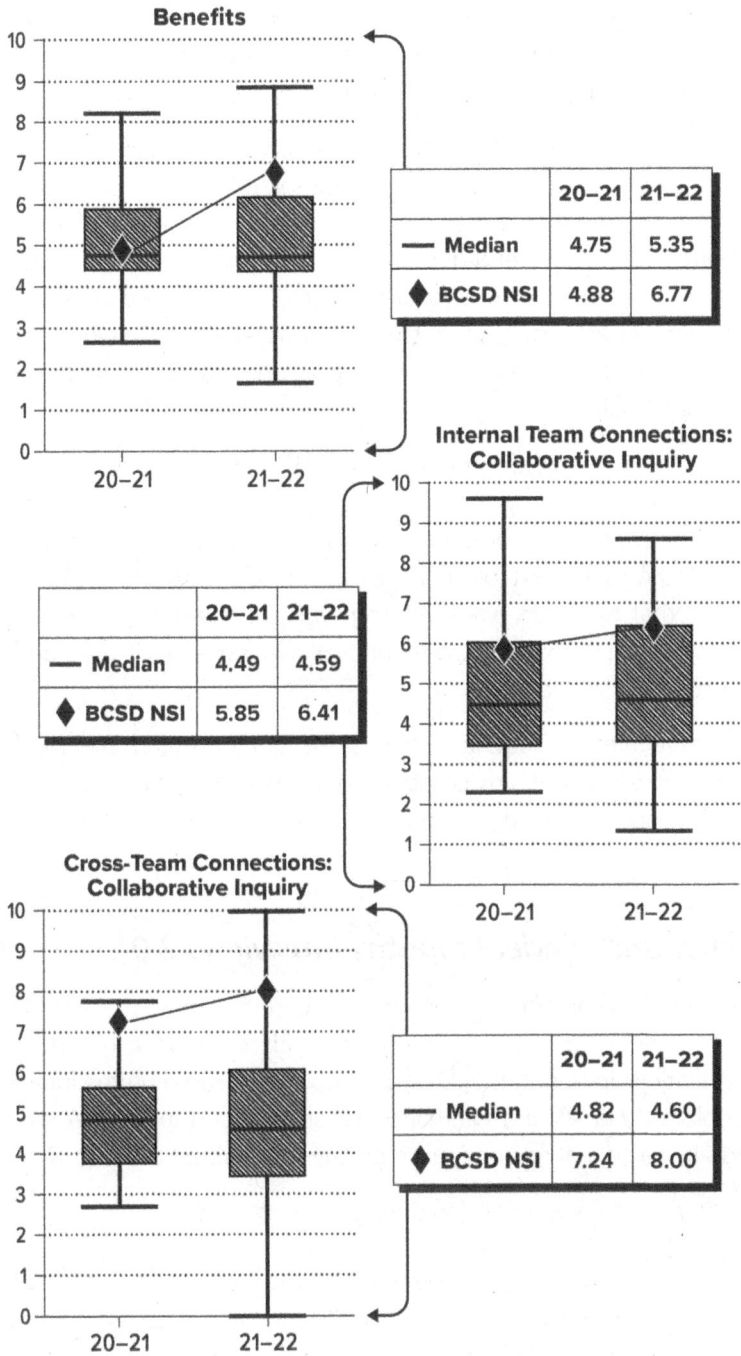

Figure 2.5 Boxplots of three key health survey measures: benefits of Network participation, school team collaboration, and cross-school team collaboration.

and (2) a sense of belonging to a larger community united by a common purpose. These benefits suggest that the Network was successfully fostering a collaborative and supportive environment for its participants.

The second boxplot reveals that the Network effectively promoted substantial collaborations among school-based teams, particularly as a way for members to use collaborative inquiry to solve problems. This collaboration is characterized by teachers working together to identify promising changes in instructional practices and collective efforts to test and implement approaches to instruction. This level of teamwork indicates a strong commitment to continuous improvement and innovations within individual schools.

Perhaps the most notable strength of the NSI was in its ability to facilitate cross-school collaborations, as shown in the third boxplot. The Network excelled in creating opportunities for educators to learn from colleagues in other schools and established itself as a leader within the broader NSI initiatives that were surveyed. This emphasis on inter-school learning and collaboration set the NSI apart, positioning it as a model of effective network-based educational improvement.

These three areas of strength collectively demonstrated the Network's success in creating a vibrant, collaborative ecosystem that promoted shared learning, innovation, and continuous improvement in instruction across multiple schools.

Teacher and Leader Empathy Interviews 2.0

To better understand the experiences of participants in the NSI, the IFL coaches conducted empathy interviews with teachers and school and district leadership during the 2021–22 school year. Based on the interviews, we published our second internal bright spots report in 2023. A thematic analysis revealed that respondents regularly spoke about the following:

- Prioritizing comprehension during ELA instruction:

    Just to see them genuinely engaged with the text and be curious about it was really great for me.... We had a text that was accessible to them, a task sheet that focused on comprehension first, and we spent two

class periods—one on just understanding, the other one on analysis of the language—and it was really one of the bright spots ...
—High School Teacher

- Using student-centered practices to focus the classroom on student learning

    When I do observations and things like that, I am looking for student-centered [practices]. *I see a difference in lessons with the student-centered [practices]*, like when students are taking ownership of their learning and they're demonstrating things and they're having conversations with each other.
    —High School Administrator

- Using and adapting IFL tools for their classrooms, including adaptations for high-quality, rigorous, virtual instruction:

    [I]t was a little rough at first, but they kept working on it.... And then on the task sheet questions—I actually started making all of them open-ended because, as you know, we had to do multiple choice 90 percent of the year.... *And that was how I eased them into it ... where it's one or two sentences to tell me your thoughts, and then it kind of revolved into "Okay, now I need full paragraphs. We're going to start planning essays."* And so that really helped their confidence because they got to start small and go bigger and bigger and have bigger goals.
    —High School Teacher

- How students responded to new texts, tasks, and ways of teaching:

    I think you got to see a side of them that they probably would not have shown if we were not reading a text to where *they can really make those connections. We got to see it, even like in their quick writes*, how they felt about borders. And those borders didn't even have to pertain to the wall; it was like borders that limit them in things they're trying to accomplish. So, we took it as like this cultural piece, but then they were able to expand on it ...
    —Middle School Teacher

> Through some of the IFL work, it's really great to see in my classroom, to watch kids get in where they fit in. And then *they feel empowered to see themselves or engage in the work in whatever way works for them*.... And I feel like a lot of that is tied to the IFL work, and by just allowing kids to have entry points into the text and the work in the best way for them. You really get to see that happen with the kids when you're going through some of those routines and things like that.... If it's not my biggest success, it is my favorite success because it allows kids to learn and engage in a way that is relevant and meaningful to them. And that's, that's really what I'm here for, so watching that happen is awesome.
> —High School Teacher

- The power of the Network to drive individual professional growth and build a shared culture around continuous improvement:

  > I truly believe we're going to have shifts in mindsets that are collaborative and not one-offs. That we engage in this work that we do from a collaborative standpoint. That *you see the impact that leaders are having in the work. You see the impact teachers are having in the work and then, most importantly, students in the work* and so that has been my approach and it helps with the design of professional development. But more importantly, it is a clear direction on where we're going, and that we are committed to continuous improvement, so we have opportunities for feedback, but we're speaking the same language and there is a clear vision set.
  > —High School Teacher

As with the first set of empathy interviews that we conducted in 2021, these fourth-year interviews also point to the importance teachers placed on giving students opportunities to begin their work with texts with comprehension, before the typical analyses of such things as structure or organization, the use of literary devices, and grammatical sentence constructions. We again see praise for the student-centered practices opening up space for students to take ownership for their learning, have conversations with each other, and feel empowered to engage with texts in ways that make sense to them. The statement about the Network fostering collaborative mindsets reflects what we saw in our network health survey data on the strengths of the Network to drive collaborations and cross-team collaborative inquiry.

Key Fifth-Year Outcomes

The Key Components of the Evaluation

The NSI analytics team's fifth-year outcomes report from 2023 provided comprehensive data on the performance of NSI schools compared to similar district and state schools. As with our other evaluation reports, we shared the 2023 report with the NSI teams and district colleagues.

The report featured three key analyses. First, it compared ELA SA outcomes for NSI schools across three academic years: 2018–19, 2021–22, and 2022–23 (in 2020–21, the state did not administer the assessment). This longitudinal analysis allowed for tracking progress over time, including during the period affected by the COVID-19 pandemic. Second, the report included teacher implementation data gathered through surveys assessing the frequency, ability, and willingness of teachers to implement the NSI's test of change—the student-centered practices. Our analysis examined the relationship between the depth of implementation of the practices and growth in student SA performance, helping to establish the link between the implementation of the practices and student outcomes. Lastly, the report compared NSI schools to carefully matched district and state urban schools.

Key Takeaways from the Evaluation

The report reveals several significant findings. NSI middle and high schools demonstrated exceptionally strong implementation of the practices during Years 4 and 5, with the highest level observed in NSI high schools during Year 5. Most teachers reported implementing these practices at least three to four times per nine-week period and expressed willingness to continue with leadership support.

> "A clear positive relationship was found between high implementation of the practices and student performance on the outcomes we measured."

A clear positive relationship was found between high implementation of the practices and student performance on the outcomes we measured. Students in classes with high implementation consistently scored higher across all 2022–23 outcome measures, including MAP reading comprehension, DCA, SA ELA, and SA 9th grade English, compared to peers in low-implementation classes.

Furthermore, students in NSI schools demonstrated significantly higher performance compared to their counterparts in closely matched district non-NSI schools and other urban schools across the state. Their outperformance suggested that the NSI had a positive impact on student achievement.

Following this summary of the key components and takeaways of the evaluation, we will now describe in more detail (1) the implementation of the student-centered practices, (2) passing rates on the 2022–23 SA by grade level, and (3) comparison of NSI schools to comparable district and state schools.

Implementation of the Student-centered Practices

Data from the fourth and fifth years showed exceptionally strong implementation of the practices, with a higher level in Year 5 than in Year 4 as well as higher regular implementation in high schools than in middle schools. Although growth in implementation might be expected in a continuing project such as the NSI in its fifth year, that year we also saw many new teachers—both new to the profession and new to the district—join the project. Table 2.3 presents Years 4 and 5 data on the NSI teachers in middle and high schools who regularly implemented each of the student-centered practices.

As you can see, even though fewer middle school teachers responded to the implementation survey in Year 5, the differences in the percentages of teachers using the practices are dramatic. While the number of 9th grade teachers who responded from Year 4 to 5 is fairly consistent, here again the differences in the percentages using the practices is substantial. It's likely that during both of these years, a core of teachers and schools emerged as leaders in integrating and adapting the practices, and it's likely that they were the ones who responded to the survey. By the fourth year, three of the NSI middle schools saw their commitments to the NSI waiver or drift away for a

Table 2.3 Percentages of teachers who regularly implemented each student-centered practice by middle school and high school in the 4th and 5th years

	2022 (Year 4)		2023 (Year 5)	
NSI Student-Centered Practice	MS (n=32)	HS (n=10)	MS (n=23)	HS (n=13)
Rigorous text selection	75%	50%	87%	85%
Task sheets	41%	70%	70%	92%
Comprehension first	69%	90%	91%	100%
Quick writes	69%	60%	91%	100%
Text annotation	75%	90%	96%	100%
Pair/trio / charting	62%	70%	100%	85%

number of reasons, so the explanation that what we're seeing in these data are responses from the NSI core has some weight.

Passing Rates on the Assessment in Relation to Levels of Implementation

In this section, we discuss the relationship of teachers' implementation of the student-centered practices to their students' Year 5 assessment scores. To test whether the high performance of the NSI schools could be attributed to the focus of the NSI effort (versus other things going on in those schools), we examined the connections between relative growth in student performance and depth of implementation of the practices.

In Figure 2.6, using z-scores to standardize 2022–23 MAP Reading scores (MOY and EOY) and fall ELA DCA and ELA SA data, we show the relationship between teachers who regularly implemented the student-centered practices and their students' outcomes.

From Figure 2.6, across all outcome measures, we see that students in classrooms with teachers who implemented practices more frequently scored higher than their peers whose teachers were low implementers. These analyses control for minor differences in beginning of year reading levels. Z-scores (converted to a mean of 0 and standard deviation of 1) were

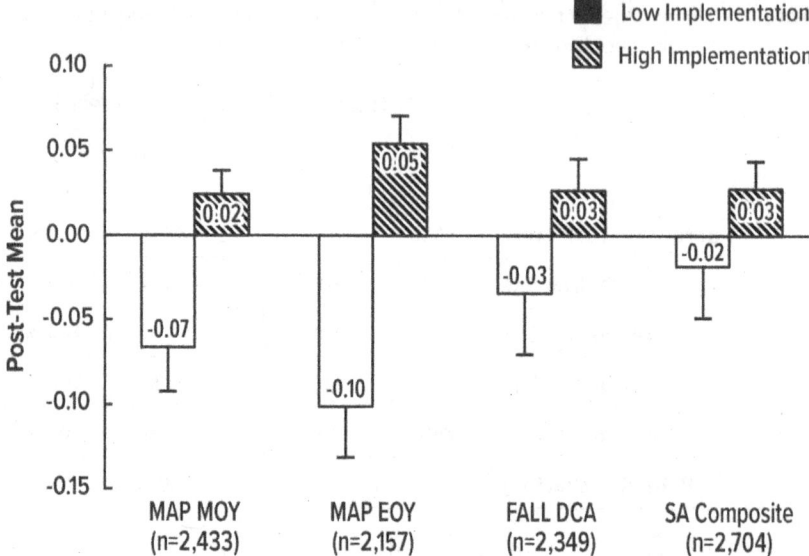

Figure 2.6 Post-test means and standard errors for students in low- vs. high-implementation classrooms across 2022–23 Reading/ELA assessments: MAP MOY, MAP EOY, DCA, and SA (using z-scores for standardization).

used for each measure to allow for easy comparison across the measures. Effects are statistically significant for all measures. Larger effects were seen using the MAP data. The MAP-based effects were likely to be a better estimate of the true effects of the NSI on students' underlying skills (and therefore success in high school and college) given the broader range of skills being assessed.

Passing Rates on the State Assessment by Grade Level

We also examined the proportions of students who were proficient and above on the 2022–23 ELA SA, which counts as passing. Figure 2.7 presents the proportions of students who scored in the passing range by low- and high-implementation classes.

Reading Figure 2.7, we see that consistently, when teachers more regularly implemented the student-centered practices, their students were significantly more likely to obtain a passing score. We see larger effects at the high school level, which may reflect the broader range of skills being measured on the 9th grade English assessment, the stronger implementation levels reported

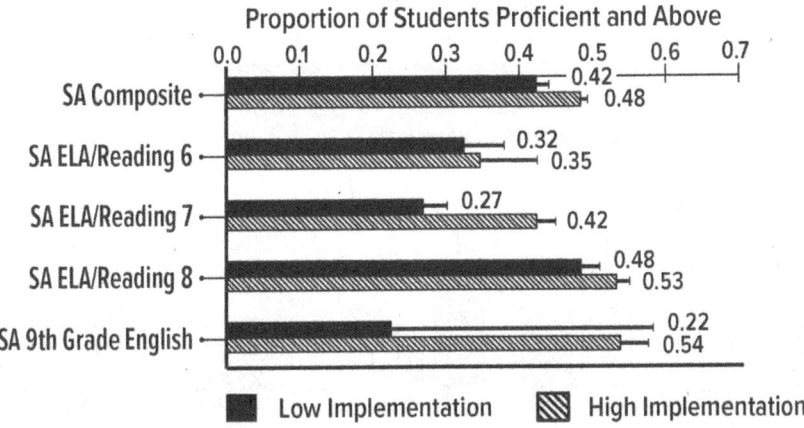

Figure 2.7 Proportions (with SE bars) of students who scored proficient and above on the 2022–23 ELA 6–8 and English I SA in low- vs. high-implementation classrooms.

by 9th grade teachers, and the number of years most 9th grade English students would have been exposed to the practices.

NSI Schools versus Similar District and State Urban Schools

To evaluate whether NSI schools had better overall ELA scores on the SA, our analytics team developed an algorithm for finding appropriate comparison schools. They focused on schools that had been rated C or lower in 2018–19 (when our project began, before school teams started making changes in instruction). For each NSI school, they found a set of closely matching "twins" with similar ELA performance in 2018–19 and student demographics. In this analysis, they dropped schools for which there was no twin. They ran the algorithm twice, first using only other BCSD secondary schools, and then using all urban (non-charter) secondary schools. They tracked the changes in ELA SA performance (i.e., the percentage of students proficient and above) into Years 4 and 5. Across these analyses, students in the NSI schools outperformed carefully matched schools, especially at the high school level (Figures 2.8 and 2.9).

Reading Figure 2.8, we see that the NSI schools had double the overall growth from Year 1 to Year 5 when compared to other BCSD secondary schools and three times the growth when compared with similar urban schools in the

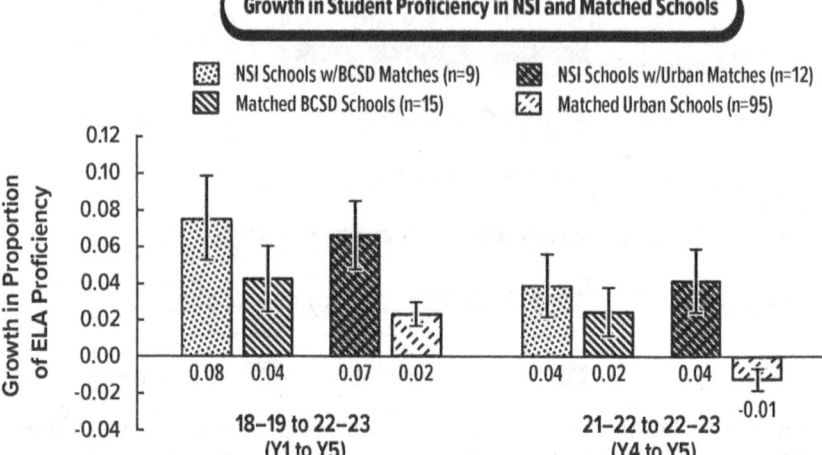

Figure 2.8 SA growth (Year 1 to Year 5 left; Year 4 to Year 5 right) in NSI high schools compared to matching BCSD and urban high schools.

state. Further, there were meaningful differences in growth within just the fourth and fifth years of the project (i.e., from Year 4 to Year 5; right side of Figure 2.8). In the next chart, you'll see that NSI high schools had greater gains than the middle schools relative to their BCSD matches, and both high schools and middle schools had greater gains relative to their state-wide matches.

Reading Figure 2.9, we see comparable performance on the SA in NSI middle schools and their district matches, but greater gains in NSI high schools relative to their district matches. We also see greater gains in the NSI schools relative to their state matches in both middle and high schools.

When we shared these data with the teachers and administrators, they speculated that the stronger performance of the 9th grade students could be related to the number of years that they were exposed to the student-centered practices. If they were in NSI classes in middle school (which is likely because the NSI middle schools somewhat imperfectly feed into NSI high schools), they could have come to 9th grade with three years of student-centered instruction at least three to four times in one to three nine-week periods. Middle school students' performance could be relatively flat because that population included a substantial number of EML 6th grade students.

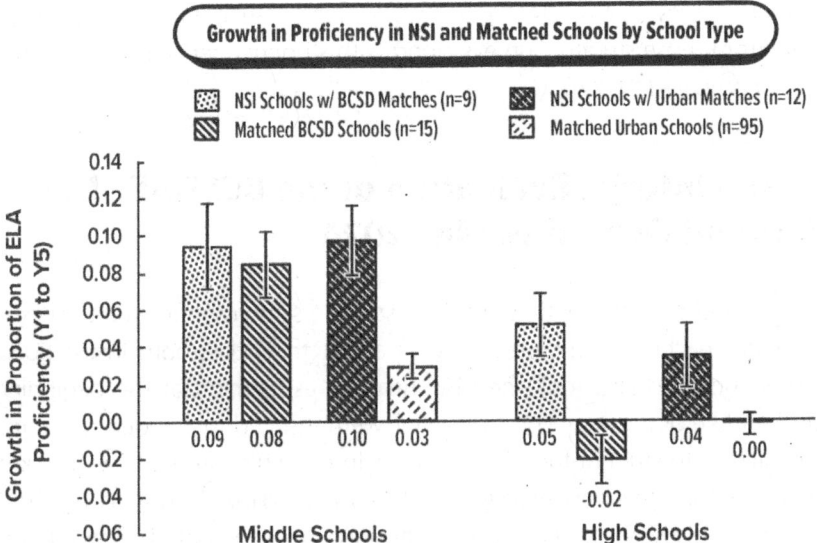

Figure 2.9 Year 1 to Year 5 SA growth in NSI middle schools (left) and high schools (right) compared to matching district and urban schools.

According to district policy, students no longer receive bilingual instruction when they reach 6th grade, and from 6th grade on, they take all their assessments in English.

Key Sixth-Year Outcomes

In the sixth and final year of the NSI, the NSI analytics team didn't issue its usual annual evaluation report. We reconfigured the monthly middle school teacher meetings, so that we could focus on building capacity with instructional district coaches and building-level mentor teachers to carry on leading the use of the student-centered practices and making instructional adaptations at schools after the IFL NSI coaches left. Because of this change in the Network meeting attendance, we didn't administer the teacher implementation survey. And so, we didn't analyze for high and low implementation or relate implementation with students' performance on MAP or the SA.

However, when we negotiated a data sharing contract with the district, it allowed us to survey students. In the sixth year, we administered our first student survey. In May 2024, our analytics team issued its evaluation using data from those student surveys along with students' performance on MAP MOY compared to BOY.

Year 6 Interim Evaluation of the BCSD/IFL NSI Student Outcomes May 2024

Three hundred and twenty-four middle schoolers (representing three schools, thirteen teachers) completed surveys about their classroom instructional experience and also took the MAP Reading assessment at the beginning and middle of the year. For the survey, we translated the student-centered practices into student-friendly language. In particular, students were asked whether their teachers usually asked them to: follow steps—as in a task sheet—using slides or a handout, write/talk about the big ideas or authors' purpose first, highlight/annotate the text, write initial ideas about the text in a quick write, and discuss the text with a partner.

As shown in Figure 2.10, 25 percent of the surveyed students regularly experienced all five student-centered practices, and almost half experienced four or five. Relatively few students only experienced one or none.

We then examined whether there was a relationship between how many student-centered practices students reported regularly experiencing

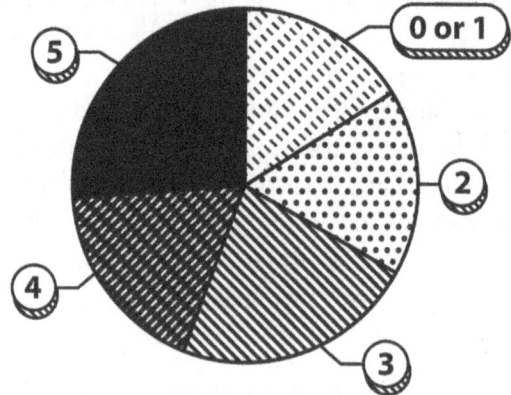

Figure 2.10 The relative frequency of total regularly experienced student-centered practices.

and the growth they showed on the MAP assessment from beginning to middle of year. There was a statistically significant relationship. Figure 2.11 presents the MAP MOY scores for students as a function of how many practices they regularly experienced, controlling for small differences at the beginning of the year. There is a near linear relationship between the two. Further, the difference across the range is meaningful. Over that time period, students gained on average three points (just below national means), but the difference shown in outcomes between zero/one and five practices is greater than that. Table 2.4 shows the relationship to mean MAP gains.

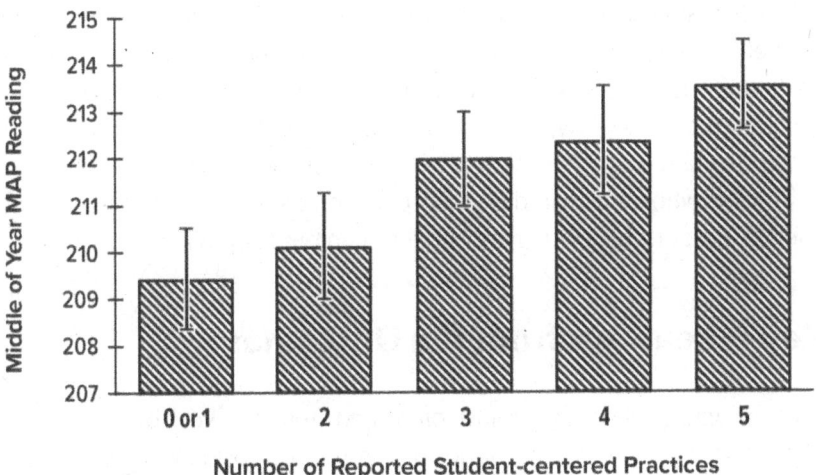

Figure 2.11 MOY MAP Reading as a function of number of experiences of student-centered practices, controlling for BOY MAP.

Table 2.4 The relationship of the number of practices students experienced and mean MAP gains

Number of Practices	MAP Gain
0 or 1	0.1
2	-0.1
3	1.7
4	3.2
5	4.3

> *"The most significant gains were seen in students who participated in all five of the practices. This points to the high effectiveness of a fully integrated student-centered approach."*

More Is Better

When we read these data, we see that more student-centered practices led to better performance. Students who regularly engaged in more of the student-centered practices showed greater improvements in their MAP reading comprehension scores. The more of these practices students experienced, the better they performed. Minimal to no engagement led to stagnation or decline. Students, that is, who engaged in only one or none of the student-centered practices showed almost no improvement or even a slight decline in their reading comprehension scores. The most significant gains were seen in students who participated in all five of the practices. This points to the high effectiveness of a fully integrated student-centered approach.

Key Takeaways from the Outcomes

Looking across the data we just presented from the year-by-year review of outcomes, we see six big trends. These trends provide key insights into the implementation and impact of the student-centered practices—the NSI's tests of change—in the NSI schools, highlighting areas of success and improvement.

1. High-implementation classes consistently outperformed low-implementation classes. From the third to the sixth year of the NSI, students in high-implementation classes consistently and significantly outpaced their peers in low-implementation classes across various assessments: MAP reading comprehension, the DCA, and the ELA and 9th grade English SAs.

2. High schools showed higher implementation compared to middle schools. From the third to the sixth year, high schools showed consistently higher implementation of the student-centered practices and stronger achievement gains compared to middle schools. This is

particularly true of the fourth year when high-implementing classes in middle schools had flat SA scores in comparison to low-implementing schools. As we discussed, the possible reasons for this flat middle school performance compared to the rising high school performance include the changed SA formats and the online administration. High schools also had greater flexibility for adapting the practices to their curriculum, the relative freedom to use supplemental texts, and access to more worthy texts in their curriculum and in their supplemental materials.

3. Teacher interest and confidence in the student-centered practices increased every year. By the fifth year, on the implementation survey, 95–100 percent of the teachers across all NSI schools reported their interest in continuing to use the student-centered practices, whether they developed the materials or whether they were provided with them. Even with this interest, many teachers—particularly middle school teachers—continued to express lower confidence in assigning rigorous texts. From our meetings with teachers, we learned that they seldom had time to search for appropriate texts within the resources available to them in the district, so they had to rely on a curriculum that presented them with texts with varying levels of interest and rigor. Teachers in low-achieving schools, and with principals whose support for the NSI drifted, pointed to the systemic issues that required them to teach from district-supplied scripted lessons that shifted the intellectual work from students to teachers.

4. NSI schools outperformed carefully matched district and state urban schools. On the SA, students in the NSI schools outperformed their counterparts in carefully matched district and state urban schools, especially at the high school level. Students in the NSI middle schools had gains that were similar to their district-matched schools, but significantly larger gains compared to matched state urban schools. A possible interpretation of high schools' greater gains when compared to middle schools on the district matches is that those students benefited from years of exposure to the practices in their feeder middle schools.

5. Students' performance on the MAP reading comprehension assessment benefited from the quantity of the practices they experienced. Students who reported regular engagement in more of the student-centered practices showed more improvement on their MAP reading comprehension scores from the beginning of the year to the middle

of the year. Students who regularly engaged in all of the practices showed MAP Reading gains at the national average, while students with minimal or no engagement showed stagnated and declining scores. We conjecture that baseline ELA instruction with none or few of the practices likely focused on skills other than comprehension, which is supported by what we saw in classrooms. When teachers, for instance, taught mostly to the district-identified "power standards"—those likely to be tested on the SA—we observed little to no opportunities for comprehension or meaning making. The texts used in those kinds of lessons are simply vehicles for teaching a particular standard or a skill. Lessons seemed to us to be fragmented, jumping from one standard to another.

6. Improvement is a zigzag walk rather than a linear run. As you will have noticed, improvement did not move smoothly forward in an orderly progression. We came the closest to consistent progress in 9th grade classes where students already had several years of work with high-level comprehension tasks and the student-centered practices. Rather than building comprehension muscles, the work in high school was about continuing to refine comprehension skills and using those skills to support analytic and interpretive tasks.

As we have shown above, the middle school data were more variable. We believe that variability was caused by significant shifts in the curriculum and the ways teachers took up NSI support to understand and adapt curricular materials. Just before the project began, the district began to develop a new ELA curriculum for grades 6–8, and administrators continued to tweak expectations as time went on. By the third year of the NSI, middle school teachers had been working with the curriculum in different iterations for two years; they adapted the texts and tasks as needed and had solidified a set of comprehension tasks that they found to be effective for their students. We expect this benefited students' performances on MAP in the third year. In Year 4, teachers were still figuring out how to get students back to learning fully in person—as much of the country was. The Network provided support and space to share and discuss those challenges, especially as teachers worked to return students to using talk to develop and share their thinking. Middle school teachers who fully engaged in Network meetings tended to be the high implementers at that point. They continued to include the student-centered practices in their instruction and made evidence-driven adjustments along the way. In class observations and discussions with middle school teachers, we saw and heard about the struggles all teachers faced in getting students to talk to each other in productive ways, which we believe may have affected the effectiveness of the practices for a time.

In Year 5, the NSI middle schools pilot tested what we're calling the New Curriculum and in Year 6, they implemented that curriculum. This posed significant challenges for the NSI schools. In some schools, the ELA teams had developed their own units of instruction that embedded the student-centered practices into lessons. One school, for example, developed a Harlem Renaissance unit that included literature, historical reports, art, and music from that period. They developed this unit over the course of two years of engagement, much of it with their NSI colleagues, and were excited to have it to teach in the fifth year. That year, however, they felt they had to drop it and pilot test the New Curriculum. Another NSI middle school had developed a novel-based curriculum that also included thematically aligned nonfiction and poetry. The team from that school felt that they too had to drop it and pilot test the New Curriculum.

When we look at the difference in MAP scores for high- and low-implementers, we see that comprehension work matters. High-implementing middle school teachers were more likely to continue to use rigorous comprehension lessons before engaging in additional work with any text. Low-implementing teachers were more likely to engage students in the first lesson for a text in the district curriculum. Those lessons, especially in the scripted curriculum—the version of the district curriculum that low-performing schools were required to use—were unlikely to focus students first on meaning making. We learned this in our discussions with principals and through our own observations of middle school classrooms. Through our own analysis of the curriculum, we know that what the curriculum labeled as a comprehension task was either formatted to reflect a question on the SA or took students directly into analytic work, which meant the tasks were either multiple choice questions or focused on small segments of texts, for example, to learn an aspect of the author's craft or to analyze a character's actions. When the scripted lessons included comprehension questions, they tended to be low-level questions that didn't require synthesizing of ideas in the text as a whole. This meant that students in low-implementing classrooms were not getting opportunities to build their comprehension muscles in any meaningful way. Instead, they were exposed to the format of questions on the SA. MAP questions, on the other hand, can't be answered through identifying key words in a text. They require synthesizing information from an entire text, a skill that high-implementing teachers worked to develop in their students through rigorous comprehension work before any analysis or interpretive tasks. Because the students of high-implementing teachers, as we see consistently in the high school data, had practice engaging in the evidence-based thinking and reasoning required of high-level comprehension and required on MAP, they were more likely to show improvement on that assessment over time.

Questions for Reflection

1. How would you describe what you learn from the year-by-year data from the third year to the sixth year?
2. What do the data from the third and fourth years, during the COVID-19 pandemic, seem to be saying about teacher implementation and students' performances on MAP and SA?
3. How would you summarize the NSI's accomplishments and failures?
4. What do the types of data that the NSI collected and reported leave out of the picture of what was accomplished and what was not accomplished?
5. If you were giving advice to the NSI now about the types of data it should collect, or should have collected, what would you say?

3 How the Network of Teachers Became an Improvement Community of Practice

This chapter tells the story of how the NSI's network of teachers became a genuine community during the COVID-19 years of the project, when they took ownership for using the regularly scheduled monthly meetings to solve the myriad instructional problems of suddenly teaching online and then in hybrid environments. This shift transformed the Network from something akin to a series of professional learning workshops into a true community. We'll argue in this chapter that the shift to becoming a community enabled the teachers and the IFL NSI coaches to work together to solve new instructional problems created by the COVID-19 pandemic when instruction went online. We'll describe how the problems of practice associated with online instruction enabled them to create novel ways to embed the student-centered practices in their online and hybrid teaching. We'll tell the story of how the NSI middle school teachers supported each other when the district shifted to what we're calling the New Curriculum by adapting their NSI meetings to focus on implementation while integrating the student-centered practices into lessons. We'll also show how the Network of principals worked to support teachers and how it became a committed but looser community.

Networks, Networked Improvement Communities, and Communities of Practice

Networks that become communities of practice,[1] what Tony Bryk and others call networked improvement communities (NICs),[2] can be powerful spaces for participants who collaborate on problems of practice and over time identify with the community and its goals. In these networked communities, members benefit from community building, instructional improvement, and professional learning.

Community Building

Regular networked meetings of teachers from multiple schools working on the same problem of practice—such as ways to create student-centered instruction—can over time enable participants to learn from one another and become genuine communities. Etienne Wenger,[3] a researcher who has devoted his career to studying communities of practice (CoPs), distinguishes networks from communities. In Bryk's research, NICs are more structured and goal oriented, aimed at solving specific problems through systematic improvement. Wenger's CoPs are more organic, focusing on social learning and identity formation within a community. Bryk's approach is driven by the need for measurable improvement in practice while Wenger's approach is broader, emphasizing how participation in a community shapes knowledge and the identities of participants. Bryk advocates for using data and disciplined inquiry to drive improvements while Wenger emphasizes the importance of shared experiences and informal learning processes. Table 3.1 is adapted from a table in Wenger's book[4] that summarizes the distinctions between networks and traits that CoPs and NICs share.

Networks, in Wenger's thinking, are "systems of connections," usually created to give their participants access to information. Think, for instance, of a district network created to keep a group of people up to date on the uses of artificial intelligence. Professional organizations, such as the National Council of Teachers of English (NCTE) and the National Council of Teachers of Mathematics (NCTM) are also examples of networks. In networks, participants check in when they can, perhaps when the topics interest them, but they aren't meeting as a community to solve a specific problem or to measure its solution.

Table 3.1 Networks, communities, and improvement communities

Networks	CoPs & NICs
Defined by connections among people under a broad umbrella of receiving and sharing information	Defined by identification with a shared domain of interest that participants commit to and hold themselves accountable to (i.e., what the community is about and what members identify with)
Do not require a collective identity or collaborative problem-solving	Commitment to collective, collaborative problem-solving and progress in practice
Enable information to flow in broad unpredictable ways—often in one direction	Information flows in focused and predictable ways because of shared commitments and regular exchanges among members
Allow easy entry into and exit out of membership as needed by participants	Membership is significant to the identity of those in the community, so participants join and stay because they're accountable to the problem-solving and to each other

CoPs, established by their members, create a space where collaboration on domains of interest—such as professional learning on teaching ratio and proportion with 8th graders—define what the community is about and shape members' problem-solving and identities. NICs go one step further than CoPs in that they use improvement science methods to solve problems of practice, and have shared, measurable goals. In contrast to NICs and CoPs, traditional professional learning, as we'll argue later on in this chapter, is usually developed to pass along information or ways of doing things. Think, for example, of sessions for teachers on ways to give students feedback on their essays that aligns with state writing standards. An outside or district expert presents information, there's time for questions, and next steps might involve teachers trying out what they learned. It's a session, or perhaps two, and there's no intention of forming a community whose members collaborate to systematically solve specific problems they've identified and to measure the results of their solutions.

It turns out, then, as Bryk and others argue,[5] that everyone collaborating on the same problem of practice is very important both for establishing a community—whether it's a NIC or a CoP—and for the work of its members. It matters, too, that everyone in the community has the capability to work on the problem and a willingness to take responsibility for the community's learning, so that there is, as Wenger puts it, "collective progress in practice." The shared focus brings with it coherence and the incentive to dig deep into the problem. The shared commitment assures that the deep dig into practice and new learning matters to the community's members and sets the stage for them to drive and assess their own learning, even when they may have the benefit of outside experts such as the IFL NSI coaches.

When participants meet regularly in a NIC or CoP, they develop a predictable cadence that contributes to their taking ownership over time for their problem-solving, becoming accountable to each other and to the task, and developing identities as community members. Predictable gatherings bring with them the time for and social structures of collaborative learning, including intentional sequencing of topics of inquiry for common knowledge building.

These communities can bridge professional and logistical barriers and create internal coherence. They offer teachers rare opportunities to form relationships with colleagues from other schools that promote shared understandings and the collaborative development of resources such as lessons and units of study. As they evolve over time, networked communities harness participants' agency and create safe spaces to center on and contribute to one another's learning. Participants benefit from the social nature of learning and its sequential layering. They build their own capacity to improve and carry their learnings to others.

A Brief Segue into the NSI's Data on Community Building

Before discussing the benefits of communities—NICs and CoPs—for instructional improvement, let's take a quick look at some data to support our claim that the NSI teachers thought of their meetings as the work of a community. Every year in the spring, a group of researchers from a third-party project administered a network health survey to the participants in thirty-four NSIs. One of the big takeaways for the IFL/BCSD NSI is that year by year, but especially from the pandemic onward, teachers and leaders strongly valued the Network meetings—more than anything else they did within the Network. As you read how they responded to survey questions in Table 3.2, which provides a sample of their 2024 responses, notice how they align with

Table 3.2 NSI participants' responses to survey questions on the NSI

Percent Who Responded Positively	Survey Item
89%	Think our work together is important
88%	Think we are working toward a common goal
87%	Value the opportunity to be a part of the network
86%	Feel support from other network members
82%	Believe the work is making a difference for the students we serve
81%	Feel a part of a community aiming to accomplish something important together
81%	Think our work is collaborative

the definitions of NICs and CoPs: identifying with the community and its work, collaborating, believing their work is important, and so on.

These positive data have to be tempered by other data from the 2024 survey that reveal the extent to which participants thought the district culture supported and aligned with the NSI's work. In response to those questions:

- 63 percent agreed that the district culture supported their NSI work.
- When asked if school leaders prioritized their work enough to allocate resources to it, 52 percent agreed.
- Only 50 percent of respondents agreed with the statement that "district leaders know what is going on in the IFL/BCSD NSI."

Year over year, the data show pretty consistently that participants thought the district's goals and those of the NSI didn't align well. As low as the percentages were in 2024, they had actually increased compared to other years.

When we probe into the open-ended questions on the issues of alignment and district support, we see responses that point to the district's emphasis on preparing students, especially in the NSI schools, to be successful on the state's high-stakes assessment. This is an issue that we discuss at length elsewhere, so we won't belabor it here. The NSI also was a small project involving fourteen schools in a district with many initiatives and over 200 schools. No matter how much we learned or had to say, it was difficult to get district-level attention.

On the other hand, when we probe into the open-ended responses from 2024 on what participants valued most about the Network, we see a picture of colleagues who value one another, as well as the IFL NSI coaches, and attach emotional meaning to their work together. As one teacher wrote, anonymously voicing what many said, "I loved the collaborative nature of the Network, and the excitement and willingness of every member to make themselves and their materials available to each other."

Back to the Benefits of Networked Communities: Instructional Improvement

It's not surprising that teachers value collaboration. They have very little time during the day to plan lessons. The NSI middle school teachers used a fairly scripted curriculum, which may lead to questions about how much time they needed. Isn't all the planning done for them? Don't they have a planning period?

Yes, the NSI teachers did have a daily planning period. It was usually forty-five minutes. That may be enough time to study test data to see which items and standards their students struggled with, but it's not enough time to plan lessons, even with grade-level teams working together. Imagine that they're teaching a text that's eight pages long. They have to read it, annotate it as their students will, and internalize the tasks the curriculum has for students, while making adaptations to the lessons to account for their actual students and their pacing. Each team member must know the text, the lesson, its sequence of tasks, and how they'll teach (e.g., whole class task completion, turn-and-talk, pair/trio sharing, and so on).

There are layers of lessons, as well, within curriculum units in high-quality curricular materials such as the New Curriculum for middle grades that was piloted by the NSI schools during the fifth year of the project. Very few digital or textbook curricula, if any, have been pilot-tested in classrooms. From teachers' points of view, they're over developed, often because state adoption committees require that a curriculum meet all the state standards in addition to other adoption criteria. As a result, materials need to be reconfigured for the pacing of schools' schedules and for teachers' students. This is difficult work to do without sufficient time. It often requires that teachers reconceptualize and/or combine tasks to align to multiple standards and backwards plan from unit assessments to determine the core tasks they'll actually have time to teach to support students on those assessments.

In the monthly Network meetings during the fifth year, teachers learned from one another how to reconfigure and prioritize lessons in the New Curriculum while maintaining alignment to standards and the unit tests. The support those meetings provided for teachers resulted in lessons paced according to teachers' and students' needs. Digging in with colleagues to understand and adapt lessons and units also helped teachers internalize the lessons and increased their confidence in planning and teaching. As we saw in the responses to the network health survey, community members felt they could reach out to the group for help with these sorts of specific problems. Everyone in the community benefits when those common tasks become the focus.

"Teachers' examples, their stories or videos of lessons, and the discussions that surrounded these artifacts built knowledge. These discussions, in turn, grew trust and established the community as a safe space to speak about successes and struggles."

Along with collaborative planning, seeing colleagues' lessons and their students' work improved instruction, especially when teachers saw alternatives to what they were doing. Teachers' examples, their stories or videos of lessons, and the discussions that surrounded these artifacts built knowledge. These discussions, in turn, grew trust and established the community as a safe space to speak about successes and struggles. Each success raised the bar. For example, when a teacher told the community that her students couldn't stop talking with each other about a text, while they worked with a task that her team had tweaked by integrating multiple tasks from the curriculum, she helped reset everyone's expectations by showing them another pathway to developing integrated lessons.

Professional Learning

Networked communities can address the variability typically found in train-the-trainer professional learning models used by almost all professional learning providers and by districts for internal training. In such a model, a provider works with district trainers who then take the provider's materials to the teachers. Teachers have little opportunity to collaborate and to build knowledge; the provider and the district trainers have most of the agency. The learning model generally lacks the time, the social structure, and the intentional sequencing of topics based on teachers' needs, that would allow common understandings and cross-school collaborations to develop.

Remarkably, the landscape of professional learning[6] still looks like a landscape of sit-and-get presentations, often conducted by popular, charismatic speakers, despite efforts toward change. For example, the Research Partnership for Professional Learning, founded by PL providers to study and produce research-based best PL practices, has issued a number of important reports that reflect their commitment to build an evidence base on teacher learning.[7] Thomas R. Guskey, an international scholar in evaluation design and educational reform, developed and tested an assessment model[8] of PL that has long been the gold standard for leaders to assess their schools' professional learning. Yet much work remains for PL providers to assess the effects of teacher learning on student outcomes.

In addition, very few districts evaluate professional learning against student outcomes. The standard fare of professional learning session evaluations tells district leaders and presenters little beyond whether the participants liked the session and what they think they've learned from it. In the larger picture of professional learning, evaluation should be concerned with (1) whether teachers actually take up what they learned and use it in their instruction, (2) whether students are positively affected by the interventions or changes in instruction that teachers learned during professional learning sessions, and (3) whether high implementation by teachers of what they learned affects students' growth and achievement, as shown by what can be observed in their work samples and what can be inferred from their performance on assessments that matter to the district.

The NSI's Early Meetings (2018–20): Not a Community Yet

Our work began in 2018, as you might recall, when three or four representatives of each of the fourteen NSI schools gathered for the first time. The meeting was designed for participants to study a packet of achievement data for the fourteen schools from the previous three years of state assessments, disaggregated by race, gender, and special needs. The packet also included data on attendance, grades, suspensions, and school climate. The session followed our typical workshop structure, focusing on individual data study, school team discussions on what they noticed and wondered about from their studies, and whole group share-outs.

We noticed the participants' agility with the data. While they were used to analyzing their school's data to identify performance gaps and corresponding standards-based skills, explaining their noticings and wonderings across multiple schools was new to them. Looking across data from multiple schools helped teams feel comfortable using a critical lens, as opposed to wanting to identify or explain perceived weaknesses in their schools' data. This broader perspective fostered a new focus on identifying patterns and potential problems of practice.

Monthly Meetings and Shifts in Focus: Working in a Professional Learning Space

Throughout the first half of the 2018–19 school year, we held monthly data study meetings. During this period, the composition of participants shifted from being leadership-heavy to including more school literacy leaders. The focus of data analysis also evolved, moving from quantitative data to prioritizing qualitative data to better understand students' experiences with literacy instruction.

To gain deeper insights, participants conducted empathy interviews with literacy colleagues and students about the state of writing and reading instruction in the NSI schools. They also collected and analyzed typical student tasks and work samples. From these artifacts, school teams created charts of observations and inquiries, referencing the underlying quantitative data findings. This work aimed to identify and prioritize problems of practice in preparation for developing driver diagrams (i.e., Figure 1.1 in Chapter 1 that shows the goals and the actions to engage with the problem of practice). A key feature was the collaboration among schools within geographic clusters, functioning like mini networks—a novel practice for the NSI schools. Many participants met colleagues from other schools for the first time in these meetings.

Guided by IFL NSI coaches, these small groups began to form a larger network, evolving in what we referred to as an early stage networked community. The tasks that we defined for them meant there wasn't yet a repertoire of ideas or approaches to negotiate, and the teams worked on goals we set. To truly become a community, the participants would need to lead the community and set its agendas. The nature of these meetings put the work squarely in a professional learning space rather than in that of a networked community.

The Network's Evolution into a Community

During the 2019–20 school year, after the root cause analysis was complete and the problems of practice identified, the school teams met together in person once a month. They engaged in professional learning during each meeting to build their understandings and uses of the student-centered practices. By mid-year, when a handful of early adapter teachers were using the practices with their students, they brought work samples and described students' responses.

Meetings began with school teams sharing stories of the work they did and artifacts of their implementations of student-centered practices, whether successful or not. We encouraged concluding discussions with their next steps and the questions the teams wanted help thinking through. Cross-school conversations began around these experiences as teachers found utility in sharing instruction and problem-solving. They also began to experiment with the practices they learned about from each other, especially after they learned that some of their colleagues had successfully brought lyrics from music familiar to their students and culturally relevant texts into their instruction.

By mid-year, we began to see adaptations to the practices, often to accommodate the texts that were being used, and just as often to accommodate teachers' understandings of what their students would respond to. They took up the simple rearrangement of classroom desks into trios, for example, when they learned how this could change the feeling of the room and increase students' willingness to engage with each other.

Those samples and stories prompted exchanges, sometimes critical, often inquisitive. As a result, we noticed changes in the group. Because some team members were comfortable taking risks with their teaching, the group began to recognize the meetings as somewhat safe spaces. Team members questioned each other, and shared their successes and some failures of texts to engage students with the practices. Teachers who had been silent for most of the meetings began to participate. Participants were building what Bryk[9] refers to as relational trust that's "marked by a genuine sense of listening to what each person has to say," and personal regard, "a sense that others really care ... and a willingness to extend themselves beyond what is formally required." Developing relational trust with the IFL NSI Fellows and the changes to instruction that we suggested took many of the NSI participants a year.

Teachers Owning the Network for Solving Their Virtual Instruction Problems

By March of 2020, the Network was on its way to becoming a community. Then the pandemic brought us together only online from March to June of 2020. We all had a lot to learn about working in this new environment. As we discussed in Chapter 1, our focus shifted from developing task sheets and using the student-centered practices to learning about the district's digital platforms and what each could offer for virtual classrooms and meetings. We thought that the online environment would derail the Network, but the opposite happened. Team members, you might recall, dug into the platforms, shared their experiences using them with students, and slowly identified a small repertoire that worked.

> *"The teacher-driven activities had an immediacy that brought a new depth and breadth to our monthly meetings. Teachers were now regularly leading them, first by taking the initial hour to share their work and their students' work, and then through their comments and questions."*

They identified online tools to present students with task sheets that allowed them to compose quick writes and engage in pair/trio discussions. Together we learned that students didn't want to talk with each other in online breakout rooms or in class meetings, but they did surprise us all by taking to writing to each other about their readings. The search for platforms shifted to finding those that would allow students to write to each other and see and respond to each other's writings.

The teacher-driven activities had an immediacy that brought a new depth and breadth to our monthly meetings. Teachers were now regularly leading them, first by taking the initial hour to share their work and their students' work, and then through their comments and questions. Teachers' learning from each other about the digital platforms and how to adapt them for the student-centered practices played the most significant role in our becoming a community. Getting these platforms to work for them and their students were their genuine and immediate problems to solve. They took risks and quickly became experts. We learned from them how the platforms and tools could be used as vehicles for student-centered instruction.

Collective Progress: Hybrid Instruction Brings More Problems to Solve

During the COVID-19 year (2020–21), as mentioned in Chapter 1, the district gave parents the option of having their children attend class in person or online. For teachers, this created the need to transition to hybrid instruction. The initial thinking in the district was that students online could participate through Google Meets during the in-person instruction and move to online breakout groups when the in-person students moved to small group work.

Hybrid instruction turned out to be difficult in two ways. First, day to day, teachers were never sure who would be in class and who would be online. This made planning specific collaborative structures difficult. Second, online students expressed frustration with tracking the in-person instruction and using the participatory platforms even if they had sufficient bandwidth. Online students were not required to, and therefore did not, turn on their cameras. Students continued to shy away from auditory conversations in breakout rooms, opting instead to use the chat feature or to leave each other comments in collaborative documents. They also continued to write and to respond in writing to each other's quick writes.

The IFL NSI coaches put their energy into collaborating with teachers during the monthly meetings rather than leading them in professional learning, since teachers were experimenting and solving hybrid instruction problems. They were teaching us and each other.

A Teacher-led Design Team Brings More Collective Progress

In August of 2020, we invited six teachers and one principal to join the IFL NSI coaches in what we called a Design Team to set the agendas for the work of the monthly meetings. They knew what supports the teachers needed, and they knew from experience the challenges of hybrid instruction.

With the Design Team leading agenda setting, and with the NSI teachers leading the monthly meetings by sharing their experiences with hybrid teaching and the ways they embedded the student-centered practices into their instruction, the Network meetings evolved into intense presentations and exchanges. Attendance continued to be strong and consistent. Although the need to solve immediate and ever-present problems continued to drive the work of the meetings, by mid-year teachers landed on a handful of platforms to use for hybrid instruction that students grew accustomed to. The monthly discussions shifted to success stories, to sharing students' work from the various platforms, and to critical exchanges focused on what was and wasn't possible in the hybrid environment and what was and wasn't working to engage students in student-centered practices.

The 2021 network health survey data on the NSI show us a NIC whose members are deeply engaged with one another's work, sharing lessons, and doing so in a space where they are critical friends who discuss how their work leads to equitable and just instruction. In the survey, 76 percent of the respondents said they used what they learned from other NSI teams to advance their teams' improvement work. Eighty-one percent said they shared what their team was learning with other NSI teams, and 83 percent said they regularly received meaningful feedback on their work. Seventy percent reported that their team dug into data to make decisions, and 68 percent said their team had explicit conversations about how their work could directly address equity and justice. In Wenger's terms, the members demonstrate that they are a community of practice learning from and with each other.

Learning from an Executive Director's Network Meetings

As the NSI coaches and teachers worked together to solve these problems of practice, another group of NSI schools—led by their executive director and her staff—was implementing regular cross-school Network meetings in ELA, math, and science. They used Google landing pages to organize and present their work, so they could engage teachers and school leaders in the actual lessons they developed before teachers taught them.

We received an invitation to attend these Network meetings and to discuss them with the executive director and staff. We saw the brilliance of their use of templated and predictable landing pages to bring coherence to their Network's tasks. Google Meets allowed for their teachers' and leaders' real-time engagements with the lessons, along with opportunities to question and discuss those lessons before they were taught to students. Their approach helped participants develop common understandings and internalize the lesson content and ways of teaching. We brought these initiatives back to the NSI teachers and the Design Team. Though we had started using landing pages for the Network meetings in September 2020, they saw the value of using landing pages in these ways and began within their school teams to standardize landing pages, their formatting, and the digital tools they housed in those pages.

The Hallmarks of the Teachers' Community

Looking back at the NSI networked community, we see the hallmarks of a NIC and a CoP in the teachers' commitment to solving the challenges of virtual and hybrid instruction, their adapting and learning to use the student-centered practices in virtual and hybrid environments, and their collaborative sharing and critiquing of their learnings.

We saw:

- Teachers continued their commitment to expand opportunities for students to engage in high-level instructional tasks in spite of the challenges posed by hybrid instruction. Teachers remained committed to participating in monthly meetings and were deeply involved in the common projects of learning about and testing online platforms.
- Teachers took responsibility for the successful adaptation of student-centered practices by other teachers in the Network as well as the growth of their own knowledge about adapting the practices, learning to teach students in person and online simultaneously, and also adapting to students' reluctance to show themselves or talk online.

- Teachers made sense of the benefits and drawbacks of their uses of various online platforms and tools. They built their capacity and competence to adapt the student-centered practices to various platforms and tools while highlighting the ways that multiple digital tools, such as Pear Deck and Google Docs, could be used together to mitigate limitations and bring coherence to students' experiences. Teachers maintained the conversation of "how do we provide high-quality teaching and learning experiences for all students" while being flexible in how they understood effective instruction as it evolved with shifts from in person to online to hybrid and back again.
- Teachers reinvented their teaching practices. They found common ground as they focused on platforms and tools. They found new, imaginative ways to present the content of task sheets with digital tools and platforms, and they took risks by trying new digital tools and by sharing the stories of their successes and failures with their colleagues and with us.

It should be clear by now that while the NSI tests of change—the student-centered practices—were the focus of our Network, they were not always the center of the work.[10] Every new year brought new challenges for the NSI teachers that shifted the community's focus. The teachers were always adapting the tests of change to constantly changing contexts in the district and in their schools.

The Middle School Teachers' Community Shifts Its Problem of Practice: Pilot Testing and Implementing a New Curriculum

During the 2022–23 school year, the Network split into two groups to address the diverging needs of middle and high school teachers. Middle schools began piloting a new ELA curriculum. The high schools continued to use the district curriculum with the addition of lessons and units that they developed over the previous two years. The high school networked community continued its ongoing work of teachers sharing their lessons built on the student-centered practices.

The middle school networked community began its meetings that year by focusing on teachers' understandings of the New Curriculum units and lessons. Through conversations with the middle school teachers, we found that the Network meetings were the primary opportunities they had to work in collaboration with other teachers around the New Curriculum, solve problems, and share their adaptations. They experimented with the digital curriculum using the Promethean boards in their classrooms, with students working on their computers, and with in-person versions of the student-centered practices. The meetings that were focused on the New Curriculum took on an immediacy similar to the community's reset to focus on online instruction. Teachers led the meetings. They owned the problems posed by the New Curriculum, and everyone, including the IFL NSI coaches, was a learner.

Another Shift in the Problem of Practice: The Middle Schools' Roll-Out of the New Curriculum

In the 2023–24 school year, with a newly negotiated district contract to continue the NSI to build district capacity, we once again adapted the Network meetings to changes in the schools and in the teachers' community. After a few initial meetings of the middle school teachers, it was clear that they were under enormous pressure now to use the New Curriculum they had pilot tested the year before.

During the pilot testing, schools and teachers had considerable flexibility in how they used the curriculum. They pared it back, added supplemental texts when that made sense, and embedded the student-centered practices in lessons.

The beginning of the district-wide roll-out year of the curriculum brought considerable confusion and mixed messages about how it was to be taught. Some executive directors, for instance, insisted that it had to be taught with complete fidelity. In classes where teachers attempted to do that, instruction began to look like an assembly line, as an observer not affiliated with the NSI remarked. Teachers and students rushed through readings, annotations, and exercises to the rhythm of timers set to give students minutes to complete their work. Other executive directors thought of the curriculum more as a resource than as a script to be followed. With that flexibility, teachers in those schools backwards planned from the unit tests to make decisions about what they would teach from a very over-developed curriculum. There was also a middle ground, where executive directors appeared to leave it to the schools to decide. In those schools, we often saw confusion in planning and a reliance on protocols to design lessons. These often translated into classes that were traditional teacher-centered spaces with lots of teacher talk in preparation for students doing workbook-type exercises.

Teachers and principals told us that it was just too much to ask of the middle school teachers to attend the Network meetings. They were struggling. So, with a green light from the executive directors, we adapted and changed the middle school Network meeting membership to include the school ELA coaches (referred to this year as the demonstration teachers), lead ELA teachers as designated by the principals, and the instructional district coaches. The rationale was simple. These were the people who were already scheduled to meet regularly with the teacher teams in their schools during Professional Learning Community (PLC) time to support their implementation of the curriculum. They were also the people charged with supporting the teachers to embed the student-centered practices into the curriculum when it was appropriate. From our point of view, these were the people who were committed to working with us to build capacity to carry on the NSI.

For the final year of the NSI, then, with a changed meeting membership, the new participants took up the problem of implementing the New Curriculum and how best to embed the student-centered practices.

The Principals' Networked Meetings

We didn't expect all the principals to become a community the way the teachers did. However, the once-a-month, two-hour meetings of the NSI school principals did help the group evolve into something of a community. Depending on the year, a core group of seven or eight principals regularly attended these meetings. They became important advocates for the NSI within their schools and within the district. As we discuss in Chapter 5, principals play an enabling role for their teachers and coaches. Without their visible support for the NSI, it would have been impossible for NSI teachers to bring the student-centered practices into their instruction. When addressing the role of principals, Bryk writes that it's essential for principals "to promote the growth of a professional community around a shared system of teaching and learning and also stay the course, guided by a coherent, strategic plan that aims to advance the entire enterprise over time."[11] The active NSI principals supported the teachers to attend the NSI monthly meetings and dealt with barriers to their work. They attended the monthly meetings themselves, participated in PL on the student-centered practices, shared information from their observations, and developed action plans for supporting teachers.

A number of schools came into and out of the NSI project. Some had year-over-year changes in leadership, and others had more pressing issues to deal with at various times. We understood what it took for teachers in those schools to continue to participate in their Network meetings and to do what they could with student-centered practices in their classrooms.

In situations where building leadership support was either missing or lukewarm, teachers felt frustrated and hesitant to use the practices. In the network health survey, responses to an open-ended question on "what gets in the way of your school making progress on the work of the Network," a teacher wrote anonymously that "the administration gets in the way. The principal requires us to keep the same pace as the curriculum even if our students have not mastered ... a skill." Almost all of the respondents said "time" or "time constraints/competing initiatives" got in the way. Leaders in low-implementing schools didn't prioritize the use of the student-centered practices. Teachers reported that given competing initiatives, leaders didn't make time for them to take up the work in school team meetings.

The Range of Activities in the Principal Meetings

The following is a brief overview of the kinds of content we developed for the principals' sessions. Our goals were to support them to (1) understand the NSI, (2) understand the work of teachers with the student-centered practices, (3) share examples of teachers' lessons and their students' work samples (often with videos of students discussing texts), and (4) share and discuss the evaluation data, some of which compared high- and low-implementing classes' performances on district measures.

We conducted these sessions as professional learning workshops with the networked community of principals, and we regularly surveyed the principals during the meetings to understand what they wanted to know and discuss about the NSI and their teachers' participation in it. Their interests cohered around the importance for them of seeing examples of teachers' and students' work and their desire to know how the work supported students on the district and state exams.

During the first two years, we focused on engaging principals as learners with the student-centered practices, including discussions of texts used in the classroom and task sheets that invited them into the practices. Such learning sessions usually lasted forty-five to sixty minutes. We always followed with step-back debriefings in which we invited a discussion of what engaging with the texts and the practices themselves had shown them about what students would learn.

We generally brought texts that were being used by teachers. One of those was "Ain't I A Woman?," by Sojourner Truth,[12] along with a task sheet collaboratively developed by the teachers. Right before COVID-19 sent us online, we brought an NPR broadcast, "Scientists Start To Tease Out The Subtler Ways Racism Hurts Health," by Rae Ellen Bichell,[13] along with a task sheet we had developed. During one virtual meeting, we engaged them with the poem "Curanderismo," by Ariana Brown,[14] with a task sheet developed by the high school team who first used that text with students. We also brought them a text called "Beyond the *English Learner* Label: Recognizing the Richness of Bi/Multilingual Students' Linguistic Repertoires," by R.A. Martínez,[15] to discuss using one of our task sheets.

We regularly shared videos of their teachers engaging their classes with the student-centered practices and shared with them task sheets that we developed for the videos that invited them to discuss what they noticed and wondered about. We typically asked what they thought it took for the teacher to conduct a class that was focused on students working with students. We asked, too, what evidence of students' learning they could see in the video.

Once our meetings became virtual, we shared how teachers were using virtual platforms and tools with the student-centered practices, tasks, and lessons. Twice a year, we shared the evaluation reports, which included the teacher implementation survey results, the relationship of implementation levels to students' growth and achievement on district and state tests, a summary of students' responses on the exit tickets, and the 8th and 9th grade on-track for college and career measures. We also focused on engaging principals and assistant principals in *learning walks* of classes in their buildings to observe teachers using the student-centered practices with lessons in the curriculum.

A Concluding Reflection

What did we learn about the NSI's work and the principal meetings? A good place to begin is with the differences between NSIs and more typical professional learning. As an organization, we have focused for decades on providing professional learning to teachers and leaders in urban schools. Through the NSI's work, we learned the importance of collaborative learning and agenda setting—if not directly with the teachers with whom we work, then with their building and district leaders. The change in our thinking and behavior might best be represented by a change in the language that we use. We used to say that we would "provide professional learning." We now say that "we collaborate with district colleagues to develop professional learning in which teachers collaborate with IFL Fellows" on specific bodies of work. In other words, we learned the importance of teachers collaborating with teachers on problems of practice and principals collaborating with principals to support teachers. We deal ourselves into that equation when teachers and principals also collaborate with us. We act on this approach by working with district leadership to establish networked communities of teachers within and across schools to make professional learning the work of a community.

Other big lessons we learned concern the contexts of the districts and schools we work with, and the ways we evaluate professional learning. We now collaborate with district leadership to develop an understanding of the context within which they've requested particular work from us. We then propose to study disaggregated district data collaboratively and to conduct asset walks and class observations together to gain shared experience with instruction in a sample of schools and classes. When possible, we ask teachers to collect students' assignments so we can see the types of tasks presented along with the curriculum. To evaluate the professional learning, we suggest teacher and student surveys to gauge how the teachers' learning is being implemented in classrooms. We also request access to students' test data, so that we can see whether the level of implementation predicts students' success on growth and achievement measures. We're not always successful with our requests for these actions, but we continue to build them into district contracts and look to collaborate with leadership to adapt to what might be possible. That intent to collaborate matters. Developing action plans to do so gets us to where we want to go.

Questions for Reflection

1 Why would you initiate a NIC in a school or district?

   a What foundations or conditions would you want to have in place before initiating it?
   b Who would be the key participants in the NIC?
   c How would you engage leadership in the NIC?
   d What steps would you follow to initiate and then establish it?
   e How would you propose to measure the outcomes of the NIC's test of change?

2 How would you distinguish the school or district conditions that would lead you to initiate professional learning workshops instead of a NIC?

   a How do the goals of PL workshops and NICs differ?
   b How do the roles of the participants, including leadership, differ in PL workshops and NICs?
   c How would you propose to measure the outcomes of the PL workshops?

Notes

1. Etienne Wenger-Trayner, Beverly Wenger-Trayner, Phil Reid, and Claude Bruderlein, *Communities of Practice Within and Across Organizations* (Sesimbra Social Learning Lab, 2023), 11–20.
2. For accessible essays on NICs see: Anthony S. Bryk and Louis M. Gomez, "Networked Improvement Communities: The Power of Improvement Science in Education," *Educational Leadership* 74, no. 2 (2016): 36–40; Paul G. LeMahieu et al., "Networked Improvement Communities: The Discipline of Improvement Science Meets the Power of Networks," *Quality Assurance in Education* 25, no. 1 (2017): 5–25; Jennifer Lin Russell et al., "The Social Structure of Networked Improvement Communities: Cultivating the Emergence of a Scientific-Professional Learning Community" (report, Carnegie Foundation for the Advancement of Teaching, 2021). For an in-depth study of improvement in Chicago schools see Anthony S. Bryk, Penny Bender Sebring, Elaine Allensworth, Stuart Luppescue, and John Q. Easton, *Organizing Schools for Improvement: Lessons from Chicago* (Chicago: University of Chicago Press, 2020).

3   For a readable introduction to CoPs, see Etienne Wenger, *Communities of Practice: Learning, Meaning, and Identity* (Cambridge: Cambridge University Press, 1998).
4   Wenger-Trayner et al., *Communities of Practice Within and Across Organizations*, 16.
5   Jennifer Lin Russell et al., "A Framework for the Initiation of Networked Improvement Communities," *Teachers College Record* 119, no. 5 (2017): 1–36.
6   Sam Sims, Harry Fletcher-Wood, Alison O'Mara-Eves, Sarah Cottingham, Claire Stansfield, Josh Goodrich, Jo Van Herwegen, and Jake Anders, "Effective Teacher Professional Development: New Theory and a Meta-Analytic Test," *Review of Educational Research* 93, no. 6 (December 2023): 1048–92, https://doi.org/10.3102/00346543231217480; Bill & Melinda Gates Foundation, "Teachers Know Best: Teachers' Views on Professional Development," December 2014, https://eric.ed.gov/?id=ED576976; TNTP, "The Mirage: Confronting the Hard Truth about Our Quest for Teacher Development," August 4, 2015, https://eric.ed.gov/?id=ED558206.
7   Research Partnership for Professional Learning, "RPPL Insights Hub," accessed March 5, 2025, https://rpplpartnership.org/insights-hub/.
8   Thomas R. Guskey, "Does It Make a Difference? Evaluating Professional Development," *Educational Leadership* 59, no. 6 (March 2022): 45–51, https://tguskey.com/wp-content/uploads/Professional-Learning-4-Evaluating-Professional-Development.pdf.
9   Bryk et al., *Organizing Schools for Improvement: Lessons from Chicago*, 135–50.
10 For a concise discussion of improvement teams making adaptations to interventions (or tests of change), see Alicia Grunow, Sandra Park, and Brandon Bennett, *Journey to Improvement: A Team Guide to Systems Change in Education, Health Care, and Social Welfare* (Lanham, MD: Rowman & Littlefield, 2023), 191–93.
11 Bryk et al., *Organizing Schools for Improvement: Lessons from Chicago*, 133.
12 Sojourner Truth, "Ain't I A Woman?" (Speech, Women's Rights Convention, Akron, Ohio, 1851).
13 Rae Ellen Bichell, "Scientists Start To Tease Out The Subtler Ways Racism Hurts Health," NPR, broadcast audio, November 11, 2017.
14 Ariana Brown, "Curanderismo," in *Sana Sana* (Boston: Game Over Books, 2020).
15 R. A. Martínez, "Beyond the *English Learner* Label: Recognizing the Richness of Bi/Multilingual Students' Linguistic Repertoires," *The Reading Teacher* 71, no. 5 (2018): 515–22.

4 PLCs that Support Instructional Inquiry: Building In-school Improvement Capacity at Arlington High School

This chapter offers a vision for what collaborative instructional inquiry can look like at the school level. We focus on the work of veteran teacher Brian Drew, who was an NSI coordinator, and a team of 9th grade English Language Arts (ELA) teachers at Arlington High School. In the previous chapter, you read about the NSI meetings and how they supported the project. Arlington's story illustrates the importance of continuing the work of improvement as a school community after teachers leave the Network meetings.

In this chapter, you will learn about:

- Professional Learning Communities (PLCs) as drivers of inquiry to
  - support planning for instructional change
  - facilitate evidence-based reflection on instruction that leads to adaptation or adoption of instructional practice
- the qualities needed in an instructional leader guiding change
- the changes a principal can make to create a system that invites teacher collaboration through PLCs

We focus here on one in-school structure—PLCs—because of the importance of teachers and school leaders taking responsibility for students' learning outcomes. When teachers and school leaders collectively own instructional problems of practice and commit to working collaboratively to focus on student learning, schools are more likely to experience sustained improvement.[1]

Instructional Change in Context: Arlington High School

Arlington High School is a large school south of downtown Big City. It is the oldest high school in the Big City School District (BCSD) and serves approximately 1,500 students in grades 9–12. During the 2023–24 school year, most students at Arlington identified as Hispanic (95 percent), with 3.5 percent of students identifying as Black and 1 percent identifying as White. Ninety-seven percent of students were economically disadvantaged. In 2018, when the NSI began, Arlington was classified as a "C" campus, with 34 percent of students scoring proficient and above on the ELA portion of the state assessment. Arlington was part of our Network from the beginning. After our first visit in 2018, the school experienced both leadership and staffing changes; however, strong internal structures and mentorship had been a constant for the 9th grade English teachers at the school, whether they were new or returning.

We met Mr. Drew when the Network came together for the first time to understand the literacy problem of practice we would be undertaking. He had been a member of the faculty at Arlington for the entirety of his 24-year career and was teaching 11th grade when he joined the Network. In a project that was working to improve students' ELA proficiency by the end of 9th grade, the NSI team was surprised to have him join our first meeting as the point person for Arlington. Mr. Drew explained that he felt the instructional improvement work was important for all of Arlington's students and did not hesitate to volunteer when his principal asked who might be interested in participating.

Over the years of the Network, the outcomes data coming from Arlington highlighted the school as a bright spot. Even as COVID took hold, teachers were grappling with hybrid classrooms, and many schools in our Network were dealing with staffing shortages, Arlington's students continued to benefit from the improvement work guided by Mr. Drew. Our Network data show that from Year 1 to Year 5, Arlington saw an overall increase of 12 percent in the number of students scoring proficient and above on the 9th grade literacy portion of the state assessment. When compared to similar schools in the state, students at Arlington showed 14 percent more growth than their matched peers during those five years.[2] In fact, Arlington was ranked as the top comprehensive high school in Big City at the start of the 2024–25 school year.

We see the data from Arlington as a model for schools and districts ready to take on the heavy work of instructional inquiry. We hear so much lately about students not having positive classroom experiences, or teachers leaving the profession in droves because students have become unmanageable and the expectations districts place on teachers have become unworkable. Arlington shines a light on what can happen in a school community that creates and sustains space for collaboration and prioritizes student-centered learning over pressure to align instruction to state testing. It's a school where teachers want to collaborate, where students show up and engage with the content, and where leadership understands the value of removing barriers to high-quality instruction.

In the next section, we discuss PLCs as important tools for in-school instructional change, followed by a description of how Mr. Drew leveraged the existing PLC structure at Arlington to focus teachers' collaborative planning on cycles of instructional inquiry.

Professional Learning Communities as Drivers of Instructional Inquiry

PLCs bolstered the enactment of improvement for our Network schools. These were key structures for the Network because they became the space where teachers internalized the process of Plan, Do, Study, Act (PDSA) cycles and made the steps of the cycle part of their regular planning practice. Research on both education-focused improvement networks and PLCs has found PLCs to be fruitful sites for collaborative improvement.[3] The literature on PLCs paints a variety of ways they can be structured, from content area groups of teachers meeting together to discuss instruction to whole school faculty meetings focused on book study.[4] Recent work on effective PLCs has coalesced around some version of what has come to be known as the "DuFour model" and on using PLC time to respond to a series of questions:

- What do we want students to learn?
- How will we know if they have learned it?
- How will we respond when learning has not occurred?
- How will we respond when learning has already occurred?[5]

We have found that the questions used in effective PLCs mirror the types of questions that an instructionally focused PDSA form asks teachers to respond to during inquiry cycles, which is why we see this PLC structure as an effective tool for instructional improvement. In an instructionally focused PDSA, teachers first consider what they want students to learn by doing the task themselves and discussing the standard for performance. When we say the standard for performance, we are not talking about the state standards, although aligning to state standards is important. We are talking about the performance a teacher would need to see or hear from students to know that they have met the learning goal. The discussion then moves to how students will work toward that standard using practices teachers learned about during Network meetings, and the evidence they will collect to analyze the impact instruction had on student learning (the "plan" step). Teachers then use the instruction with students (do), and come back together to analyze the student-generated artifacts (study). They use what they learn from those artifacts and their own reflections on their practice to adjust instruction for the next task (act), and the cycle begins again. It is this collaborative work that moves instructional planning away from isolation to collegial work that has positive outcomes for student learning and teacher well-being.[6]

"Knowing that teachers who are able to engage in instructionally focused collaborative planning find it effective and that students' academic performance benefits, school and district leaders should carefully consider how to open more time and space in the schedule for teachers to engage in collaborative instructional inquiry."

Nationally, about half of all K–12 teachers report having time built into their schedules to potentially engage in PLCs that could be used for instructional inquiry. Large-scale surveys have shown that about 45 percent of teachers have collaborative planning time at least once a month that is dedicated to instructional planning. In addition, 63 percent report that they find collaborative planning time effective in helping to plan for instruction that meets the needs of their students.[7] Knowing that teachers who are able to engage in instructionally focused collaborative planning find it effective and that students' academic performance benefits, school and district leaders should carefully consider how to open more time and space in the schedule for teachers to engage in collaborative instructional inquiry. The case story of the Arlington team shows one way that teachers and school leaders have worked to create an effective PLC structure that supports instructional inquiry similar to a PSDA cycle.

Leading Change with a Planning Tool

The monthly Network meetings were never meant to be a place for Network teachers to do all of the work necessary to lead instructional change. This is true of any network. Convenings of network members, whether they are monthly or at any other cadence, are typically meant for taking stock of progress toward a shared goal, learning about promising practices, and sharing successes and challenges across schools both to build additional knowledge around promising practice and to collectively problem solve. Our Network meetings functioned mostly as cross-school professional development time that focused on content, incorporated opportunities for teachers to engage in tasks as learners, supported collaboration, modeled effective use of change ideas, provided coaching and expert support, offered opportunities for peer-to-peer feedback and reflection, and built learning across time.[8]

> *"When teachers come to collaborative planning time willing to engage in instructional tasks to experience the learning they want their students to experience, share the successes and challenges happening in their classrooms, analyze artifacts of student learning, learn about instructional practice from each other, plan for instructional shifts, enact the planned changes, and come back and do it again next week, collegiality grows and benefits everyone at the school."*

The real work of improvement was always going to happen back at the schools with teacher teams developing their collective insight and instructional capacities through shared planning experiences. As Grunow, Park, and Bennett note, these teams thrive when teachers "show up as learners with humility, transparency, and curiosity, ready to roll up their sleeves and dig in."[9] When teachers come to collaborative planning time willing to engage in instructional tasks to experience the learning they want their students to experience, share the successes and challenges happening in their classrooms, analyze artifacts of student learning, learn about instructional practice from each other, plan for instructional shifts, enact the planned changes, and come back and do it again next week, collegiality grows and benefits everyone at the school.

We found pretty quickly that for NSI teachers, the idea of showing up as learners to a planning meeting at their school, as Grunow, Park, and Bennett suggest, rubbed against teachers' previous experiences in PLCs. While the work of planning instruction should be a normal part of most PLCs, we found that it was happening in an abbreviated way at the schools in the NSI. As mentioned in Chapter 3, all fourteen of our schools had dedicated collaborative teacher planning time built into their schedules. The protocols shared by the district provided two structures for the PLCs, one for instructional planning and one for studying data, both quantitative data and student-generated exemplars from the previous lesson.

The first district-created protocol was called "Look Forward" and was intended to support teachers in collaborative lesson planning. The sixty-minute protocol dedicated thirty minutes to unpacking the state standards listed on the instructional planning calendar, the document that paced teachers' use of the curriculum. "Unpacking the standards" is explained by the document as naming the "to do" based on the standard. So, teachers were working to answer the question, "What do students have *to do* to show that they are hitting the standard?" During our observations, this often sounded like a listing of phrases based on verbs in the standards (i.e., students have to comprehend, students have to use evidence, students have to draw conclusions). Once the "to dos" were named, the next direction was to review or create assessment-like questions based on those "to dos." These were meant to be the formative assessment pieces that would be discussed during the data meeting. The final thirty minutes of planning asked teachers to script a portion of the lesson they would teach to hit the standards that were unpacked and if time permitted, to rehearse the script they created.

When compared to the questions addressed by effective PLCs noted earlier in the chapter, the Look Forward protocol addresses the question of "What do we want students to learn?" through asking teachers to discuss the skills students should demonstrate to hit particular standards. The protocol leaves open opportunities for teachers to connect the standard to the text being used in the lesson and to discuss the performance standard—what teachers would need to hear and see from students to know they are making progress toward the learning goal. This was the space where Mr. Drew saw an opportunity to include discussions focused on instructional inquiry.

Mr. Drew and the Arlington team provide a successful use case of how small shifts in the existing protocol could create in-school space for collaborative inquiry and instructional change in a process that was already part of their standard planning practice.

The changes he introduced to the PLC protocol flowed directly from his experiences in the monthly Network meetings. In the early meetings, we (the Network coaches from IFL) focused on a set of practices and tools that NSI coordinators could use and adapt to guide in-school collaborative instructional inquiry. (Chapter 3 provides extensive details on the work that happened in our Network convenings.) From that work, Mr. Drew integrated into the district protocol the process of engaging his peers as learners with the texts they were using with students. He used several tools from our Network meetings, including a student-facing task sheet to orient teachers to the student-centered practices, a tool for determining if a question is high or low level, and a set of guiding questions for thinking about the complexity of a text. The PLC Planning Protocol that Mr. Drew created is shown in Table 4.1.

> *"Once Mr. Drew began holding them accountable for preparing for the PLC, and teachers saw how the preparation directly impacted the work they did with their students, they began to show up to the weekly meetings prepared."*

You will notice that the protocol takes teachers through three stages: Pre-work, Discuss, and Planning for Debrief. Given the limited time available, Mr. Drew found it critical to send a copy of the text(s) that teachers would

Table 4.1 PLC Planning Protocol

Prepare Before PLC	**Individual Work: Prepare** • Read and annotate the text for the big ideas in an informational text or the theme of a literary text. • Draft responses to the question: ○ What's the text's big idea or theme?

Discuss	**Whole Group: Target Response**
	• What are the target responses about the big ideas/theme?
	• What are the target responses for the author's purpose?
	• Students can give target responses that are different from the responses you developed and be ok.
	
	Whole Group: Task Considerations
	• Study the instructional task with these questions:
	  ○ How does the task guide students to understand the big ideas/theme?
	  ○ What are some other possible responses?
	  ○ What scaffolds might need to be put in place for students who need extra support?
	
	Whole Group: Other Considerations
	• What do you think students will have trouble with in the text?
	• How can you prepare students to deal with those trouble spots? Consider:
	  ○ Building background knowledge before reading
	  ○ Having students talk with a peer
	  ○ Providing Spanish cognates where necessary
	  ○ Reading the text aloud
	  ○ Chunk the text and ask questions

> **Planning for Debrief**
>
> **Collecting Artifacts**
>
> - Collect student work for your next meeting:
>   - Writing artifacts
>   - Pictures of charts
>   - Video of student discussion
> - What do the artifacts tell you about what students can do?
> - What do the artifacts tell you about what students still need to know?

be using for lesson planning ahead of time. He also asked teachers to write down what they understood the text to be about, so they would come to the PLC ready to discuss from a shared starting point. This step took some time for teachers to carry out consistently. As previously noted, they were not used to showing up to a PLC as learners ready to dig in; rather, they were often required to be passive receivers of information. They had not been expected to prepare materials for a PLC or to be held accountable for doing the work. Pre-work proved to be a critical commitment for teachers. Without this step, the majority of the PLC time was spent reading the text. Once Mr. Drew began holding them accountable for preparing for the PLC, and teachers saw how the preparation directly impacted the work they did with their students, they began to show up to the weekly meetings prepared.

The Discuss phase of the protocol is where teachers would spend the most time. Mr. Drew facilitated discussion first around what teachers understood the text to be about, working with them to refine a target response that would indicate students got the gist. They also generated responses they might hear from students that were in the target space but may also have shown misunderstandings. Through generating this list, teachers would narrow in on a performance standard.

The Task Considerations step in the Discuss phase has evolved since the creation of this protocol for Arlington. When Mr. Drew first began engaging teachers in planning instructional changes around comprehension, he created the comprehension task sheets for teachers and, as the protocol reflects, asked them to analyze the work of the task sheet. He asked them to think through how the steps in the task helped students get to the target responses of "What is this text about?" He also set the expectation that what he was sharing was the starting point for adaptation. He helped teachers think through where they might need to scaffold the work for the different students in their classrooms. Since that time, the work has evolved to teachers planning out the task sheets themselves during PLC meetings and taking shared responsibility for creating various aspects of the lesson (see the *Whole Group: Other Considerations* step in the protocol in Table 4.1), which you will see in the case story that follows.

The final five to ten minutes of the meeting is spent discussing when teachers expect the task will be used with students and agreeing on the student-generated artifacts teachers will bring back as evidence of both successes and challenges. Successes here might be defined as students being able to engage with the task and show progress toward a learning goal. Challenges might be defined as the task not providing enough support to help students access the text, students being confused about what a task is asking them to do, or responses being far removed from the learning goal. This information is used during a debrief PLC to discuss possible instructional shifts.

The protocol takes teachers directly into studying the questions that DuFour and others note as being hallmarks of PLCs that lead to sustained instructional change. Mr. Drew's PLC protocol addresses the question of "What do we want students to learn?" by engaging teachers in reading the text and discussing the target responses/performance standard for the task question. Teachers then talk about how the task should be structured to guide students to work collaboratively to get to that target response, including discussing the skills that students need to engage in the task. The group then addresses the question of, "How will we know if they have learned it?" by anticipating students' responses, both responses that let them know students are moving toward the target and misconceptions that students might surface along the way. At the end, teachers commit to bring student-generated artifacts of learning, such as quick writes and charts, to the next PLC meeting, to help answer the questions "How will we respond when learning has not occurred?" and "How will we respond when learning has already occurred?"

In the six years since Mr. Drew began leading the 9th grade PLCs, the protocols have been internalized by teachers to the point where it is just their way of working. Mr. Drew was not always the holder of the instructional pieces that guided the PLC work; he shared the responsibility of adapting curriculum and developing tasks with his peers. As you will see in the case story, he facilitated the discussion, but other teachers brought instructional texts to the group and took on responsibility for developing the task sheets.

Case Story: Planning Protocol in Action

It was a December night in 2021 when we returned to Mr. Drew's classroom for the first time since March of 2020. During that last visit, Mr. Drew had been prepping laptops. He had looked at us and said, "I don't think we're going to come back from break." He was right. On this December night, most of the people seated in the circle of desks had changed since that March day. Matt Gage was the new assistant principal over literacy. The 9th grade ELA team was composed of three new faces, Bea Paulo, a second-year teacher, Luke Dinh, a third-year teacher, and Ian Alvarez, who had been a history teacher in Puerto Rico for thirteen years and was teaching ELA and in the continental United States for the first time. We were a little late to the meeting and could hear Mr. Drew's voice as we walked toward his classroom. His tenor and southern twang carried into the hall as he asked the group if they had read the poem and were ready to engage in a comprehension discussion, the process that is called for in the Pre-Work section of the PLC Planning Protocol. Sounds of agreement and rustling paper could be heard through the classroom door.

We quietly made our way to the seats that had been kept for us within the circle. We had been asked to attend the PLC to help the Arlington team collaborate around planning a test of change for instruction on the poem "Curanderismo,"[10] by Ariana Brown, which Mr. Dinh had suggested for instruction during a previous PLC. Teachers agreed that the poem would be a good instructional text because of its complex ideas, and for its potential relevance to the school's largely Mexican student population. The poem also resonated with the topics of healing and empathy, which had been the focus of the instructional texts during this school year. As students and teachers continued to deal with the realities of a global pandemic in a state that largely denied mitigation protocols, teachers were using carefully selected texts and writing as ways to help students express their fears and feelings of loss. Mr. Drew asked the teachers and us to compose a quick write to respond to the question, "What's Brown saying in this poem?"

We explained, we interpreted, and we argued about the ideas in the poem and the content that was worth asking students to dig into (see the *Discuss* phase and *Whole Group: Target Responses* in Table 4.1). Mr. Drew led the discussion and took notes. He asked teachers questions to help them think through which content was worth asking students to study without imposing his beliefs about what was "worthy" of instruction. He asked questions such as, "What do you all notice about the methods that Brown uses as a poet when she writes?" prompting teachers to think about how Brown weaves together history and her present reality, and then to pose their own questions about the structure of the poem. Mr. Drew was methodical in how he asked the team to first understand the poem and what it offered, but then to backwards plan. What did they want students to produce as the culmination of their work with the poem? He asked the team to think through the student-centered tasks that needed to happen to deepen students' understanding of Brown's poem and to support students to be successful with that culminating task.

By the midpoint of the ninety-minute PLC, the Arlington team had created the framework for an instructional arc of tasks that would support students to respond to the prompt:

> Arianna Brown, who wrote the poem "Curanderismo," says that she is the "girl who washes herself with poems & finally gets to the therapist." Sometimes people need to heal, mentally or emotionally, after difficult situations or life experiences. Think carefully about this statement. Write an essay explaining how people heal from mental or emotional pain.

At that point—when teachers would begin thinking about the details of the comprehension work for students—Mr. Drew asked them to reflect on how they had taught another poem that was part of the district's curriculum, "My Ceremony for Taking,"[11] by Lara Mann. Teachers had engaged in instructional planning similar to the planning you've read about here for the Mann poem several weeks earlier. They committed to collecting and bringing back student work related to that poem, and were prepared to reflect on what the work told them about what students knew and were able to do.

We want to take a moment to note that large grain instructional improvement often looks different from traditional improvement. Rather than rapid change that might happen in the moment (and does happen at Arlington when appropriate), the "study" piece of the PDSA cycle might take place a few days after the "do" part. This can be because of the nature of the test of change. ELA teachers aren't going to switch out an instructional text in the moment when students aren't getting it but will note, for example, that students struggled to move from literal meaning to understanding figurative meaning. They then can use that information to inform subsequent rounds of instructional planning for similar texts. It might also take more than one data point to understand if it's the text or the task that is causing the issue.

Ms. Paulo, Mr. Dinh, and Mr. Alvarez concluded that while the sequence of tasks for the Mann poem had helped students to grapple with the poet's words, students, especially those still classified as Emergent Multilingual (EML), would benefit from a short background piece prior to engaging with the Brown poem. The goal would be to help them go beyond the literal and start making inferences about the poem's broader ideas. They also decided that students should have a chance to read the poem once and think about the ideas, and then watch a video of the poet reading it to help deepen their understanding of the meaning.

To help students access their background knowledge, teachers decided they would start with a short quick write in response to the question, "What do you know about curanderas?" This question would allow Spanish-speaking students to be the experts, and help others develop a shared understanding of the word. Here, we were still engaged in the Discuss phase of the planning protocol and starting to shift the conversation to Other Considerations.

The Arlington team was familiar with creating, testing, and adapting task sheets. Mr. Dinh and Mr. Alvarez volunteered to draft and share the task sheets for "Curanderismo," get feedback from Mr. Drew, and share with Ms. Paulo, who would work on the background piece that would be their instructional change (see Appendix A on page 253 for the task sheet).

Toward the end of our time, Mr. Drew moved into Planning for Debrief as he led the team in developing a timeline of when they planned to try out each task sheet, what they wanted to see and hear from students to understand the impact on student learning, and when they would come together to share what they learned and consider how they would adapt the task sheets for when they taught poetry again. He also committed to visiting each

9th grade classroom in his role as NSI coordinator and instructional leader to help teachers track the impact the work had on students, and to provide some instructional coaching and in-the-moment instructional problem-solving when needed. As a classroom teacher, this work is not a normal function of Mr. Drew's job; however, as an improvement leader, he felt responsible to the 9th grade teaching team and to their students.

Over the next several weeks, teachers worked to implement the instruction they had planned around "Curanderismo," and Mr. Drew worked with teachers to make adaptations as needed. In reflecting on having Mr. Drew as an improvement lead, Mr. Alvarez said, "Mr. Drew is amazing.... We're learning the whole time we're planning. [He] pushes us to ask why, what's the purpose of the work.... It's a really cool process when you build [instruction] … it's a lot of work but it's worth it when you have the results in the classroom."[12]

Debriefing with Teachers after Task Implementation

You saw an integration of the Debrief protocol as part of the PLC planning in the preceding case story. Mr. Drew found it useful to discuss the work teachers did with another poem during that PLC to inform the planning and potential instructional changes for the work around "Curanderismo." However, debriefing an instructional change or a co-planned lesson does not always happen during the planning of the next lesson, especially when the texts or tasks are distinctly different. It can happen as its own PLC and it is a process that can be revisited with content that is taught every year. The Debrief Protocol (Appendix B, pages 254–5) is an outline of the steps for a PLC dedicated to debriefing the outcomes of an instructional test of change.

You will notice that this protocol picks up where the planning protocol left off—with collecting and sharing artifacts of student learning. During our monthly Network meetings, NSI coaches modeled studying student work for teachers, and in annual surveys, teachers reported finding the process valuable. For thirty minutes at the beginning of the meeting, each school coordinator shared a task and student work with other Network coordinators. Their discussions focused on how the task was adapted from the original task, what they hoped to hear and see from students based on the adaptation, what they learned from engaging students in the task, additional information they learned from studying the student work, and what they wanted to keep, adapt, or abandon with the next instructional task.

Mr. Drew used this structure as he created the Debrief Protocol for Arlington. The Planning Before PLC phase ensures that student work is being collected and shared among the members of the PLC. During his facilitation of this work, Mr. Drew found it helpful for teachers to bring copies of work from their own students and share packets of that work with one another. This meant each teacher had a chance to learn something about their instruction through the lens of their own students but could also reflect on the impact of instruction across the 9th grade student body. Keeping the students anonymous helped to remove some of the bias or preconceived ideas that teachers may have had about students, preventing statements such as, "This is good work for X ...," and keeping the conversation focused on evidence from students' responses in relationship to the learning goal/performance standard for the task.

The IFL uses a protocol for studying student work that provides a process for teachers to study and then talk about the student work in relationship to the task. The process can be a hard shift for teachers in the beginning because it requires describing student work in relationship to the main trait of the task. This practice sometimes sits in opposition to the standard grading practice that requires evaluation of the work. When teachers study student work, they might say that the work included a claim, but the claim did not include a big idea from the poem. This signals that students don't yet understand the poem and need some additional comprehension work. If teachers were grading, they might mark the paper down for lacking a proper claim and move on.

Arlington teachers regularly studied student work to ensure that instruction was building students' knowledge about a text. For example, in a debriefing meeting that took place a year after the case story and after teachers' second implementation of the work on "Curanderismo," teachers looked at a recent batch of student work for the first comprehension task. Students were asked to write in response to the question, "What do you think Brown is saying in this poem? In other words, how would you explain Brown's central idea to someone who has not read this poem? Draw on evidence from across the poem to support your response." When Mr. Alvarez shared his students' work, teachers found that students typically were able to talk

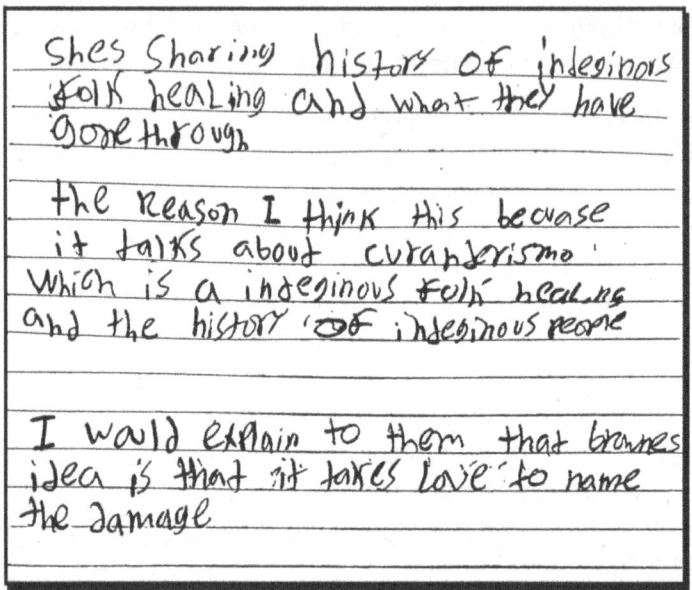

Figure 4.1 Sample of student work.

about Brown's ideas in the first section of the poem, but did not connect what they understood from section one to the other two sections of the poem (see Figure 4.1 for an example). Teachers used this information to make adjustments to the next task in the sequence, asking students to focus in on each section to develop a coherent understanding of the poem as a whole.

In the excerpt of a transcript that follows, Mr. Drew leads a PLC reflection and discussion of instructional changes that may improve students' understanding of the poem. The practice of discussing and adapting going forward should happen during implementation of instruction, but teachers should continue to adapt as they return to tasks, which, in education, may only happen a semester or a year later. The transcript shows how the conversations around the "Curanderismo" tasks have continued and how teachers discussed adaptations based on evidence from their instruction.

Excerpt from PLC Discussion at Arlington High School

1	Mr. Drew	Let's talk about the next task. Do we do it like we did last
2		time? Or are we going to? Is there something that we want
3		to change, that we want to make better?

4	Mr. Alvarez	Because of timing. I have a question. We don't have to do it. But I kind of would like to try. So, we have three different sections in this poem. What if we tried to divide our entire class into three different groups? One handles section one, one handles section two, one handles section three and then they do the guided or the whole group discussion. And they guide that discussion and we're there to facilitate it. But they really take ownership of "hey, this is what's happening in stanza one, stanza two and this is why. What do you think?" And like, I guess they teach it. I mean, I don't know if that's the correct terminology.
15	Mr. Diaz	Yeah. Like, they can go into that with their group, like, section one, and then they share it with the whole group. And then when they are sharing with the bigger group, like the other people that didn't have that one, they can make notes about what they're saying.
20	Mr. Drew	I think that's a really cool way to do it. The only thing that you always have to think about, okay, is that whenever they do that, you give somebody like, you know, he has section one, you have section two, you have section three, right? Whenever he teaches section one, sometimes what'll happen is that nobody else has read section one or put a whole lot of thought into section one. And so you have to hold them accountable to make sure that they do that. You know what I mean? Because we do that, teachers do that all the time. They give us, you read this chapter, and you read that chapter, and you read that chapter. Well, then I never read chapter two or three because I only focus on one.
32	Mr. Alvarez	Right.
33	Mr. Drew	I'm listening to him, but I'm beholden to what he believes and what he saw there. Right? And so then that becomes a problem where the kids aren't making their own decisions on some of these questions, but are like, what's happening here, what's happening there. We have to make sure that they can talk about the whole thing.
39	Mr. Alvarez	Yeah. And so we could do, um, so we have them work on section one, section two, section three. And then now you're taking these five minutes to go through section

42		one, because group one is going to present and then
43		we're walking around facilitating, making sure that they're
44		reading and thinking.
45	Mr. Drew	They're where those other groups can kind of at the very
46		least consider these. Where it takes them so that they'll be
47		more ready to argue about what the sections say because if
48		we can get them arguing then we've got them.

You'll notice in line two that Mr. Drew begins the conversation by asking the question, *"Is there something that we want to change, that we want to make better?"* This question invites and sets the expectation that conversation will focus on instructional improvement rooted in teachers' experiences. He then opens the floor for discussion. In lines four to fifteen Mr. Alvarez acknowledges that the length of a class period worked against the time the task required for students to deeply engage with each section of the poem and suggests an adaptation to try. Mr. Drew, drawing from his own experiences, encourages the adaptation in line twenty. He goes on in lines twenty-one to thirty-one and thirty-three to thirty-eight to ask teachers: how do they ensure that students do not singularly focus on their assigned section and miss the rest of the poem? Mr. Alvarez then shifts to thinking about how the task can ask students to revisit each section of the poem before student groups facilitate discussions.

Mr. Drew does not take over the thinking in this quick exchange but surfaces a potential issue that might arise. We often talk about teachers' ability to move the conversation forward without taking over the intellectual work in classrooms rich in academically productive talk. It's also a skill that's needed in an effective PLC. The ability to facilitate thinking during a discussion in this way comes with content knowledge and teaching expertise. From working with texts and studying the poem, Mr. Drew understands the importance of students seeing how ideas build throughout a text. He also knows from his own teaching experiences that students may only attend to their assigned sections and that instruction needs to consider and mediate for that possibility. Rather than telling the teachers in the PLC exactly what they should do, he opened space for Mr. Alvarez to talk through a possible solution. By doing so, Mr. Drew is building Mr. Alvarez's instructional capacity and continuing to set the expectation that Arlington is a collaborative community that is constantly working to improve for students. He is working as an effective improvement instructional leader.

Characteristics of Effective Teacher Leadership

The case story provides a glimpse into work that happens at least once a week at Arlington, and begins to highlight the power of a teacher leading collaborative improvement work during a PLC. We have found, and the research supports, that there are several characteristics that can make teachers effective instructional leaders. Teachers who are primed to lead improvement (1) demonstrate a deep understanding of their school context including knowing who students are both as people and as learners; (2) have deep teaching and content knowledge, which allows them to help new teachers blend instructional improvement and content-based instruction; and (3) demonstrate a desire to improve teaching and learning at the school through an inquiry stance.[13] In this section, we will look more closely at each characteristic.

A Deep Understanding of School Context

Mr. Drew has history in the Arlington community—he has spent all of his teaching career working with students at the school—and he grew up a member of the community that surrounds it. He knows the Hispanic students well. He has worked to develop an understanding of what students need to access and be successful with instructional tasks in 9th grade, as well as the knowledge and skills that students need to develop to be successful when they arrive in his classroom during their 11th grade year.

While Mr. Drew is fortunate to work in the community where he was raised, that is not the only way teachers can develop a deep understanding of their school context. Understanding can be developed through sustained interaction and involvement with the school's community. Mr. Alvarez is a great example of someone who has become an improvement leader himself, as you'll see toward the end of the chapter, but did not join the Arlington team with strong community ties. He moved to Big City from Puerto Rico in 2021. His knowledge of the Arlington community comes from his involvement with student organizations at the school, his desire to collaborate with other teachers, and his willingness to participate in neighborhood events.

Mr. Drew's and Mr. Alvarez's experiences have helped them to understand who the Arlington students are as people and as learners. They have seen students grow when teachers ask them to work in collaboration—when they are able to talk about their ideas and understandings with their peers and learn from one another, actions that happen with purposeful implementation of the student-centered practices. It goes back to the idea that we highlighted in the introduction, that learning is social, and intelligence grows from socialization. However, to facilitate those interactions, teachers need to understand and acknowledge who their students are—both inside and outside of the classroom—and leverage and build on students' assets during instruction. Teachers with deep understanding of students and context develop classroom communities where students are comfortable expressing confusion, are invested in helping each other learn, and are committed to working hard to get their understanding right. The same can be said about leading teachers during a PLC. An effective instructional leader will have an understanding of the teachers in the room, acknowledge who they are as individuals, and create space to leverage the collective experiences and knowledge those teachers bring to the learning community.

Understanding the school context also creates opportunities to leverage culturally relevant texts for instruction. The authors, characters, ideas, and language that are prioritized and held up as "ideal" in the texts students are asked to read and to write about sends a message to students about whose experiences matter and whose thoughts and experiences are seen as being worthy of study and discussion. Mr. Drew and the team at Arlington prioritized the voices of authors who reflected the students in their classrooms, creating opportunities for students to see themselves as being worthy members of the literacy community. Students who find value and relevance in instructional materials are more likely to improve as readers and writers over time.[14] Selecting culturally relevant instructional materials goes beyond making sure Hispanic or Black authors are included here and there. Teachers are purposeful about choosing specific authors and texts. For example, the Arlington team selected "Curanderismo" because the poet's background is similar to their students' backgrounds and the poem cohered with the themes teachers were working on. This process of text selection also means making sure that texts represent the diverse range of experiences within cultures. Recently, a Big City teacher expressed her frustration that all of the texts in the curriculum by Black authors were slave narratives. Students took note and openly wondered why that was. They were yearning to see Blackness in writing in other ways—ways that represented the joy, triumph, and defeat that they experienced in their own lives and the ways in which they wanted to write about their own experiences.

In the case story, we don't see how Mr. Drew laid the foundation for Mr. Dinh to bring the Brown poem to the group as a potential text. Early on in the PLC teachers had completed an audit of the texts in the curriculum, a process that NSI coordinators also had engaged in as part of the Network's root cause analysis. Teachers began by using a rubric to analyze the complexity of the texts. They then took a step back and asked, "Whose experiences are truly being represented in these texts?" During that analysis it became clear to teachers that Arlington's students were not being centered in the authors and experiences the curriculum put forward as being worthy of study. Teachers found that in the first six months of the school year, students were only asked to read one text by a Hispanic author—a satire about political events in Argentina. The texts in the curriculum represented a mostly White, mostly male group of authors. This is typical in middle and high school curricula across the United States, despite calls to diversify the curriculum going back decades.[15] Recognizing the need to add more relevant texts, but also the need to choose purposefully so that texts cohere with the themes and standards of the current units, Mr. Drew led teachers through the text selection process. They prioritized texts that provide relevant mirrors for the students at Arlington, but also made decisions about which texts to keep from the district's curriculum that offer worthy lenses into the lives and cultures of other people.

Deep Teaching and Content Knowledge

Second, instructional leaders have deep teaching and content knowledge in ELA, which allows them to help new teachers blend instructional improvement with content-based instruction. We often talk about cognitive overload for students, making sure that instruction doesn't require students to take in, process, and retain too much new information at once because science shows that, inevitably, something will get missed. We don't often talk about it in terms of teachers. When we ask new teachers—teachers new to the profession, new to ELA, or new to the school—to dive into blending instructional planning with improvement methods, a concept that is often unfamiliar to new and veteran teachers alike, we risk putting them into cognitive overload if they don't have a peer to help scaffold and guide the process. We saw that happen at the beginning of the project as we heard teachers reference doing "IFL instruction" on a particular day of the week and the district curriculum the other four days. An instructional leader with deep knowledge of ELA content and effective teaching practices can facilitate instructional change planning by using protocols, as Mr. Drew did, for the study and discussion of texts that will serve as a framework for instruction. As they guide the planning work of the PLC, instructional leaders model the process of surfacing the major understandings from a text, identifying the evidence teachers expect to hear from students to know that students "got it," and developing student-centered tasks that help students first comprehend a text and then dig into author's craft and interpretive work.

Mr. Drew entered into the PLC meeting described previously knowing what the poem offered for instruction, how the content in the poem cohered with other texts the 9th grade team was working on, and the standards that the district expected teachers to address during that particular week's instruction, much the same way a prepared teacher would enter a classroom. We noted in the story that Mr. Drew asked purposeful questions during the PLC to help teachers think through what they wanted students to learn through their work with the poem without imposing his own personal beliefs about what should be taught. Teachers had agency in deciding what they wanted students to know and understand from the poem, but Mr. Drew kept them focused on the English content that the poem exemplified—the work that would grow students' knowledge and provide them space to talk, as opposed to thin work that leaves little room for talk and that students would not value. As teachers wrestled with Brown's use of language and the aspects worth studying, Mr. Drew helped the team keep the focus on how various language aspects of the poem were rich enough to talk through and learn something about, how they helped students deepen their understanding of the poem, and how they supported students to be successful with the final essay.

Mr. Drew kept the full year curriculum in mind as he planned for his work with teachers. He was keenly aware that this was a second instructional change focused on poetry. He engaged teachers specifically in talking about and sharing artifacts from their first experiences with poetry because that experience was relevant to informing the instruction they designed around "Curanderismo." Both from experience and his work during our Network meetings, Mr. Drew knew that if he had not asked the teaching team to come with the artifacts they had kept from their work with "My Ceremony for Taking," they risked experiencing the same instructional challenges they had faced with the Mann poem. They may not have explicitly considered and analyzed students' experiences that lead to more surface-level understanding rather than deep interpretation of a poet's ideas.

Improving Teaching and Learning through Inquiry

Instructional leaders demonstrate a desire to improve teaching and learning at their school. This characteristic can be hard to find in a system where teachers are compensated for having students who outperform students from other classrooms on standardized assessments or where teachers are penalized on evaluations for not marching through scripted curriculum. These conditions often create teachers who are siloed, opting to work independently to protect themselves from potentially negative attention. We needed to do a lot of work at the onset of our collaboration with teachers to develop the Network as a safe space where teachers could share what was happening with their instruction without the fear of reprimand (see Chapter 3). One benefit of creating a network where schools and teachers opt-in to participating is that, for the most part, schools and teachers are part of the network because they want to be. They recognize that something about instruction isn't working for students and they want to do better. This doesn't mean that teachers join the network with an improvement mentality already in place, but it does mean they are ready to engage in the hard work of being open about their practice, both the good and the not so good, and they want to discuss the successes and challenges other network teachers face.

In a conversation with Mr. Drew, he reflected on his decision to opt in to leading improvement at Arlington. He told us that he saw learning becoming stagnant and felt the compounded effects of that as students entered his 11th grade classroom. They were often underprepared for the rigor of the work he asked them to engage in. And students seemed to agree. When teachers at Arlington conducted empathy interviews during Year 1 of our improvement work, students asked to experience student-centered, collaborative learning. Teachers heard comments such as, "In the beginning of the year I felt very uncomfortable, and the topics seemed confusing at first. I didn't think I could talk to anyone about what I thought."[16] Students were sitting in silence at points of confusion rather than talking with peers to clarify thinking and grow their understanding.

When the principal brought the prospect of joining the Network to the entire ELA team at Arlington, Mr. Drew saw an opportunity. He told us,

"Though what the 9th grade team was doing [in 2018] wasn't bad, we weren't really moving forward. We were up a few points one year then down a few points the next year. We were maintaining, but we weren't changing much."[17] His principal asked if he'd be willing to join the department coach in attending the meetings and bringing the information back to the relatively young 9th grade team of teachers. Mr. Drew welcomed the chance.

This disposition carried forward into the teaching and learning Arlington planned for coming out of COVID-19 when many other schools were still planning what we referred to as "online learning in person." Mr. Drew supported the 9th grade teachers to move back to paper, pencil, and student-to-student collaboration. He helped teachers plan instruction that was student-centered and talk-based. The task sheet teachers planned for "Curanderismo" invited students to write, talk, refine their thinking, and talk some more about the ideas in the text. These are practices that teachers knew, from studying their instruction and the artifacts of their instruction, that students could handle even after COVID-19, and that students wanted to engage in.

The trust that teachers had in Mr. Drew and in the process of instructional change comes from the way he positioned himself as a learner with the group of teachers. Both the case story and the PLC Discussion transcript show that Mr. Drew encouraged teachers to reason through and then try out instructional decisions with the expectation that they would bring back evidence of instructional practices on student learning and make additional adjustments as needed. It's this supported cycle of Plan, Do, Study, and Act, along with conversations about effective instructional practice, that provides a framework for teachers to adapt curriculum and other instructional materials to meet the learning needs of their students. It also builds the capacity for teachers to begin to spread promising practice.

Moving to a Whole-School Culture of Improvement

While Mr. Drew started as the sole improvement leader at Arlington and was an early adopter of the work of instructional improvement, the ELA team has become a truly collaborative force. In a recent conversation, Mr. Alvarez told us that he chooses to stay in the profession and continue to work at Arlington because of the collaborative culture at the school and because Mr. Drew and Sophia Ruiz, who took over as principal of Arlington in 2019, are committed to helping both teachers and students grow. The desire to create a culture of improvement has led Principal Ruiz to implement whole-building changes that removed barriers to collaborative planning and to developing teachers across grade levels and disciplines as a community committed to improving their practice for the benefit of their students. The biggest change she undertook was rearranging the master schedule so that grade-level content teachers have the same planning periods. When we asked her about the challenges of making such a massive change, she told us, "It meant that there were fewer options for when students could take something like ninth grade English, but the returns are worth it, and you can see that in the growth that our students have made."[18] In addition to teachers sharing time, they are now also sharing space. Rather than having some teachers in one wing or another, teachers who teach the same grade and content share hallways, allowing for even more collaboration.

Proximity has proven to be an important feature for Arlington. Timewise, it allows teachers to get to PLC meetings in a large building more quickly. Outside of PLC, teachers can talk and problem solve in the hallway. Recently, Dan Ibsen, a first-year teacher during the 2023–24 school year, told us about an experience he had making a small change to a task for the text "Joyas Voladoras,"[19] by Brian Doyle. During his first period, he noticed that many students weren't participating during a whole group discussion of the comprehension question. Between periods he met Mr. Alvarez out in the hall and explained what happened. In the moment, Mr. Alvarez suggested that they engage in a shared gallery walk (both classes were working on the same text) to see if that improved conversation. During the next period, both teachers asked pairs to create charts of their ideas about the text and then post the charts on the lockers between the two classrooms. Mr. Ibsen reflected that he learned two things from that experience: that students need multiple opportunities to nail down their understanding before they are comfortable going public individually, and even then, it may be more comfortable for students to talk about what they noticed about another student's ideas. He also learned that he valued being able to co-facilitate the gallery walk with Mr. Alvarez to better understand his own role as facilitator.

The Power of "What do you think?"

We recently asked Mr. Alvarez to check in with his students to see how they are experiencing the literacy instruction in his classroom. We were curious about how students are feeling, given the agency and collaborative work teachers at Arlington put into developing meaningful instruction. We wondered whether they still felt left behind or if they felt differently from the students Mr. Drew spoke with in 2018. In an email, Mr. Alvarez let us know that he thought checking in with his students was important and an exciting opportunity for them to have their voices heard about the instruction they engage with at Arlington. One 9th grade student said the following: "I like coming to Alvarez's class because I know I'm not going to just sit there. Sometimes I think teachers don't want to hear what we think or think kids are just dumb. Mr. Alvarez isn't like that. He's always asking us 'what do you think?' and I like that."[20]

Questions for Reflection

1. How might you leverage a Planning and Debriefing protocol similar to what Mr. Drew uses at Arlington?
2. What is one big takeaway that you have about the role of PLCs for instructional improvement after reading this chapter?
3. Leaders, where do you see opportunity to empower teachers at your school, like Mr. Drew, to lead instructional change?
4. What systems might need to change or be put in place to create space for instructional improvement at your school?

Notes

1. Paul V. Bredeson and Jay Paredes Scribner, "Statewide Professional Development Conference," *Education Policy Analysis Archives* 8 (2000): 13.
2. Chapter 8 provides additional details on how Network schools were matched with non-Network schools to better understand the impact that teachers' instructional inquiry was having on students' academic growth.
3. Richard DuFour, Rebecca DuFour, Robert Eaker, M. A. Mattos, Anthony Muhammad, and ProQuest, *Revisiting Professional Learning Communities at Work: Proven Insights for Sustained, Substantive School Improvement*, 2nd edn. (Bloomington, IN: Solution

Tree Press, 2021); J. L. Russell, A. S. Bryk, D. Peurach, D. Sherer, E. Khachatryan, P. G. LeMahieu, J. Z. Sherer, and M. Hannan, "The Social Structure of Networked Improvement Communities: Cultivating the Emergence of a Scientific-professional Learning Community," *American Educational Research Association Annual Meeting*, Toronto, ON (April 2019); Rebecca H. Woodland, "Evaluating PK–12 Professional Learning Communities: An Improvement Science Perspective," *American Journal of Evaluation* 37, no. 4 (2016): 505–21.

4 Ray Williams, Ken Brien, Crista Sprague, and Gerald Sullivan, "Professional Learning Communities: Developing a School-Level Readiness Instrument," *Canadian Journal of Educational Administration and Policy* 74 (2008): 1–17.

5 Rick DuFour and Douglas Reeves, "The Futility of PLC Lite," *Phi Delta Kappan* 97, no. 6 (2016): 69–71; B. W. Cottingham, H. J. Hough, and J. Myung, *What Does It Take to Accelerate the Learning of Every Child? Early Insights from a CCEE School-Improvement Pilot* (Policy Analysis for California Education, December 2023), https://edpolicyinca.org/publications/what-does-it-take-accelerate-learning-every-child.

6 Susanne Owen, "Professional Learning Communities: Building Skills, Reinvigorating the Passion, and Nurturing Teacher Wellbeing and 'Flourishing' within Significantly Innovative Schooling Contexts," *Educational Review* 68, no. 4 (2016): 403–19.

7 Sy Doan, Joshua Eagan, David Grant, and Julia H. Kaufman, *American Instructional Resources Surveys: 2024 Technical Documentation and Survey Results* (Santa Monica, CA: RAND Corporation, 2024), https://www.rand.org/pubs/research_reports/RRA134-24.html.

8 Linda Darling-Hammond, Maria E. Hyler, and Madelyn Gardner, *Effective Teacher Professional Development* (Report, Learning Policy Institute, June 5, 2017), https://learningpolicyinstitute.org/product/effective-teacher-professional-development-report; K. J. Roth, C. D. Wilson, J. A. Taylor, M. A. M. Stuhlsatz, and C. Hvidsten, "Comparing the Effects of Analysis-of-Practice and Content-Based Professional Development on Teacher and Student Outcomes in Science," *American Educational Research Journal* 56, no. 4 (2019): 1217–253.

9 Alicia Grunow, Sandra Park, and Brandon Bennett, *Journey to Improvement: A Team Guide to Systems Change in Education, Health Care, and Social Welfare* (Lanham, MD: Rowman & Littlefield, 2024).

10 Ariana Brown, "Curanderismo," in *Sana Sana* (Boston: Game Over Books, 2020).

11 L. Mann, "My Ceremony for Taking," in *My Ceremony for Taking* (Champaign: University of Illinois at Urbana-Champaign, 2009).

12 Interview with Ian Alvarez by Sara DeMartino, October 2022.

13 Sara DeMartino, Glenn Nolly, and Anthony Petrosky, "Teacher Leaders Help Change Ideas Stick," *The Learning Professional* 44, no. 2 (2023): 46–50.

14 Pedro A. Noguera, "The Trouble with Black Boys: The Role and Influence of Environmental and Cultural Factors on the Academic Performance of African American Males," *Urban Education* 38, no. 4 (2003): 431–59; R. Gutiérrez, "Framing

Equity: Helping Students 'Play the Game' and 'Change the Game,'" *Teaching for Excellence and Equity in Mathematics* 1, no. 1 (2009): 4–8; Gholdy Muhammad, *Cultivating Genius: An Equity Framework for Culturally and Historically Responsive Literacy* (New York: Scholastic Incorporated, 2020).

15. Tanji Reed Marshall and William H. Rodick, "The Search for More Complex Racial and Ethnic Representation in Grade School Books," The Education Trust (2023); "Guess What? There's Already Under-Representation in School Curricula," The Education Trust, accessed January 8, 2025, https://edtrust.org/blog/guess-what-theres-already-under-representation-in-school-curricula/.
16. Interview with Arlington student by Brian Drew, November 2018.
17. Interview with Brian Drew by Sara DeMartino, December 2022.
18. Interview with Sophia Ruiz by Glenn Nolly, March 2024.
19. Brian Doyle, "Joyas Voladoras," *Now I'm Just a Shot in the Dark* (blog), February 7, 2008, http://nowimjustashotinthedark.blogspot.com/2008/02/joyas-voladoras-by-brian-doyle.html.
20. Interview with Arlington student by Ian Alvarez, April 2024.

5 Leadership for Instructional Change: Rose-Wood High School and Zora Neale Hurston Middle School

In the fall of 2019 and the beginning of Year 2 of our Network, we arrived at Rose-Wood High School (RWHS) to discuss the student-centered practices with English teachers and an assistant principal. We had been invited by the principal, Jackson Turner, after he engaged in a student-centered task at our first principal-focused Network meeting. The plan was to facilitate a conversation with the team to develop a small instructional change they could immediately enact with students. At the next Professional Learning Community (PLC) meeting, teachers would bring artifacts and share what they had noticed about the impact of the change on student learning. The plan was for these actions to be part of an inquiry cycle for teachers, supported by Mr. Turner.

We were greeted by the assistant principal, who informed us they would have to reschedule the meeting; their executive director had asked teachers to engage students in a practice exam that morning. We agreed to reschedule. Adaptability was one of the team's guiding principles when working with Network schools and teachers. School schedules are constantly in flux, and we learned to be flexible when the unexpected occurred.

On our way to the exit, we saw Mr. Turner. We stopped to say hello and let him know we would gladly reschedule the session. Mr. Turner greeted us like he always did, with a big smile and tremendous enthusiasm. "It's so good to see you. How are you doing? We had to change our schedule to accommodate district testing so things might be a little off today. You are here to meet with the admin team and some teachers. We have you meeting in the theater conference room."

When we told him that the meeting had been postponed, he asked us to hold on while he called one of the assistant principals on the two-way radio. He told the assistant principal we were there waiting for the meeting to start. Though we didn't hear the response, we heard Mr. Turner say, "Please get the teachers together and all other parties and proceed as we planned." To us, he said he was sorry about the mix-up. "We don't waste resources around here," he said. "Give us a few minutes, and we'll get started." Mr. Turner escorted us to the conference room, and soon we were fully engaged in conversation.

Through this one action of focusing teachers' work on rigorous instruction, Mr. Turner set the expectation for teachers and the assistant principal that teaching and learning were a priority at RWHS.

We use this story to center the importance of principals who create school cultures that value collaboration around a shared vision of rigorous teaching and learning. We learned early in our work with Big City School District (BCSD) about the role principals play in setting the conditions for teachers to engage in instructional inquiry, and in promoting academic growth beyond the acquisition of skills aligned to an assessment. In this chapter, we share the leadership of Mr. Turner, who led RWHS, and Tonya Coates, who led Zora Neale Hurston Middle School (ZNHMS). We will look at how both leaders opened doors for instructional improvement to take place. Both principals leveraged the knowledge they built during Network leadership meetings about improvement processes and instructional changes to help teachers find coherence and safety in their own instructional inquiry work. Both encouraged teachers to create spaces for students to experience complex texts and tasks with scaffolded support and high expectations. Overall, in this chapter we highlight the specific ways both principals demonstrated leadership for improvement.

We begin by describing each school to set the context. Next, we look at student outcomes over time at the two schools. We briefly consider what the research on effective principals shows, followed by a discussion of how we worked with principals and how the Network supported them. From there we discuss the individual moves the featured principals made at their schools in two general areas: building productive school climates and focusing their work with teachers on instruction. We close the chapter with the lessons we learned about leadership that give us hope for the future, and with a tool to support the assessment of a school's readiness to take on instructional change.

School Contexts

Rose-Wood High School

Like many schools that serve predominantly Black students, Rose-Wood High School has a history rooted in segregation, underfunding, mismanagement, and government takeover. Rose and Wood are two small cities south of Big City. In 1927, they were incorporated to form the Rose-Wood Independent School District (RWISD). Like most districts, RWISD was segregated. The original Rose-Wood High School was established for White students. Black students attended the Colored High School on the second floor of the Colored Elementary School. The district had a standing practice of often closing the Black schools to enable students to pick crops.

Government policies made it easy for Rose-Wood to maintain the practice of separate and unequal. After desegregation in 1967, the now predominantly poor Black district was plagued with fiscal mismanagement, dilapidated buildings, declining enrollment, and inadequate performance on state assessments. In the 1970s, the State Education Agency appointed monitors to oversee the district, ultimately closing it for the 2005–06 school year. After all other surrounding school districts had declined the opportunity to receive students of the Rose-Wood community, BCSD absorbed all assets and students.

The superintendent of BCSD promised to rebuild RWHS. In 2011, the new RWHS, fully renovated and partially rebuilt, rose from despair to thrive again and provide hope for new generations. As of 2024, RWHS served almost 1,000 students: 47 percent Black, 49 percent Hispanic, 1 percent White, and 2 percent Asian, Indigenous, or Pacific Islander. Ninety-eight percent of students were classified as economically disadvantaged.

Zora Neale Hurston Middle School

Zora Neale Hurston Middle School is located in the southwest of Big City, in a neighborhood known as Hillside. The area has gone from being predominantly White to primarily Hispanic and Black. During the 2023–24 school year, the student population was 93 percent economically disadvantaged, 64 percent emergent multilingual, 94 percent Hispanic, and 4 percent Black. Built in 2012 to house the growing population of Hispanic students, the school is a modern structure featuring ceiling-to-floor windows.

After the first principal left, the executive director at the time mentioned the challenge she had identifying principals who were interested in leading ZNHMS. Many candidates declined because at the time, it was an underperforming school. Principal Coates willingly accepted the opportunity.

Student Outcomes

Data show that the early work of Principal Turner to establish a culture rooted in rigorous grade-level instruction paid off as RWHS emerged from COVID-19. Many schools, including those in our Network, saw state exam scores dip during the 2020–21 school year. RWHS saw a 7 percent decline (from 30.1 percent in 2018–19 to 28 percent in 2020–21) in the percentages of students scoring proficient and above on the 9th grade English state assessment. Other schools not in the Network, but matched to RWHS based on size, demographics, and students' literacy proficiency rates, saw a 31.9 percent to 22.1 percent decline (from the 2018–19 SY to the 2020–21 SY) in students who scored proficient and above on the same exam. (See Chapter 8 for an explanation of how schools were matched.)

Data also show that students at ZNHMS benefited from instructional change led by Principal Coates. When compared to matched middle schools, the percentage of ZNHMS students who scored proficient and above on the reading portion of the 8th grade state assessment was almost identical at the end of Year 1 of the Network (ZNHMS: 28.6 percent, matched: 28.1 percent). Principal Coates joined the school in Year 2. Across her four years of Network support, the percentage of students scoring proficient and above on the tests grew by more than 17 percent (from 28.6 percent in Year 1 to 33.5 percent in Year 5). Matched schools, in comparison, saw an 11 percent change during the same period (from 28.1 percent to 31.3 percent on the same assessment. The improvement in scores was particularly strong during Year 4 when students at ZNHMS outperformed their matched peers by nearly 6 percent. Scores decreased in Year 5, perhaps partially due to a shift to a new middle school curriculum at the beginning of that year.

The Qualities of Highly Effective Principals

Principals play various roles in a school—lead learner, culture builder, advocate, mentor, supervisor, manager, politician, and conductor.[1] One study indicates that highly effective principals raise the achievement of a typical student in their schools by between two and seven months in a single school year; ineffective principals lower achievement by the same amount. What makes a principal highly effective? Mastery of organizational, people, and instructional skills underpin strong principal performance. Research shows those skills all come into play when principals carry out the following four key behaviors:

- Focusing their work with teachers on instruction. This covers a range of activities, from instructional coaching and evaluation to smart use of data to inform improvements.
- Building a productive school climate.
- Forging collaboration and professional learning (PL) among teachers and others.
- Managing personnel and resources well.[2]

Qualities of Effective Network Principals

We worked to strengthen these behaviors in the leaders of the Network schools. For example, we helped leaders focus on providing teachers with non-evaluative feedback on their use of the student-centered practices, both when they taught the district curriculum and when they taught supplemental texts. We did this by engaging principals with the student-centered tasks teachers were using with students. We provided them with opportunities to analyze the demand of the texts and tasks, helped them align district-mandated PLC protocols to support the work of instructional inquiry, and helped them plan and enact *learning walks*. By developing a common understanding of the work of the Network and the planning required of teachers to enact inquiry cycles with the student-centered practices, principals were able to help teachers see the alignment between the NSI work, the state standards, and various other district initiatives, such as AVID and the middle school tutoring and support initiative we have called Reaching New Heights (RNH), creating a more productive school environment. Principals rearranged master schedules to facilitate more opportunities for teacher-to-teacher collaboration and for bringing IFL NSI coaches in for additional professional learning and observations. Human capital became a priority as leaders sought out new hires committed to a culture of improvement. Principals also provided school teams with additional resources, from supplemental texts to time, that would support teachers in their collaborative improvement efforts.

> *"Our goals were to help principals understand the student-centered practices; how the practices look in classrooms when they are implemented with rigorous, appropriate, grade-level texts and tasks; and the types of supports teachers would benefit from to engage in instructional inquiry."*

Knowledge about instruction was especially critical for principals supporting Network teachers. In the view of Leithwood et al., "To successfully guide continual professional learning, principals must become intimately familiar with the 'technical core of schooling' and all that is required to improve the quality of teaching and learning."[3] The "technical core of schooling" includes collaborating with teachers to develop a shared vision for teaching and learning, keeping track of and participating in teachers' professional learning, and closely monitoring how practices learned during professional learning manifest in the teaching and learning happening in classrooms. Our goals were to help principals understand the student-centered practices; how the practices look in classrooms when they are implemented with rigorous, appropriate, grade-level texts and tasks; and the types of supports teachers would benefit from to engage in instructional inquiry.

How Principals Support Teaching and Learning

As we said, using examples from each school, we will discuss how Mr. Turner and Ms. Coates established supports and conditions for teachers and their students to be successful with student-centered instruction driven by the Network practices. These supports included setting high expectations about and for students with worthy texts and academic give-and-take in classrooms that put students' thinking and reasoning at the center. Teachers also benefited from time and scheduling changes that allowed them to collaborate on and view high-quality instruction.

Using the Network to Create a Shared Vision of Teaching and Learning

We spent a good part of the first year asking teachers to analyze the instruction happening in their classrooms and at their school. They used shared tools to analyze the questions in tasks, a shared rubric to understand the complexity of texts, a protocol to study artifacts of student learning, and transcripts and audio recordings of interviews with their peers and their students about instructional experiences. By the spring of 2019, when students had been experiencing the practices for some months, these analyses highlighted students' desires to be intellectually challenged in the classroom and to work with each other to make sense of the content and ideas they were studying. During an empathy interview conducted by a teacher, one student stated, "I want [the teacher] to know that I am good enough to answer his questions and I like to hear other people's thoughts on the prompt so that I can relate or disagree on what [my classmates] believe is being portrayed."[4] Other students also noted that they wanted to be engaged with their peers' thinking about the texts they read.

The analysis of instructional artifacts showed that the curriculum offered opportunities for teachers to adapt and build on the prescribed instruction to increase instructional rigor. It also revealed a tension. Teachers saw opportunities to make instructional changes. They hypothesized that these changes would allow students to engage with content through academic writing and talk with their peers. However, they hesitated to make them. They didn't know if their principals understood the current state of teaching and learning in their classrooms, or the reasoning behind the instructional shifts under discussion.

The teachers' concerns about what principals understood surprised us, not because we did not expect teachers to have concerns, but because we *had* been working with principals in between our Network convenings. We invited principals to come to Network meetings with teachers, and several took up the charge. In the first few months of the Network, we would see Mr. Turner from RWHS, Ms. Waverly from Big City High School, and Ms. Hanes from Star Middle School join their teachers during our Thursday meetings. However, others were not able to come or couldn't stay the full two hours. We realized that the inconsistency of this contact made it difficult for some principals to understand what was being asked of Network teachers and to fully understand the impact the student-centered practices could have on students. To accommodate principals' schedules, and to create more regular contact with them, we met with those who couldn't attend the Network meetings at their own schools. There, we discussed the teachers' work and engaged with them in *The Learning Walk* process described in detail below.

At the beginning of Year 2, we began to schedule monthly convenings with principals. These meetings became an important space for principals to make sense of how shifts in their leadership behaviors could have a big impact on instruction and to discuss among themselves how they could support their teachers who wanted to incorporate the practices.

We began by asking them to focus their work with teachers on instruction. As we had done with teachers, we engaged principals as learners, using a comprehension task with a complex text and the student-centered practices. Our first goal was for principals to build a shared lens for what teaching and learning could look like with small instructional shifts. Second, we wanted principals to think of themselves as instructional leaders who used non-evaluative coaching and data to support the collaborative improvement efforts happening at their schools.

We were strategic about our approach. We drew from our experiences working in other districts across the country. At the same time, we knew that the most compelling examples of the impact of any change would come from their own district. We asked Cate Newbaugh, an 8th grade teacher at Pietro Middle School and one of the early champions of instructional improvement, to engage the principals in a comprehension task that she used with her students. The task used an NPR broadcast titled, "Scientists Start To Tease Out The Subtler Ways Racism Hurts Health."[5]

> "Principals were struck with how the simple practices drove the collaborative development of knowledge with their peers. One reflected that she was excited about 'the way students can finally become active participants in their learning' when they are invited to engage in the practices."

After they had completed the task, she asked them to reflect on how the student-centered practices affected their learning. Principals were struck with how the simple practices drove the collaborative development of knowledge with their peers. One reflected that she was excited about "the way students can finally become active participants in their learning"[6] when they are invited to engage in the practices. Principals wanted to know how they might support their teachers to study and adapt their own instruction. Ms. Newbaugh explained the process teachers went through during Network convenings to analyze their own instruction, and she told them that the task they had just engaged in reflected small changes the Network teachers had decided to try out. She pointed to the quick write as an instructional change that had made a big difference in the quality and amount of her students' conversation, and she tied the change in conversation to the improvement she saw in her students' writing. Students were verbally explaining their ideas and she was starting to see that translate into longer written explanations.

The principals were interested but also expressed concerns. They wanted to know how the work supported students to meet the state standards, and how it cohered with other district initiatives, specifically RNH, a program that had garnered a lot of attention for its potential to increase students' overall academic success.

We were prepared for these questions. They were not all that different from the questions teachers had asked during Year 1. We had aligned the task and the practices to the state standards and to the standards on the district's instructional planning calendar, and we shared that information with principals. We gave them the district's PLC planning guide, created to reflect the core principles of RNH, and asked them to work in trios to think through how they could use the guide to support teachers in planning a task like the one they had experienced. They talked about creating collaborative time and space for teachers but also surfaced the need for additional support and more classroom examples. They were interested in seeing the impact these changes had on the work that students produced in class. In her reflection after that first meeting, Ms. Coates stated, "I would definitely like to see a video of Ms. Newbaugh conducting the exact lesson she did with our group with students."[7]

Successive meetings with principals focused on deepening their vision of teaching and learning and aligning it to the vision that our Network teachers built through the root cause analysis process, the driver diagram (see Chapter 1), and their engagement in their own collaborative instructional inquiry. As one example, during a session that turned out to be particularly powerful, we asked principals to work in small groups to analyze texts and comprehension tasks that Network teachers had developed and shared. Principals used the same task analysis guide and text complexity rubric that teachers used in Year 1. They were then asked to describe the work students had produced from the task, a process different from grading, which centered them on strengths and areas for improvement. Several themes were common in the big takeaways principals generated for themselves during the meeting, as follows:

- Leaders would benefit from classroom observations with a shared protocol that focused observers on describing what they noticed about classroom tasks.
- School leaders and IFL NSI coaches across schools should continue to facilitate communication beyond the sharing at Network meetings.
- Leaders would benefit from making time to engage with teachers' PLCs and to help teachers use their Network tools to support instructional change.
- Leaders could support normalizing student-centered instruction at NSI campuses.[8]

In the discussion that follows we focus on Mr. Turner and Ms. Coates, who made those takeaways part of their leadership practice. We look at two aspects of their leadership: building productive school climates and focusing their work with teachers on instruction.

Building a Productive School Climate

Studies of what makes a school ready to engage in instructional improvement often cite capacity for change as a critical element of any successful initiative.[9]

Capacity for change can be measured by how a school is structured to receive and support a specific program. This includes whether there is a culture of trust, a shared vision for change, and an open channel of communication between teachers and leadership.[10] In the case of our Network, we asked how school communities were prepared to support, plan for, and implement student-centered practices. Both Mr. Turner and Ms. Coates created school communities where teachers collaborated around and supported a school-wide plan for change, shared a vision for the practices that supported grade-level instruction, and had ongoing opportunities to build an understanding of the practices. As you saw at the beginning of the chapter, Mr. Turner engaged in instructional planning in collaboration with his teachers in their PLCs. This was part of a plan he developed to build a school climate conducive to improving instruction. What follows is a description of Mr. Turner's plan for school-wide change.

Mr. Turner: Creating a Plan for School-wide Support

In the spring of 2020, after taking some time to engage with other principals, engage with the IFL NSI coaches, and work with his teachers, Mr. Turner called a meeting to create a school-wide plan for developing a culture of improvement. He invited us, Daniel Jones, the teacher who was leading the 9th grade instructional inquiry work, and Rochelle Thompkins, the literacy coach. His desire to make a school-wide shift was prompted by his classroom observations. Before instruction moved online because of COVID-19, Mr. Turner had noticed a positive change in students' interactions with each other around content. He wanted to spread those changes vertically to other grades and across content areas.

The plan we developed included a road map for where the instructional inquiry work would move, who would be responsible for moving that work, and what additional supports teachers would need. Ms. Thompkins was identified as the person who could champion the spread of the work to social studies and science, which fell under her coaching work. Those teachers trusted her and would follow her lead to develop an understanding of the student-centered practices and how they could use inquiry cycles to support and adapt them. She had participated in inquiry cycles during ELA PLCs and attended Network meetings with Mr. Jones. Mr. Turner decided to consult with the mathematics team before developing a plan for that content area. Overall, the expectation was that the improvement plan would be a collaborative effort across teachers at the school, underscoring Mr. Turner's commitment to creating space for teachers to own the improvement work.

The team also considered how new teachers would learn about the work. We saw an opportunity for Mr. Jones and Ms. Thompkins to run professional learning for new hires. This would include taking them through a student-centered task as learners, asking them to reflect on the instruction they experienced, and asking them to reflect on how they might use the practices in their own classrooms. New teachers would engage in small instructional changes using the practices in their PLC work with the support of teachers experienced in instructional inquiry. Along with new hire learning, the team planned to continue working with veteran teachers by using a sequence of school-wide PL on additional instructional practices that could be used as part of an inquiry cycle, such as studying student work, selecting texts that could carry the rigor of the student-centered practices, studying and testing out different types of questioning to elicit Accountable Talk®[11] (student-driven talk that is accountable to the learning community, knowledge, and rigorous thinking), and modeling supports for students to move from their quick writes to more complete essays. These PL sessions would be run by RWHS faculty and, when needed, supported by IFL NSI coaches. Mr. Turner protected three hours of time during the four district-mandated PL days to accommodate whole-school learning related to instructional inquiry.

In addition to the learning happening at RWHS, he welcomed opportunities from outside of the NSI that he and the teachers saw as beneficial to continuing to grow veteran Network teachers and contributing to building a productive school culture around inquiry. From November 2020 to May 2021, 9th grade teacher Susan Knight, along with several of her students, collaborated on a voluntary design project involving a nonprofit to develop a sequence of reading and writing instruction that centered students' identities, with Mr. Turner's support. Mr. Turner was one of three NSI principals who took up the invitation for his school to participate. Ms. Knight had a deep commitment to equity and the academic empowerment of her students. Working with the outside group, she extended her understanding of the inquiry process, learning about additional ways to use empathy interviews and surveys to understand students' instructional experiences and the content they were interested in learning. During the project, Ms. Knight and her students worked from the themes that emerged from the data to develop a two-week lesson on identity, with a focus on empowering students to think of themselves and for themselves.

As part of an inquiry cycle in the spring of 2021, Ms. Knight tested the assignment by having students explore aspects of their identity after she modeled her own journey of identity development for them. She shared the project at the final Network meeting of the school year. During that meeting, Ms. Knight commented that she had learned new things about her students during the project. In addition, she noted that students produced more writing for that particular assignment than they had for any other essay she had assigned that year. Mr. Turner asked her to share the project with teachers during school kick-off in August of 2021, hoping to seed another promising instructional change that would get students writing and help teachers get to know them better.

Ms. Coates: Improving Relationships to Foster Collaboration

We know that teacher effectiveness and student growth on tests increase considerably when there is an established school culture of academic excellence.[12] At ZNHMS, Ms. Coates saw whole-school staff ownership of teaching and learning as key to creating a school climate focused on instructional change. In a conversation she had with us in the spring of 2023, Ms. Coates stated that the success the school was seeing in shifting students' literacy outcomes "didn't happen because I crouch over my people. It happens because of what happens in the classroom. I trust my teachers to take risks with their instruction and support them in making evidence-based decisions."[13] This shared ownership of teaching and learning has empowered teachers to lift students up and invite them to engage in rigorous instruction in ways that were not happening prior to Ms. Coates joining ZNHMS.

The process of sharing ownership of teaching and learning began each school year before students entered the building. Ms. Coates asked teachers to read (or reread) and discuss "Improving Relationships Within the Schoolhouse," by Roland Barth.[14] Barth points out that the nature of relationships among the adults within a school has a more significant influence on the character and quality of that school and on student accomplishment than anything else. "It talks about the four major types of relationships that we see among staff members within a campus and which ones you want to build, which ones you want to stay away from—parallel play, adversarial relationships, congenial relationships, collegial relationships,"[15] Ms. Coates explained. At the beginning of her work at Hurston, Ms. Coates noticed that the adult relationships in the building were a barrier to student learning. She asked teachers to reflect on the types of relationships they had with their fellow teachers. Listening and being responsive helped her move teachers from congenial relationships, where teachers were personal and friendly, to collegial ones, where they discussed and exchanged ideas about teaching and learning and the staff felt empowered to mentor and support each other.

After checking in on school culture, Ms. Coates engaged school staff in a version of a root cause analysis to set goals for the upcoming school year that all faculty and staff were expected to support. In an interview, she recalled that the process began with participants analyzing several data points including assessment data, attendance data, and survey results from teachers, students, and parents on climate and culture.[16] She then asked the staff to study the data in groups of four. These were mixed groups with teachers from different content areas, guidance counselors, secretaries, and other school staff. They used a process that Ms. Coates described as "discovery learning." During this process, staff individually note what they notice about the data and then work in their groups to ask questions about what they saw, where they could improve, and where they wanted to be as a school community at the end of the school year. Groups shared out their thinking and the school's coaches and assistant principals consolidated ideas and suggested goals for the year, working with the staff to refine and shape them.

By the end of teachers' first week back in the building, shared goals were posted throughout the school for teachers and students to see. Coaches then met with content area teachers to discuss how instruction might support reaching the goals, which could range from increasing students' feelings of belonging to the ZNHMS community to moving from a "C" campus to a "B" campus on the state school grading system, and how school initiatives aligned with each one. Ms. Coates acknowledged that the work that took place that week required a lot of pre-planning, but she found it was a critical component of shifting a school culture.

She had spent her first year at the school "listening and just showing up,"[17] as she said in an interview, learning the existing culture while building relationships with teachers and the community. She acknowledged the previous progress made by the school and asked stakeholders what they thought the critical issues were. She adhered to the established norms and rituals of the school, such as celebrating its rich history. This kind of respect and honor are critical to the impression a new principal makes on a school community. Often behavior demonstrates more profoundly than words what we honor and respect. It was the relationships that Ms. Coates built during her period of listening that allowed her to start Year 2 with tough conversations around adult relationships in the school.

Leading Teachers to Focus on Instruction

Once principals lay the groundwork for a productive school climate, which could be through creating a school-wide plan for change as you saw with Mr. Turner or by building relationships and creating whole staff ownership of goals as you saw with Ms. Coates, they can then establish high-quality instruction as the school's overriding priority for improvement, a crucial feature of schools where teaching and learning positively impact student achievement.[18] Both Mr. Turner and Ms. Coates were heavily invested in their teachers' instruction. They both believed, for example, that teachers should prioritize rigorous, grade-level instruction over assessment practice, as you saw with Mr. Turner in the opening story, and over teaching skills with no content. (Teaching skills without content can show up in a curriculum as a learning goal like "students will be able to turn and talk to a partner about their ideas." Generic goals such as these can lead teachers to think that a lesson was successful simply because students had partner conversations, but without specific, content-focused learning goals and tasks, student talk could be all over the place.)

The Network teachers had begun to recognize opportunities within the curriculum to center comprehension and content as they engaged in the root cause analysis work in Year 1. Another reason to engage school leadership in understanding the Network vision of teaching and learning was that teachers wanted to adapt both the curriculum's lessons and the student-centered practices for their own students. They began looking at the provided curriculum with a critical eye to see where those adaptations would be appropriate, but they needed their principals' support to make them. Once principals understood the small instructional shifts that teachers were learning to make and the rationales behind the adaptations, they could openly engage teachers in conversations about their potential instructional changes. As you'll see in the stories that follow, Mr. Turner did this by making himself an active member of the instructional inquiry PLCs held by the 9th grade team at RWHS. Ms. Coates took a slightly different approach. She helped teachers focus their work on instruction through non-evaluative feedback provided through the lens of what she noticed about the use of student-centered practices in classrooms she observed.

Mr. Turner: Focusing on Instruction as a Collaborator

In the spring of 2021, we asked Ms. Knight and Mr. Jones, the two 9th grade teachers championing the improvement work at Rose-Wood, to talk to us about the planning process they designed with the full support of Mr. Turner. Ms. Knight began by discussing her initial reluctance to make any instructional change. Her previous school's principal had expected adherence to the district curriculum and planning protocol. She stated that it took two or three meetings before she realized instructional inquiry did not mean that she needed to deviate completely from the district curriculum. Instead, the process asked her to think about the texts students were assigned and consider whether they were genuinely complex enough to promote thinking and discussion. She cited the collaborative work she engaged in with Mr. Jones and Mr. Turner as the catalyst that helped her realize they should tweak the district protocol. "[T]he process the district set forth really wasn't working for our students, so we began to backward plan," she said. "[We would ask] what did the district want students to know? And then, how would the texts we knew we wanted our students to work with support the standards? Then we'd think through all the layers—time constraints, engagement constraints, what's going to be meaningful on a different level besides just doing well on the test."[19] (See Figure 5.1 for the document RWHS created to support their planning process.)

As shown in the beginning of this chapter, Mr. Turner opened space for conversations with his teachers through being an active participant in instructional planning. At the PLC meeting that occurred after the planning meeting, he positioned himself as a facilitator, working to answer questions and guide inquiry. When teachers explained their desire to make adaptations, Mr. Turner told them they could teach other texts if the texts were additions, not replacements, and if they would support students' knowledge-building around the content of a unit. From there, he worked with teachers to review the slides provided by the district, and took notes as teachers discussed

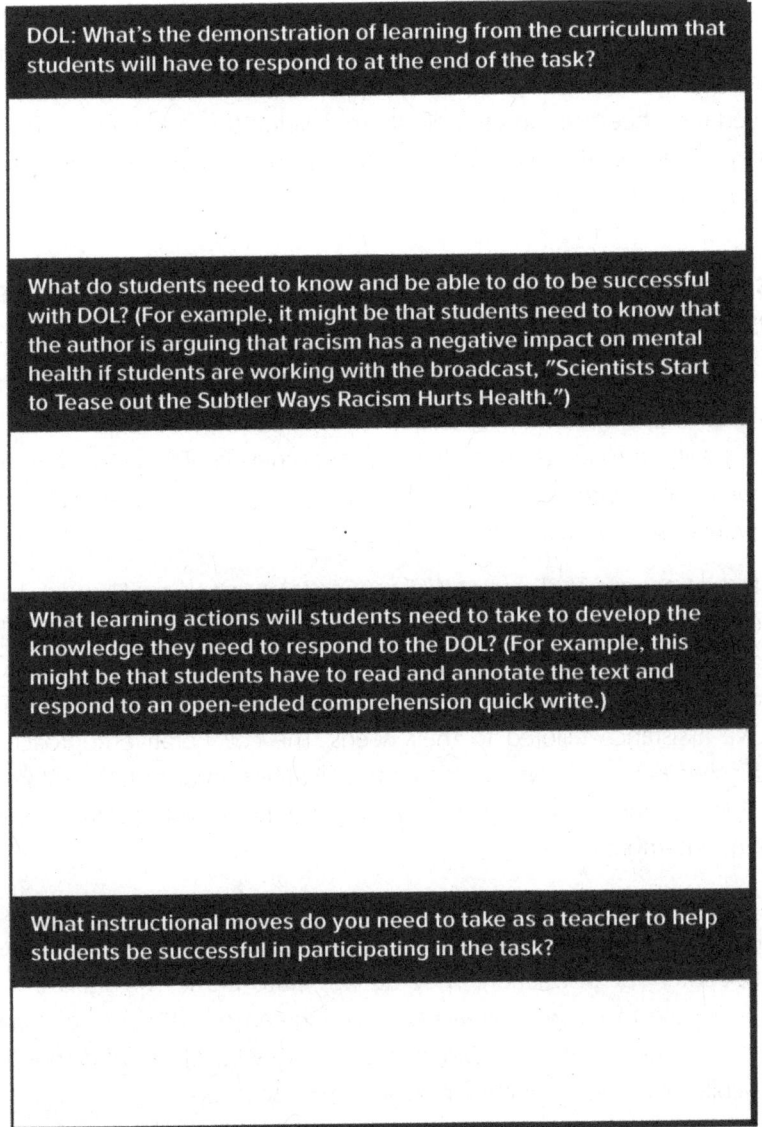

Figure 5.1 The RWHS planning process. "DOL" stands for Demonstration of Learning.

where they wanted to adapt and try out small changes they thought would increase opportunities for student-to-student meaning making.

These actions validated teachers' agency. By becoming a member of their PLC, Mr. Turner signaled that he understood the Network's vision for rigorous, grade-level, student-centered instruction and wanted to support teachers' efforts. He set clear expectations for implementing the student-centered practices in all 9th grade English classrooms. He showed teachers that he viewed task sheets as tools to help them develop the tasks and as student-facing resources that could help students understand the tasks, their purposes, and their sequence.

Ms. Coates: Focusing on Instruction through Evidence-based Feedback on Class Observations

Ms. Coates's work to focus teachers on instruction looked different from Mr. Turner's. Where Mr. Turner was an active participant in teacher planning, Ms. Coates wanted to focus on feedback that teachers could use to inform the instructional inquiry process. *The Learning Walk* became an essential tool in her work to support teachers.

We first introduced *The Learning Walk* routine to principals as a Network in the fall of 2019, using a protocol the IFL developed that we adapted for Big City. Through *The Learning Walk*, principals gather real-time data on classroom dynamics. Insights gained on walks can help principals ensure that teachers receive assistance tailored to their needs. The collaborative approach to *learning walks* helps build a community of learners among staff, reinforcing the shared vision of teaching and learning and the school's commitment to continuous improvement.

The norms for *The Learning Walk* protocol emphasize "do no harm" and "focus on learning." Teachers are aware of when the team is coming. The walkers do not interrupt instruction. They do not state praises or dislikes. They attend to the focus, which teachers have agreed on. They use objective, descriptive statements, cite evidence, and note what they are wondering. They collectively determine the next steps with teachers.

The protocol itself was a new way for principals to think about the purpose of classroom observations. We heard from most Network principals that when they observed classrooms, it was usually through two lenses. The first lens was something akin to compliance. They wanted to see that teachers were utilizing the district curriculum. The second was for an evaluation using the state rubric. Class observations weren't yet seen as opportunities to grow teacher practice and note instructional trends in a class, at a grade level, or within a content area.

Engaging principals in the Network complicated the idea of observation. After several meetings, they expressed that they wanted to see student-centered adaptations, *and* they wanted to have conversations with teachers about the rationales behind them. We shared *The Learning Walk* protocol during one leadership meeting late in 2019 (Figure 5.2), hoping it would meet both needs. The protocol unfolds in phases to ensure that teachers and leaders have time to prepare and to share the text and tasks that will be seen during the observation. Before observing in a classroom, principals asked teachers what they expected the change to do for student learning. During the observation, they took descriptive notes on their noticings and wonderings. Afterwards, they debriefed with the walking team—usually made up of the principal, a coach, and sometimes an IFL NSI coach—to synthesize what they noticed and wondered about in the lesson they observed. Amongst themselves, they then developed a plan for getting that information back to the teachers they had observed to inform the next cycle of instructional inquiry. We encouraged them to hold *learning walks* at least once a quarter.

We participated in several *learning walks* at ZNHMS during the project. During our *learning walks* in Year 2, the first year Ms. Coates led the school, she was a willing participant, listening thoughtfully to the distinction between her traditional observations and *The Learning Walk*. Though she continued to conduct traditional observations with the executive director, she and her team conducted *learning walks* two to three times per week, more than most Network principals. Over time, teachers became comfortable with *The Learning Walk* process and looked forward to having a *Learning Walk* in their classrooms.

What follows is one example of the feedback provided after a walk and how teachers used that feedback to make a change to instruction.

The walk took place in February of 2022, when teachers were transitioning from online instruction during the COVID-19 pandemic back to face-to-face instruction. By this time, Network teachers were fully immersed in student-centered practices—quick write, turn/talk, small/large group discussion, charting—and had begun to be more intentional and skillful in using the quick write and turn-and-talk to engage students. Teachers also were becoming more aware of the complexity of the texts and tasks they presented to students. However, Ms. Coates had noticed that teachers focused much of their planning on how they could enact instruction on students' Chromebooks, creating "online in person" situations in classrooms

Preparation	Steps	Norms

• The test-of-change and inquiries are specified by the teacher
• The 4–6 walkers are specified
  ◦ Content expert
  ◦ Leader(s)
  ◦ NSI coordinator(s)
  ◦ Special populations staff (EML, SwSN)
  ◦ Linguistic and ethnic diverse representation
• Visit date selected and visit schedule created
	• Pre-walk meeting
	  ◦ Set learning stance
	  ◦ Review overall focus & schedule
	  ◦ Set student foci (Black, EML, Hispanic, SwSN)
	• Walkers visit each class
	  ◦ Stay for 15 min
	  ◦ All complete Evidence-Based Collection tool
	  ◦ Hall talk for 5 min
	• Post-walk meeting
	  ◦ Chart patterns across classes
	  ◦ Create master summary chart
	  ◦ Teacher(s) joins
	  ◦ Decide next steps
	• Feedback given to the other teachers
		• Pre-meeting
		  ◦ Be on time
		  ◦ Confused? Ask!
		  ◦ Emphasize **do no harm**. Focus on the learning
		• Classroom visits
		  ◦ Acknowledge appreciation to teacher in a way that is not disruptive
		  ◦ Do not "fix" the teacher
		  ◦ Do not interrupt instruction
		• Noticings
		  ◦ Attend to visit focus
		  ◦ Use objective, descriptive statements of fact
		  ◦ Do not state praise or dislikes
		  ◦ Cite evidence
		• Wonderings
		  ◦ Attend to focus + real inquiries
		  ◦ Avoid "fix teacher" wonderings
		• Next steps planning
		  ◦ ToC decision: Adopt / adapt / abandon?
		    ▪ Adaptations for populations (Black, EML, Hispanic, SwSN)
		  ◦ Future inquiry work
		  ◦ Schedule teacher feedback
		• Next days
		  ◦ Walk contents kept private

Figure 5.2 The Learning Walk overview. "ToC" refers to tests of change, "SwSN" refers to students with special needs, and "EML" refers to emergent multilingual students.

that limited the amount of student-to-student talk, a critical component of student meaning making.[20] Students were physically there, but everything was happening digitally. For example, students might be collaborating on a presentation in Google Slides but not having an oral conversation about the content that should be added to the slides.

After walking several 8th grade classrooms with Ms. Coates and describing what we saw and what we wondered for each room, we sat down and synthesized our observations to provide ELA teachers with data to inform their next round of instructional inquiry. The following is the feedback the walking team provided:

> There is evidence of shared planning across classrooms. We saw hybrid versions of instruction where students sat in pairs/trios, read texts individually, turned to talk with each other about the big ideas and/or author's purpose, and then returned individually to their computers to compose their quick writes. Once they composed their quick writes, they shared them on their computers, discussed them, made changes, and then moved to a Google slide on which they recorded their thinking agreements and questions to share with the class. The teacher monitored the students' work on their computers. Once the students completed their slides, in both classes, they were asked to go to the front of the room together to present their thinking about the text to the class. The teacher then displayed their Google slide on a very large monitor for the class to read. In most cases, the students took turns reading their slides and answered questions posed by the teacher. This went on until all pairs/trios presented their slides. The school has over 60 percent EML students, so the reading of the slides gave those students an opportunity to practice reading, but we wonder if they might have benefited differently if, instead of reading their slides, they presented their thinking to the class in a back-and-forth exchange.[21]

Ms. Coates shared this information with teachers and the assistant principal for literacy the following day at the beginning of their planning period. Teachers discussed *The Learning Walk* feedback and their own reflections on the instruction observed, and looked at students' exit tickets from the lesson to help inform their decisions about instructional next steps. The group decided that Ms. Newbaugh, who had moved from Pietro Middle School to ZNHMS in the fall, would test the change (asking students to present their thinking to the class orally) in one of her classes for the next set of lessons. The group also decided that Ms. Newbaugh and the other 8th grade teacher, George Porter, would provide time for students to ask questions of the students who presented. Ms. Newbaugh and Mr. Porter explained that they had considered opening up space for conversation previously, but thought that after COVID-19, students might not be ready because they hadn't had opportunities to continue the development of their language skills while they were engaged in online instruction.

After the planning conversation, Ms. Coates reflected that teachers seemed relieved to have support in trying out an instructional change they had found success with prior to COVID-19. It took some time, but the 8th grade team found that with scaffolding, consistency in the expectations to engage, focusing on wait time, and starting to move back to paper-based work, students began to talk with each other again.

What We Learned that Gives Us Hope for Student-Centered Instructional Change

Both Ms. Coates and Mr. Turner saw it as their jobs (1) to promote a collaborative culture in their schools where teachers worked together to understand student-centered, grade-level instruction; used inquiry practices such as *The Learning Walk* to better understand the teaching and learning happening in their classrooms; and shared promising instructional practices with peers that led to a positive shift in students' knowledge and skills. Mr. Turner (2) worked with teachers to establish a plan that would involve the whole RWHS community in instructional change. Ms. Coates (3) put structures in place to have the ZNHMS staff actively discuss the state of teaching, learning, and community at the school in order to develop goals. She then supported teachers to work toward those goals, and toward instructional change, by engaging in rounds of instructional feedback through *learning walks*. Key to building and maintaining a learning culture at both schools were both principals' (4) willingness to dig into instructional inquiry alongside teachers. Both principals (5) approached instruction as being everyone's responsibility, which meant that neither Mr. Turner nor Ms. Coates made instructional decisions alone, but were collaborative experts at the table engaging in inquiry cycles during instructional planning.

Both principals (6) created space for teachers to collaborate in PLCs even when this meant a reworking of the master schedule at ZNHMS to allow grade-level teachers to have shared planning periods at least twice a week. (For more on how Network schools used PLCs to support the work, see Chapter 4.)

The school culture (7) created by both Ms. Coates and Mr. Turner led to their ability to attract and retain effective teachers dedicated to collaborative cultures of inquiry and improvement. This is often a challenge for schools located in communities of high need, especially in a district with bonuses connected to students' outcomes on state assessments. Research shows that a student with an outstanding teacher for just one year is likely to remain ahead of their peers for the next few years. Unfortunately, the opposite is true as well—a student with even one ineffective teacher may not catch up to peers for up to three years. One excellent teacher does not fully compensate for the effect of an ineffective one. Worse yet, students with three ineffective teachers in a row rarely catch up at all.[22]

To be instructional leaders, (8) principals do not need to be experts in every subject across all grade levels. They do need to have a vision of rigorous, grade-level instruction for each grade and content area they support. At ZNHMS, teachers and other school leaders helped Principal Coates build that vision. Every year they revisited it together before the start of school.

The story of ZNHMS gives us hope in the collaborative power that teachers and principals can share when a principal realigns her priorities and observations based on a shared vision and empowers teaching teams to adapt instruction to align to that vision. It gives us hope that schools can be sites of shared authority among teachers and school leaders. Students benefit when everyone is accountable for leading change.

At RWHS, we saw what happens when a strong leader leaves the school, and teachers lose support to continue instructional inquiry. Principal Turner left RWHS at the end of Year 3 to lead a larger school in another district. With his departure came a shift in the teaching staff at the school. Mr. Jones, who was leading the instructional change work, was offered the position of assistant principal for literacy at another of our Network schools. Ms. Knight was promoted to the role of instructional coach and was tasked with supporting three brand new 9th grade ELA teachers at the school. In Year 4, the interim principal mandated the strict use of the district PLC protocol for planning, which removed opportunities for the types of instructional inquiry promoted by the Network, endorsed by Principal Turner, and taken up by Mr. Jones and Ms. Knight in Years 1 to 3. Years 4 and 5 saw an ever-changing teaching staff and a steady decrease in the numbers of students scoring proficient and above on the state assessment.

> "Our time with the teachers, students, and leaders at Rose-Wood High School showed us that students and teachers flourished when leadership acknowledged the potential and brilliance of the school community to plan and engage with relevant and rigorous instruction."

Our time with the teachers, students, and leaders at RWHS showed us that (10) students and teachers flourished when leadership acknowledged the potential and brilliance of the school community to plan and engage with relevant and rigorous instruction. It was RWHS teachers and students, supported by Principal Turner, who stepped up to engage in creating an instructional unit that addressed issues of identity, at a time when Black and Brown people were being told by state and national officials to quiet down about equity. The years where students engaged with each other's thinking by using the student-centered practices were the years that students remained steady or grew in their literacy performance.

Next Steps: Exploring Readiness for Change in Your School

After working with leaders such as Ms. Coates and Mr. Turner throughout our time in Big City SD and reflecting on how they invited a school culture of improvement and instructional inquiry to flourish, we developed a tool for leaders to take stock of their own school's readiness to engage in change. The "Instructional Change Readiness Matrix" shown in Table 5.1 reflects structures and mindsets that we found in schools with effective principals at the helm, such as Rose-Wood High School and Zora Neale Hurston Middle School. You'll notice that the dimensions are aligned to the stories of leadership we shared in this chapter: Vision for Instructional Change, shown through principals' work with the Network to understand instructional inquiry practices and

Table 5.1 Instructional Change Readiness Matrix

Dimension	Not Ready (1)	Somewhat Ready (2)	Ready (3)
Vision for Instructional Change	No clear vision or plan for instructional change.	Vague or broad vision for change that may not be clear to the school community. There is no plan for implementing change.	Clear vision for improvement that is shared with and understood by the school community. A plan for implementation may or may not exist yet.
Collaborative Culture	Limited collaboration among staff with no structure in place to expand collaboration.	Collaboration is limited and does not include practices that support inquiry. Leaders do not participate in PLCs with teachers.	Collaboration that includes teachers and leaders happens in regularly occurring PLCs. PLCs focus on instructional inquiry at least once a week.
Shared Leadership	All decisions regarding instruction and instructional planning are given top down.	Teachers have some voice in developing a vision for teaching and learning. They also have some agency in adapting instruction to meet the needs of their students.	Teachers and leaders share in the process of drafting a vision for teaching and learning. They have agency to adapt instruction as needed using student-based evidence.
Adaptability	School community is resistant to change or feels that they do not need to change.	School community is open to change but is unclear how to start or does not feel like they have agency to change.	School community is open to change and is seeking to start making changes. The school is actively seeking change ideas that may improve teaching and learning.

align their vision of teaching and learning to the vision developed by Network teachers; Collaborative Culture, shown by principals' commitment to creating space for teachers to engage in PLCs and Ms. Coates's and Mr. Turner's participation in collaborative planning; Shared Leadership, shown through Ms. Coates's dedication to having all staff work to develop a shared vision of teaching and learning and Mr. Turner's work to engage teachers in creating a school-wide plan for change; and Adaptability, shown through both principals' commitment to supporting teachers in feeling comfortable engaging in instructional change. Neither school would have been a perfect three across all dimensions when we began our work, nor would we have expected them to be. Both leaders worked across time to shift school cultures, put schedules in place, and hire staff who would create a school community where instructional inquiry became the norm.

The purpose of the tool is to identify areas that need to grow alongside instructional change. The tool should be revisited periodically to mark progress in shifting to a whole-school culture of change. And rather than being used in isolation, it requires conversation. One clear lesson we learned from working with educators at different levels of a system is that not every role group shares the same perspective on readiness. For example, when assessing for the Shared Leadership dimension, principals may think they've provided autonomy to teachers, but teachers may not have received that message and, as a result, would use a different score point to describe shared leadership at the school. We would encourage school and district leaders to use this tool in collaboration with teachers and coaches they see as being potential early champions for change. This will provide a more rounded view of readiness and support the use of the rubric as a tool to prompt conversations rather than as an evaluative tool for rating schools.

Questions for Reflection

1 What resonates with you in the stories of Ms. Coates and Mr. Turner?
2 What are you left wondering?
3 Where is your school on the "Instructional Change Readiness Matrix" and what does it tell you about your next steps?

Notes

1 J. L. Matthews and Gary M. Crow, *The Principalship: New Roles in a Professional Learning Community* (New York: Allyn and Bacon, 2010).
2 G. F. Branch, E. A. Hanushek, and S. G. Rivkin, "School Leaders Matter: Measuring the Impact of Effective Principals," *Education Next* 13, no. 1 (Winter 2013): 62–69, https://educationnext.org/school-leaders-matter/; Jason A. Grissom, A. J. Egalite, and Charles A. Lindsay, *How Principals Affect Students and Schools: A Systematic Synthesis of Two Decades of Research* (New York: The Wallace Foundation, 2021).

3 K. Leithwood, K. S. Louis, S. Anderson, and K. Wahlstrom, *Review of Research: How Leadership Influences Student Learning* (2004), accessed December 2024, http://www.wallacefoundation.org/knowledge-center/school-leadership/key-research/documents/how-leadership-influences-student-learning.pdf.
4 Interview with anonymous high school student by high school teacher, November 2018.
5 Rae Ellen Bichell, "Scientists Start To Tease Out The Subtler Ways Racism Hurts Health," *National Public Radio*, November 11, 2017, https://www.npr.org/sections/health-shots/2017/11/11/562623815/scientists-start-to-tease-out-the-subtler-ways-racism-hurts-health.
6 Anonymous principal's written reflection, August 29, 2019.
7 Tonya Coates's written reflection, August 29, 2019.
8 Transcribed from principals' reflection charts, January 16, 2020.
9 K. Scott, G. Dawson, and J. Quach, "How Are We Measuring Domains That Influence Teacher Readiness for Change? A Scoping Review of Existing Instruments in Non-Tertiary Settings," *Journal of Educational Change* (2024): 1–38.
10 Bryan J. Weiner, "A Theory of Organizational Readiness for Change," in *Handbook on Implementation Science* (Northampton: Edward Elgar Publishing, 2020): 215–32.
11 Accountable Talk® is a registered trademark of the University of Pittsburgh.
12 Linda Darling-Hammond, "Teacher Quality and Student Achievement," *Education Policy Analysis Archives* 8 (2000): 1–1.14.
13 Interview with Tonya Coates by Glenn Nolly, August 2024.
14 Roland S. Barth, "Improving Relationships Within the Schoolhouse," *Educational Leadership* 63, no. 6 (2006): 8.
15 Interview with Tonya Coates by Glenn Nolly, August 2024.
16 Interview with Tonya Coates by Sara DeMartino, March 8, 2023.
17 Interview with Tonya Coates by Glenn Nolly, August 2024.
18 Penny Bender Sebring, Elaine Allensworth, Anthony S. Bryk, John Q. Easton, and Stuart Luppescu, "The Essential Supports for School Improvement. Research Report," *Consortium on Chicago School Research* (2006).
19 Interview with Susan Knight by Glenn Nolly, May 2021.
20 Sarah Michaels, Catherine O'Connor, and Lauren B. Resnick, "Deliberative Discourse Idealized and Realized: Accountable Talk in the Classroom and in Civic Life," *Studies in Philosophy and Education* 27 (2008): 283–97.
21 *Learning Walk* notes, February 2022.
22 Linda Darling-Hammond, "Teacher Quality and Student Achievement," *Education Policy Analysis Archives* 8 (January 2000): 1, https://doi.org/10.14507/epaa.v8n1.2000.

6 Supporting *Every* Student's Engagement in Cognitively Demanding Studies: Miles Middle School

Before discussing any engaging strategies that lead to success in my classroom, it is important to mention that I have an unshakable belief that my students can handle any text, any essay question, and any task I throw at them. Everything starts with the belief that our students can handle on- and above-grade level texts with the right supports. Nothing can flourish in your classroom until you have faith that they can do it all.[1] (Erica Racine, 2023)

In this chapter we share the story of a 7th grade teacher at Miles Middle School, Erica Racine, who took up the charge to shift her instructional practices, specifically the work of adapting instruction both to honor the language assets students bring with them to the classroom and to make sure students developed the English language skills they'd need to be successful on the state exam and beyond. In this chapter you will learn about:

- the impact teacher mindset can have on instructional planning
- a high-level adaptation to curricular material that provides access to texts and tasks that many teachers in Big City School District (BCSD) have deemed too complex for their students, especially their emergent multilingual students
- scaffolds and student-centered practices that hold students accountable for leading the learning happening in the classroom

We also use this story to illustrate how a literacy teacher moved from instruction that skipped over rigorous comprehension work to instruction that used scaffolded, high-level comprehension tasks that supported students to grow their text-based knowledge and standards-based skills. This kind of instruction creates conditions for strong academic outcomes, provides students access to high-level resources, helps students see themselves as valuable assets for learning, and provides them with the power to shape their learning experiences.[2] Through this work, Ms. Racine created a classroom space where students knew they would be held to high learning standards but would be supported to engage with the instruction along the way. Her story shows the importance of planning with the belief that students *can* access rigorous grade-level instruction, adapting high-quality resources to align with the student-centered practices, and adapting the student-centered practices to align with the support Ms. Racine's students needed.

Instructional Change in Context: Miles Middle School

Miles Middle School is situated among the tree-lined streets of the northern part of Big City. It's an older brick building surrounded by massive oak trees that provide shade to the benches sitting underneath the acorn-heavy branches. When the school's windows are open, you can hear the sounds of Spanish and English floating through the air as teachers and students negotiate what it means to be multilingual in middle school in BCSD.

Being multilingual is an asset. Students who can negotiate multiple languages develop cognitive flexibility as they move between languages to communicate and develop knowledge.[3] Moving between students' dominant language and English when speaking and writing is called "translanguaging." When translanguaging, students use all their linguistic resources to make sense of the assigned task, make sense of ideas in texts, communicate those ideas to a partner or in a whole group, and produce writing that expresses their own ideas.[4]

Teachers can leverage students' ability to translanguage and build on that asset by utilizing scaffolds that increase students' vocabulary knowledge. Vocabulary words are divided into three tiers. Tier One words are what you might consider everyday words. Tier Two words are non-domain specific words that are seen frequently in writing but aren't common in conversation. Tier Three words are domain specific words that students will not encounter frequently in writing or hear in everyday conversation. Scaffolds that help students build knowledge around Tier Two and Tier Three words create access and provide space for students to discuss content in their preferred language.

Middle school is a milestone for emergent multilingual (EML) students in BCSD. Beginning in grade six, students must take the state assessment in English. If they have exited from the district's EML program, they are often expected to fully engage in instruction in English to prepare them for the test. This expectation creates a bottleneck for students' knowledge growth because many are exited from the EML program before they are fully ready for unsupported instruction in English. But these students flourish when teachers continue to provide scaffolding that includes dominant-language resources.

During the 2022–23 school year, the student population at Miles was 94 percent Hispanic, 4 percent Black, and 2 percent White or multiple races, with 92 percent of students classified as economically disadvantaged. Seventy-one percent of the students were classified as EML.

When we first began our work in BCSD, 35 percent of 8th grade EML students in our schools were deemed on track for graduation based on state assessment scores, GPA, and credits. By the end of the 2022–23 school year, that number had grown to 80 percent. When looking across all students at Miles, our Network data show that by the end of Year 5, 8.3 percent more students scored proficient and above on the literacy portion of the state exam than students in other schools in the state that matched Miles's demographics and performance data.[5]

Access to high-quality resources is one critical dimension of equitable instructional spaces where students see themselves as having a voice in shaping language and literacy.[6] Throughout the country, schools that traditionally serve Black and Brown children are frequently underfunded and under-resourced.[7] When students consistently receive low-quality resources, they begin to get the message that the system does not want to invest in them, so why should they invest their time at school? When systems devalue students, it leads to chronic absenteeism, classroom management issues, and reduced opportunities for students to learn.

Ms. Racine invested time in preparing to meet her students' needs. She learned to adapt and add to district resources in order to value her students' language and knowledge assets. And she used the knowledge about teaching and learning that she gained through participating in the NSI.

What follows is a discussion of adaptation, including the concept of mutual adaptation, and its relationship to high-quality instructional materials (HQIM), followed by a discussion of the role HQIM play in classrooms. We then describe how Ms. Racine mutually adapted one change idea—scaffolded comprehension—to meet the needs of her students while she leveraged the instructional materials in the district's curriculum.

Adaptation Drives Change

Mutual Adaptation

Adaptation is a core principle of instructional inquiry. Teachers engaged in change work adapt processes and practices to improve an aspect of teaching and learning within a classroom. Adaptation can be, and most frequently is, one-sided, or what's known as "local." In instructional inquiry, local adaptation may occur at the change idea level, meaning that a change idea goes through an adaptation, leading to a surface-level change in practice, but the habitual practices of the person implementing the change do not shift.[8] In the context of the NSI, local adaptation might look like a teacher adding in a turn-and-talk to a warm-up question at the beginning of the class, without addressing the main intent of the change idea, which was to utilize the student-centered practices in core work with the content. While the teacher adapted part of their classroom work to include a student-centered practice, they did not discuss the practices as part of instructional planning around content. Any signs of a shift in beliefs that students need opportunities to work together to discuss content were not evident. There was no change to the core of the teacher's instructional practice.

Mutual adaptation, on the other hand, is a more complex process. It occurs when there's a change to the processes, practices, and beliefs of the teacher as well as adaptation of the change idea to help it better address the needs of students and fit the local context.[9] This means that not only has the teacher shifted their ways of thinking about and planning for rigorous instruction, but they also made informed decisions about how specific change ideas should be adapted based on the curriculum and the students in the classroom. Teachers who were motivated to engage with the NSI often mutually adapted their practice, especially when they felt supported by peers, IFL NSI coaches, and school leadership. The Network itself fostered a shift in teacher mindsets by having teachers experience what was possible with student-centered instruction and then opening space to hear from each other about the successes they had with students engaging in that work. These conversations helped teachers see that students were capable of accessing rigorous grade-level instruction with appropriate support, as stated by Ms. Racine in the quotation at the beginning of this chapter. The conversations also built and spread teachers' knowledge and shared problem-solving about how our change ideas—the student-centered practices—could support students when integrated into the curriculum.

HQIM and Adaptation

Around the time the Common Core State Standards began to take root, the phrase "high-quality instructional materials" (HQIM) began to spring up in conversations about which curricular materials met the expectations of the new standards and how well the curriculum supported teacher implementation. EdReports[10] has led efforts to evaluate materials for coherence and alignment to standards. The intention is to take the guesswork out of material selection for states and districts. Materials stamped HQIM are deemed standards based and rigorous and, therefore, ripe for classroom use.

We were optimistic in the spring of 2021 when we heard that middle schools in Big City would begin working with a published HQIM. We had conversations with the authors of the HQIM several years prior to the work in BCSD and were hopeful that the features of the curriculum would facilitate the use of the student-centered practices in ways that the district-created curriculum had not. As states have worked to develop their own education standards, states and districts have expanded curriculum evaluation efforts to include their own rubrics aligned to local contexts.[11] The middle school curriculum that BCSD adopted during the 2021–22 school year was deemed HQIM both by EdReports and the state's own board of education.

Middle school students in BCSD now had physical access to high-quality instructional resources. We quickly found out that teachers needed time and support to adapt the content and ideas to be accessible to every student without reducing the rigor of the content. They also needed support to think through what it meant to adapt the new materials to include the student-centered practices. This was not unique to BCSD. Research on teacher implementation of HQIM has found that without support, teachers are overwhelmed by curricula that are dense with content. They skip over instruction that they don't feel confident in delivering to their students, or substitute resources that teachers see as more accessible to their own students, whether or not those resources are at grade-level.[12]

Curricular materials, even those deemed HQIM, move through phases as they are used with students.[13] Rubrics, such as those used by EdReports, traditionally evaluate materials as written. However, what teachers do with the materials is equally important. When they're looking to adapt curriculum to new instructional approaches, teachers who have a system of support, whether through school leadership or a network of peers, base their decisions on their beliefs about rigorous instruction and how their students learn, and on their knowledge of research-based instructional practices developed through collegial conversations and professional learning.[14] Our Network teachers' approaches to adaptation were shaped by the social relationships developed at Network events and by their autonomy to navigate the structural conditions at their schools.

Meaningful Relationships Lead to Adaptations

The relationships formed between Network teachers and between the teachers and the IFL NSI coaches often influenced teachers' motivation to make and share adaptations to their curricular materials. As you'll see in the example that follows, Ms. Racine shared early drafts of her task sheets with other teachers in the Network because, as she later told us, she valued the Network's input and advice and wanted to adapt her work to meet the needs of her students in ways that did not remove the rigor.

The Beginning of Ms. Racine's Work with Instructional Change

The sharing of instructional artifacts became a core part of our Network meetings early on in our work with teachers in Big City. It gave teachers an opportunity to spread promising practice but also to get feedback and advice when they were struggling with developing an instructional change they hoped would lead to student growth. Teachers became motivated to try out change ideas and share their instruction when they saw the successes of their peers, as well as when they observed their peers receive effective feedback on instructional challenges. The process of sharing instructional artifacts also provided us with the opportunity to see the change in teachers' thinking about instruction over time.

When Ms. Racine began her work with the Network, she shared her first attempts at creating a task sheet for students' first read of the poem "We Wear the Mask,"[15] by Paul Laurence Dunbar, as part of the thirty minutes built into our Network meetings for teachers to share a change. As you'll see in Figure 6.1, the task sheet Ms. Racine created covers a lot of ground, with the purpose of having students make connections between the poem and characters in the novel they had been reading, *Buried Onions*,[16] by Gary Soto. If you've reviewed the sample task sheet shared in the introduction, you'll notice that Ms. Racine's task sheet borrows several components of that model. For example, students are expected to read the text, annotate it, and complete a quick write. However, those practices are only effective if the content they are working to support has grist for thinking.

The work in this task sheet reflects what we typically see in a teacher's first attempt; it tries to do everything from building background knowledge, to comprehension, to analysis, to cross-textual interpretation. This work really calls for three task sheets—one for comprehension, one for the analytic work, and one for the interpretive work. This particular task sheet was also designed to be one size fits all. It has no scaffolding or differentiation to address the needs of different learners. In conversation with Ms. Racine and the Miles team, it was clear that the production of this task and its particular lack of language supports, aside from vocabulary, was a direct result of district expectations that every student engage in the same work, and the unsaid expectation that every student engage in English.

The work in Figure 6.1 begins with something akin to a web quest. In Step 1, students were asked to dig into who the poet is, develop some conjectures about America during Dunbar's life (1872–1904), and speculate about the impact that being Black had on Dunbar. Responses to these questions require knowledge about what it was like to be Black in the United States at the turn of the twentieth century, information not given on the linked site provided in the task but that students may have learned in elementary school—the state standards focus on the Civil War and Reconstruction in 4th grade. However,

> Students will be able to make connections between the speaker in a poem and the narrator in a fictional text.
>
> ▲ Step 1: Poet Background
> ✱ Step 2: Read & annotate the poem
> ◆ Step 3: WWAM (Google Slides)
> ○ Step 4: Quick Write
>
> ---
>
> ▲ Step 1: Poet Background
>
> Use the website & your inferencing skills to fill out the chart: https://poets.org/poet/paul-laurence-dunbar
>
> | Who is Paul Laurence Dunbar? | When was he born? | What is his race? | What was American society like during his lifetime? | How do you think his race impacted his life? |
> |---|---|---|---|---|
> | | | | | |
>
> ✱ **Step 2: Read & annotate the poem** (read and highlight anything that seems significant)
>
> 1. We wear the mask that grins and lies,
> 2. It hides our cheeks and shades our eyes,—
> 3. This debt we pay to human guile;
> 4. With torn and bleeding hearts we smile,
> 5. And mouth with myriad subtleties.
>
> 6. Why should the world be over-wise,
> 7. In counting all our tears and sighs?
> 8. Nay, let them only see us, while
> 9.   We wear the mask.
>
> 10. We smile, but, O great Christ, our cries
> 11. To thee from tortured souls arise.
> 12. We sing, but oh the clay is vile
> 13. Beneath our feet, and long the mile;
> 14. But let the world dream otherwise,
> 15.   We wear the mask!

Figure 6.1a Ms. Racine's first task sheet.

given the number of EML and immigrant students at Miles, it's possible that these 7th graders had not had extensive instruction on American history.

Background knowledge plays an important role in reading comprehension.[17] By developing background in Step 1, Ms. Racine demonstrated that she

Students will be able to make connections between the speaker in a poem and the narrator in a fictional text.

Step 3: WWAM Chart with your partner. Click the link for your class.
Work together with your partner (will be assigned on Zoom). Be prepared to share your chart with your peers to explain your ideas. Include any questions you have about the poem.

1st/5th Pd

2nd/6th Pd

3rd/7th Pd

When asked, please be ready to present your chart. After presentations, we will complete the Quick Write in Step 4.

Tips
Quick writes are times for you to use writing to think on the page. Most people write them quickly, in 3 to 5 minutes, and they don't need to have correct sentences or even be complete sentences. They don't need to have correct spellings. They are your thinking on the page in writing to get your ideas down as quickly as you can.

Before you do the quick write, glance back at the passages you marked when you read. Refer to those as much as you can when you compose your quick write.

When you write this quick write, try it this way. When you're ready to write, write out your thoughts without stopping until you feel like you've said everything that's on your mind. The idea here is to push yourself to keep the writing flowing.

Step 4: Quick Write
Question: Does anyone in *Buried Onions* wear a mask? Why or why not?

Figure 6.1b Ms. Racine's first task sheet *continued*.

understood the importance of students coming to the poem with some context. However, the structure of Step 1 created the possibility that students would go into the poem with misconceptions about Dunbar because they could not find or understand the information in the link provided, or they had an incomplete understanding of the United States right after the Civil War. Ms. Racine explained that students did not talk about the poet after completing the background chart in the task sheet. This allowed students' undeveloped or unfinished understandings to stand and may have had a ripple effect in the success they had with the rest of the task.

Completion of the chart took up a good bit of class time. Students had twenty minutes of the fifty-minute period to work through the poets.org site and note the requested information. This is a step that Ms. Racine could have done quickly, especially because the text-based work didn't depend on students going back and doing extensive work with the biographical information. She could have given students the information in the chart verbally, ensured accuracy in their understanding of Dunbar, and then moved on to the reading. Students could have spent most of those twenty minutes reading and rereading the poem, which should have been the main driver of instruction.

Step 2 takes students directly into reading the poem and annotating for significance. Significance can be complicated to annotate on a first read, especially when students don't yet know what the author is saying. In conversations with teachers in the Network, they consistently said that directions such as "annotate for significance" lead to a sea of yellow. Students highlight everything because they don't yet know what's important to the text. A reader typically looks for significance during a second pass, after they've finished reading and processing what they understand the author to be saying.

You'll notice that Step 2 also offers an early look at scaffolds Ms. Racine provided for her students. For example, words are hyperlinked in the task sheet, which was shared with students digitally. The hyperlinks take readers to student-friendly definitions that include the option to hear the word read aloud. This scaffold helps to create access to the words and ideas in the poem in context for average readers, emerging readers, and English learning readers alike. You'll see later in the chapter that this is a feature Ms. Racine kept in her instruction; it was a successful small change.

The final pieces of the task sheet are where students are asked to do some heavy lifting right away. Students are asked to analyze the poem using WWAM—What, Weird, Attitude, and Message—a method we saw frequently when our middle school teachers asked students to work with poetry. The idea is that students paraphrase the stanzas (what), indicate any words or phrases that seem strange (weird), analyze the poet's tone (attitude), and then state what the poem is about (message). The enactment of the WWAM is where the intellectual work was removed for students. Ms. Racine opted to provide students with the "what." Students' slides had a summary of the poem pre-filled in, taking the intellectual work of understanding the poem away from them.

The end result of this task sheet was that students wrote very little, wrote only using the "what" summary, or wrote using information they knew about Dunbar. Figure 6.2 shows an example of the responses that Ms. Racine received for this task. Students did not get to the point of making the connection between the idea of wearing a mask and the characters in *Buried Onions*,[18] because students did not demonstrate enough understanding of the poem to continue. Instead of digging into the poem a little more, they quickly left it behind as they continued working through the novel, which was the priority in the unit.

> *"We have found in our work with teachers from all over the country that shifting teacher mindset from 'I have all the authority in the classroom,' to 'I share the authority to lead learning with students,' and giving students some agency to learn from each other, is often the biggest hurdle. Once teachers get over that hurdle, they can begin building professional knowledge around high-level instruction."*

This first task was a starting point for adaptation and improvement and an early sign that Ms. Racine was working toward mutual adaptation. She had begun to shift her planning processes to include planning for the student-centered practices and was working to make sense of how to adapt the change idea of a student-centered task sheet to support her students. Ms. Racine began her work by taking to heart the idea that students needed something to guide their work and that a task sheet could give them some independence to figure ideas out and learn from each other. We have found in our work with teachers from all over the country that shifting teacher mindset from "I have all the authority in the classroom," to "I share the authority to lead learning with students," and giving students some agency to learn from each other, is often the biggest hurdle. Once teachers get over that hurdle, they

The summary is done for you. Divide the work between the two partners for questions 1-4.	
W-What (Summary)	*The speaker states that we wear a "mask" that disguises how we really feel inside. The speaker questions whether we should show our real selves, or continue to hide behind our "masks". The world might believe we are happy even when we go through struggles, but it is all because of the "mask" we show the world.*
W-Weird (Figurative Language)	1. What is the major symbol in this poem? Why is it appropriate? Use evidence from the text to support your answer. 2. In your own words, explain what wearing the mask represents in this poem? **Hideing yourself and your true colors**
A- Attitude/ Tone How does the author feel? What does the speaker say that tells us this?	3. Describe the speaker of this poem. Use evidence from the text to support your answer. **A man who is very talented and hard working**
M- Message (Theme) What big ideas, topics, and themes are present?	4. In your own words, explain what wearing the mask represents in this poem?
Questions we have about the poem:	

Figure 6.2 One response to Ms. Racine's first task sheet.

can begin building professional knowledge around high-level instruction, understanding how scaffolds can provide access to that high-level thinking without diminishing the demand of instruction, and collaborating around instructional planning.

Deficit Thinking as a Barrier

NSI school teams initially struggled with owning the causes of our problem of practice and at first named everything but instruction as a cause. The Miles team listed school culture, classroom management, relationships, and student motivation as root causes of the decline in literacy proficiency for students at their school. When we asked the team to dig in and look at how those root causes were related, they found that school culture, classroom management, and relationships were all causing students to lose motivation and that student motivation was a product and not a cause of their problem of practice. While Ms. Racine was not a part of this initial analysis, the task sheet she shared showed signs of another perceived deficit, that students could not handle grade-level instruction. The over-scaffolding of the task came from a genuine place of wanting students to be successful, but unintentionally sent the signal that students could not handle grade-level work. She told them what they needed to know.

Deficit thinking and language, in the view of Pollack, can be normalized at both the district and school levels through informal conversations that "disseminate beliefs, attitudes, and expectations about students of color, their families, and their communities."[19] It influences teachers' expectations of their students, even (or maybe especially) when using complex texts and high-level tasks. These underlying beliefs about what students can and cannot do also influence how tasks are constructed and enacted. This means that when engaged in instructional planning, teachers need to be conscious of how planned enactment might shift learning expectations. Over time, the work of the Network helped to provide new lenses for thinking about what influences the outcomes of instruction.

As teachers, we suggest keeping the following in mind during instructional planning and reflection. To provide access to students without taking away the cognitive demand of tasks, teachers must consider how instruction can build on the assets students have. During the planning, teachers discuss the learning goal for the lesson and then work to anticipate what they need to hear from students to know that students' thinking is aligned with the goal. They plan lines of questioning that place the onus for explaining and reasoning on students. Reflection after the enactment of the task considers the impact instruction had on student learning, through analysis of student-created artifacts, observations, and student responses on exit tickets. This type of planning is especially critical for work with EML students. Instructional planning has been cited in the research on what makes a teacher effective.[20] As you saw in the case study of PLCs in Chapter 4, when teacher teams have the support, time, and drive to plan together, both teachers and students benefit. Teachers benefit because when collaborative time focuses directly on instructional planning, those conversations shift teacher thinking about what to center during the planning process and build knowledge around how adapted instructional practices support students' needs.

Ms. Racine shared her task sheet at our convening with the intention of receiving feedback after implementation. She found the task successful in that students could follow the practices and engage in the work. However, she acknowledged that students did not develop enough of an understanding of the poem before being asked to apply the poet's ideas to another text. She wanted to leverage the collective knowledge of the Network to improve. Ms. Racine's willingness to share her practice even when it wasn't perfect, and learn from and collaborate with others, led to her becoming a change leader at Miles and during our Network meetings. Both Ms. Racine and her students have benefited from the shifts she made to her instruction over time.

What follows takes place three years after Ms. Racine shared her first instructional changes. It is the story of how she worked to create rigorous, student-centered instruction for all her students.

Beginning with Collaborative Planning

Ms. Racine's 7th grade classroom was situated next to Kim Sweet's, another 7th grade ELA teacher, on the top floor of Miles, which combines old-school charm and newly renovated, collaborative spaces that are typically utilized for staff meetings. Both teachers have benefited from proximity and thoughtful scheduling. They shared the same free periods and this allowed them to work together to co-plan instruction.

Ms. Sweet joined the Miles team during the 2022–23 school year as a first-year teacher. During the prior year, Miles' principal left for a district-level position, but her replacement, Dr. Dee, continued the focus on improvement and bringing in teaching faculty who were committed to collaborative improvement and feedback. Dr. Dee hired Ms. Sweet with the expectation that she would work with Ms. Racine as a collaborative planning partner and the two would attend Network meetings together. The previous 7th grade teacher had opted not to attend the Network meetings consistently, which often meant Ms. Racine was missing a thought partner. By contrast, both Ms. Sweet and Ms. Racine embraced being critical friends willing to grow as practitioners.

Case Story: Planning for Student Success

We had previously seen glimpses of the ways that Ms. Racine and Ms. Sweet worked together. During a Network meeting in the fall of 2023, teachers were working with a new change idea for comprehension, and we hopped into the breakout room where Ms. Sweet and Ms. Racine were working. They were engaged in conversation to better understand the idea that had been introduced that would scaffold students' reading of a complex text. At the heart of the change idea was breaking down the reading of a complex text to help students process the information in purposefully chunked sections, and to reflect on how ideas or content in one section built on another. The change idea supported students to process text using open-ended questions that they could respond to in writing or orally. Listening to Ms. Racine and Ms. Sweet's conversation, we could tell they were already seeing the potential of this change idea for differentiating reading instruction in their classrooms. After that meeting, we received an email from Ms. Racine inviting us to sit in on a collaborative planning session with Ms. Sweet. Ms. Racine let us know that they would be planning with the change idea from the earlier Network meeting using an informational text from the district's middle school curriculum.

The instruction in the 7th grade classrooms at Miles was carefully adapted from the instructional units and the change ideas that teachers identified as having potential to support, shift, and elevate student learning while maintaining alignment to grade-level instructional standards. Ms. Racine and Ms. Sweet took on a change idea only after they took time to engage with the idea to understand how it might play out in the classroom, heard from others about the improvement work that had been happening in their schools, and considered how the change idea would specifically benefit their students. The team from Miles presented several times at Network meetings, sharing the successes they had adapting change ideas for the new curriculum, but also sharing the process that they engaged in as they collaboratively planned.

In discussing the planning process they used at Miles, Ms. Racine pointed directly to being able to engage with Mr. Drew, who is the subject of the case study on PLCs in Chapter 4, before the middle school and high school meetings split in the fall of 2022. In her conversations with Mr. Drew, Ms. Racine heard about his work leading the planning at Arlington High School, and that influenced the ways she and Ms. Sweet worked together.

The planning meeting Ms. Racine asked us to attend was for the development of comprehension work on *Inventing Ourselves: The Secret Life of the Teenage Brain*,[21] by Sarah-Jayne Blakemore, a text from the new district curriculum (the HQIM). They were nervous about trying out a new change idea with an informational text (they had experienced the change idea with a fictional story during our Network meeting) and had asked us to attend as thought partners. They saw the scaffolded reading change idea as potentially having a huge impact on their EML students. They thought the process of responding to questions about intentionally segmented sections of text would help students tackle a dense informational text full of Tier Three vocabulary—the words typically acquired last by English learners. Ms. Racine sent us a copy of the text and asked us to read it and think about it through two lenses; one, what the big idea of the text is, and two, where we might segment the text and ask students questions to help them comprehend the content.

The work in this particular unit was challenging for students and teachers alike. As we described in Chapter 1, teachers had been told at the beginning of the school year that BCSD would be working with a completely new curriculum. They had three days prior to the start of the school year to preview the materials. Because of the timing of the introduction, school teams had been engaging in just-in-time planning days before lessons were rolled out to students, giving teachers little time to deeply internalize the content. Students found the work challenging because the texts in this curriculum were more complex than any texts they had worked with previously. The curriculum is also knowledge building. It assumes students had been engaged in the work of that particular curriculum since elementary school and that they'd built a specific set of knowledge and skills over time. For students at Miles that had not been the case, so teachers had to do a lot of knowledge patching, building background knowledge where needed, and teaching other skills that may not have been addressed by the previous, district-developed curriculum.

Ms. Racine and Ms. Sweet approached their planning with an eye toward access and building on the assets that their students had. Both women had worked to build trust and relationships with their students from the beginning of the year. Ms. Racine built relationships in a couple of ways connected to instruction. First, she made it explicit to students that she valued their opinions. She reinforced that students' voices were important. Over time, she said, students felt responsible for sharing their voices with their classmates. Centering student voice also let Ms. Racine know that students comprehended what was happening in the text beyond just putting events in order or identifying figurative language. Second, Ms. Racine used the student-centered practices as effective tools in building relationships with her students. In conversation, Ms. Racine said:

> With some of the student-centered [practices] that we do, such as pair-trio share and whole group discussions, it helps to build rigor and relationships at the same time because it tells [students] that as their teacher, I value them as an individual, not just as a student. It shows them that as their teacher, I'm learning alongside them, not just telling them what to do or think. It's not the usual multiple-choice question. But we really value them as individuals and their thoughts. And as the teacher, I would venture to say, you get to see them blossom as intellectuals. But that's just one way I'd say that you can build relationships with students.[22]

Building from the idea that the student-centered practices effectively help maintain the rigor of a task while scaffolding instruction, Ms. Racine and Ms. Sweet's planning involved examining the structure of the instructional task from the curriculum as it is written, then considering how that structure would work for their students. They discussed how they could leverage the assets students brought with them to the classroom. They approached the instruction in their classroom as a tool to grow students' knowledge, skills, and confidence. This meant that not every student followed the same path to meet the learning goal.

Planning the Task

We met with Ms. Racine and Ms. Sweet online. The two teachers sat together at a table. Each had a heavily annotated copy of the text, indicating they had read and thought about the content extensively. They began their discussion with the text's big ideas. One is that adolescence includes more than the teenage years. Blakemore says explicitly that adolescence ends between the ages of twenty-two and twenty-five. They also discussed the three reasons Blakemore says adolescence is an important and distinct period of development: it spans cultures, species, and historical periods. They noted that hearing these ideas from students would signal that students were working with the text's content and not only drawing from what they already understood about adolescence.

> "When the discussion turned to talk about the EML students in both teachers' classrooms, the question was, 'How might we support the EML students during reading so they can engage in discussions of what's happening in this text with the whole class?' There was no discussion of providing a full text summary such as the one Ms. Racine created for 'We Wear the Mask.' Instead, they talked about ways to create access without taking any of the thinking away from students."

It was clear that students and student success remained at the center of how Ms. Sweet and Ms. Racine were planning, especially the students who were still working to acquire academic English. When the discussion turned to talk about the EML students in both teachers' classrooms, the question was, "How might we support the EML students during reading so they can engage in discussions of what's happening in this text with the whole class?" There was no discussion of providing a full text summary such as the one Ms. Racine created for "We Wear the Mask." Instead, they talked about ways to create access without taking any of the thinking away from students.

The teachers first talked about the Tier Three vocabulary words in the text that were important to understanding the ideas (they identified the words *aberration, physiology,* and *self-regulation*) and what might be student-friendly definitions for them. Ms. Racine suggested that they provide the definitions both in Spanish and in English. They also discussed possible cognates (words that have a common root) they might highlight. For example, they selected *adolescent/adolescente, aberration/aberración, socially/socialmente* from Blakemore's text, which were critical to students' understanding of the ideas in the text.

From there, we moved to talking about how to segment the text and the questions they could ask for each segment. Our advice was to look for places in the text where a key idea is brought up or where the author starts to shift the content. We also let them know that the segments of text wouldn't always be the same size and stopping points might happen in the middle of a paragraph. The first stopping point they created was after paragraph two in which the author addresses the common stereotypes she often hears about adolescents. They decided the question students would answer about that section is, "What does the author tell us here?" They wanted students to recognize that the author is saying people have a negative opinion of adolescents and how they use their brains. Ms. Sweet and Ms. Racine saw this as a good stopping point because it set the stage for why the author is writing, the author's purpose, before she gets into the actual science. The next stopping point happened to be two paragraphs later after paragraph four in which the author provides her purpose. The question for students after that section is, "How does the author respond to the ideas in the previous section?" The question for this section requires students to start putting information together in ways that expert readers tend to do unconsciously as they read.

The next stopping point came after paragraph five because that particular paragraph had a lot of information about how the author defines adolescence that students needed to tease out. The group carried on discussing and debating stopping points and questions, keeping in mind that they wanted all students to be able to respond to the question, "What does the author say in this text about adolescence and the teenage years?" At this point the conversation paused, and Ms. Racine asked us, "Is it okay if we read the text aloud with this change idea?" As they discussed the author's words and ideas, Ms. Racine recognized that her EML students needed to hear the words aloud to help with processing the technical English terms. Reading aloud with EML students models fluency and facilitates connecting oral and written language.[23]

The scaffolded reading change idea they were discussing was developed from Questioning the Author[24] (QtA), which is a process for reading and discussion of texts. Research has shown that this instructional scaffold improves students' comprehension of complex texts.[25] While QtA was developed specifically as an effective method for engaging students in a read aloud, we adapted this practice for independent reading. We introduced it to the middle school Network as a way to help students process the content in chunks of text by stopping at pre-planned points and writing in response to open-ended queries for each chunk. After reading and writing, students then talk about how the chunks build to develop an understanding of the text as a whole. The method uses strategic queries, a specific type of open-ended question, along with student discussion to make sure that all students understand the ideas in a text and how they fit together.

We thought structuring the reading of the text as a read aloud for the EML students would be a good adaptation to try, and wondered aloud how a classroom with students working with different scaffolds at the same time would look. Ms. Racine invited us to Miles to see how students took up the different ways of interacting with the comprehension task.

Engaging in a Change Idea that Provides Access to High-Level Instruction

Ms. Racine's classroom is a mishmash of old-school wood, green chalk boards, and new technology. You can hear the squeaking chairs from Ms. Sweet's room next door and the trill of birds through the open windows. At the beginning of the period, twenty 7th grade students entered Ms. Racine's room with loads of energy (more than you would expect from the after-lunch crowd), but they knew the routine. They grabbed their notebooks from their class's milk crate and the text and task sheet that Ms. Racine had laid out before making their way to their seats.

As students settled down at their tables, they began to write. They were responding to the prompts on the screen, "Can someone make 'good' choices all the time? / ¿Alguien puede tomar decisiones 'buenas' todo el tiempo?" and "What factors do you think should be considered when the punishment for a juvenile offender is decided? / ¿Qué factores cree que se deben considerar cuando se decide el castigo para un menor infractor?" There was also a reminder on the board that students could respond in whichever language they felt most comfortable using. Ms. Racine's goal with this prompt was to remind students of the previous day's discussion and to prime them for the day's work with the new text. Students were in the middle of an instructional unit that focused on texts about brain science. That day, they began working on the subunit around the adolescent brain.

Before beginning the comprehension work, Ms. Racine held a brief discussion of the questions students had responded to in writing. She then posted a description of the work they would engage in with the text and the purpose for the work. She asked a student to read the description aloud, and then asked if there were any questions. Because this was the first time students would be engaging with a segmented text, Ms. Racine modeled the process with them for the first few segments using her document camera. She read the first two paragraphs of the text and asked herself the first question, "What is the author telling me here?" She thought aloud, "I think she's telling me that many people see adolescence as a joke, something to make fun of. I am going to write that in this box." She proceeded to write that explanation in the first box, projected so students could see what she wrote, and prompted students to copy down the sentence. She then read the next segment, posed the planned question to students, got their responses, asked if others agreed with what their peers said, and added the thinking to her copy of the text. After moving through three segments, she explained to students that they would be working through the rest of the text themselves, stopping to answer the questions for each segment. She gave them fifteen minutes to read and respond and explained that they would then share their responses with a partner before they worked in pairs to respond to the comprehension quick write question. Figure 6.3 is a copy of a portion of the segmented text and questions that students worked with for each segment.

While the majority of Ms. Racine's class worked independently, she asked four boys to sit with her at the front table. When we asked her later about why she pulled this specific group together, she said:

> In the first minute or two of partner or independent work, I make note of which students need teacher support. By taking inventory, I can be strategic about which groups to sit with, for how long, and what the focus of our time will be. This is also an opportunity to modify or adapt an activity without singling students out or making them feel different.[26]

She explained that these students had been exited out of the EML program, but still struggled with academic English, so she knew that this specific text was going to be challenging for them even if she asked them to work with a partner. Ms. Racine read each segment to them, pausing afterward to ask them questions. When she needed to, she directed them to the definitions and cognates to help them process the content of the text. They responded orally and Ms. Racine added their thinking to her text. She prompted them

Text	Question
When I tell people I study the **adolescent** brain, the immediate response is often a joke—something along the lines of: "What? Teenagers have brains?" For some reason, it's **socially** acceptable to mock[1] people in this stage of their lives. But when you think about it, this is strange: we wouldn't ridicule[2] other age groups in the same way. Imagine if we went around openly sneering at the elderly for their poor memory and lack of agility. Perhaps part of the reason why adolescents are mocked is that they do sometimes behave differently from adults. Some take risks. Many become self-conscious. They go to bed late, get up late. They relate to their friends differently.	What does the author tell us here?
We now know that all these characteristics are reflections of an important stage of brain development. Adolescence isn't an **aberration**[3]; it's a crucial stage of our becoming individual and social human beings. I find teenage behavior fascinating, but not because it's irrational[4], inexplicable—quite the opposite: because it gives us an insight into how natural changes in the physiology of our brains are reflected in the things we do, and determine who we will become as adults. In this book, I want to tell you what we know about the adolescent brain. I will show you how we study the way the brain develops during these years, how that development shapes adolescent behavior, and how it ultimately goes on to define the people we become. This is the time during which much of our sense of ourselves, and of how we fit in with others, is laid down. The development that adolescents go through is central to human experience.	How does the author respond to the ideas in the previous section here?

adolescent /adolescente
socially/socialmente

1. mock: to make fun of (para burlarse de)
2. ridicule: to laugh at in an unkind way (reírse de una manera cruel)
3. aberration /aberración: something strange that doesn't always happen (Algo extraño que no siempre sucede)
4. irrational: act, talk, or think in a crazy way (actuar, hablar o pensar de manera loca)

Figure 6.3 A portion of the text Ms. Racine segmented to scaffold students' first read.

to do the same, letting them know it was okay if they wanted to write their ideas in Spanish.

Once students had completed the reading and annotation of the text, they shared the segmented responses in small groups. Ms. Racine asked the EML students each to join a group to be part of the discussions. We heard students talk about the text in both English and Spanish without hesitation. After groups came to an agreement about what each piece of the text was about and how each segment contributed to the text as a whole, they worked together to write a summary on chart paper. They posted their charts and conducted a gallery walk to read each one, spreading what they understood about the text to their peers. The gallery walk also provided Ms. Racine with some formative insight into whether students had the gist of the text, and gave her ideas about how to leverage student-to-student talk to bridge any gaps in their understanding that might prevent them from being successful with the analysis work that would come next.

Following the gallery walk, Ms. Racine engaged students in a whole group discussion to check where students were in their understanding of the text after seeing their peers' charts, and to open up the conversation to ideas that may not have been expressed when charting. An excerpt from that conversation follows.

```
 1 Ms. Racine:  So, how are adolescents different than adults? Alejandro.
 2 Student 1:   The most, they're more risk taking.
 3 Student 2:   I agree with that 'cause the author said that they take more
 4              risk when their friends are out with them, but when their
 5              friends are not with them, they don't take that much risk.
 6 Ms. Racine:  Why do you think Blakemore is so fascinated by this age?
 7              Why do you think she's so fascinated by this information
 8              here?
 9 Student 3:   You can learn more about adolescence by other people
10              interacting with kids taking more risk and stuff and actually
11              studying why people are doing that.
12 Student 4:   I was going to say she's interested in what the thought
13              process is. And when they're doing, she like wonders, like
14              what they're thinking of and stuff.
15 Ms. Racine:  Levi, did you want to add?
16 Student 5:   She's probably fascinated because the brain's developing is
17              not done.
```

18	Student 6:	I want to add on to Levi because their brains are still
19		developing and they have, like, the most difficult things than
20		any other age, so out of any age, it's a very special time. They
21		act so differently, so they're like, when we are like little kids,
22		we are like, we think we don't know nothing, right? We just
23		curious about the world when we think, when we're like …
24		Like, like other lesson? Like teenagers. We're like, so let's do
25		look to see him into the world, but we're more like crazy or
26		we're taking more risk. And when we're adults, we like, we
27		know what's good and what's bad. We know what we have
28		to do.

When compared to the student work shown in Figure 6.2 on page 180, you can see the extent of the changes in students' responses and Ms. Racine's role. She didn't summarize the text for them here, nor did she feel she had to. Instead, she became the facilitator. She asks them in line one to respond to an open-ended question, "How are adolescents different than adults?" and gives them time to respond. In line two, Student 1 provides a brief response. Student 2 agrees with Student 1 and elaborates on that response in lines three to five. Student 6 is one of the students Ms. Racine worked with in the small group. You'll notice in lines eighteen to twenty-eight that Student 6 is working to tie his ideas back to the ideas he heard from his peers and expand on what they contributed. The scaffold Ms. Racine used, in this case oral reading and discussion, laid the foundation for that student to share his thinking, and for all of the students in the small group she pulled aside to respond to the same high-level questions as their peers who read independently.

Ms. Racine's Student-facing Task Sheet

Figure 6.4 shows the task sheet Ms. Racine created to go with the scaffolded text shown in Figure 6.3. You'll notice that it looks different from the task sheet shared earlier in the chapter. The biggest difference is that this task sheet does one thing: it supports students to comprehend the text. It supports comprehension by asking students to talk about what they understood each chunk to say (Step 1), to work collaboratively to solidify their understanding of the text as a whole through creating a shared summary (Step 2), and to spread their understanding through posting their summaries and engaging in a gallery walk (Step 3). The differentiation comes in how she supported

After you have finished reading and responding to the text questions, please do the following:

1. Please share your responses to the text questions with a partner. Make sure you provide <u>evidence</u> for what you say.

2. On your chart paper, create a summary of the reading. Make sure to address the three things the author says about adolescence. (En el papelógrafo, crea un resumen de la lectura. Asegúrate de abordar las tres cosas que dice el autor sobre la adolescencia.)

   Use the box to draft your thinking before you put it on the big paper.

3. Gallery Walk

4. Exit ticket on sticky note
   What is one thing this text added to your understanding of adolescence? What makes you say that? (¿Qué aporta este texto a tu comprensión de la adolescencia? ¿Qué te hace decir eso?)

Figure 6.4 Task sheet for the steps after students read.

students to use the task sheet. Ms. Racine pulled that small group of students together to make sure they would have access to the text while not giving them something different or modified in a way that would impact the conversation they could have about the text when they joined their peers.

The comprehension task that Ms. Racine used also sat in stark contrast to the first-read work as it was written in the HQIM. For all first reads, the curriculum asked students to read independently and then answer a series of questions meant to mimic the question types they would see on the state exam. The curriculum did not invite any sort of comprehension conversation after this read; the teacher was mostly prompted to share a few correct answers and move on. The questions themselves were typical exam questions, not what we would consider high-level comprehension work, and students had confided in Ms. Racine that they could use the "find" feature in their Chromebooks to answer the questions without really digging into the text. For example, one question for *Inventing Ourselves: The Secret Life of the Teenage Brain* asked students to select a word to complete the sentence "The author thinks that adolescents are sometimes mocked because they _____ than adults." A word search for "mock" brings up a similar sentence in the text and clearly indicates that the correct response from the drop-down list is "act differently." Even if students were to read attentively and answer the questions, Ms. Racine felt (and we agreed) that the questions themselves do not help students comprehend the excerpt and do very little to support students who may need additional reading support. Comprehension of the text as a whole, especially one full of charts and scientific terms unfamiliar to students, is critical to students having success with any follow-up work.

A Framework for Mutual Adaptation

As we mentioned at the beginning of the chapter, for sustained improvement to take place, mutual adaptation must occur. From our work with Ms. Racine and other Network teachers, we've found that teachers who moved into the mutual adaptation space valued the following:

1 Collaborative time. Mutual adaptation thrived when collective knowledge was shared among colleagues and supported by leadership. This included time for collaborative problem planning and studying instruction in PLCs. Teachers felt empowered to center students' needs and make adjustments to improve students' learning experiences using both quantitative and descriptive student-based data.

2 Self-adaptation. Educators modified their planning processes, instructional practices, and beliefs based on the diverse needs and backgrounds of their students. They adapted instruction to include scaffolds and differentiation that supported students without removing the thinking required by the task.

3   Inquiry stance. Teachers gathered information about student understanding and progress through assessment, observation, and direct communication. They studied these data to inform their teaching.

4   Centering students' assets. Teachers recognized and respected the cultural and contextual backgrounds of students as essential to their successful learning. Teachers adapted their approaches to be culturally responsive, ensuring that all students felt included and valued.

The quotation at the beginning of the chapter exemplifies the expectations that Ms. Racine brought with her when she sat down to plan for instruction. It's worth repeating that for her, "Everything starts with the belief that our students can handle on- and above-grade level texts with the right supports."[27] Collaborative planning played a key role in preparing Ms. Racine to maintain the rigor of the task through her classroom instruction. She provided students with task sheets and physical texts, the tools they needed to successfully engage in the work, which communicated the purpose of the task as well as the steps students were to take. Ms. Racine engaged students in conversation about the expectations and modeled what they were expected to do. She maintained the rigor for students who needed extra support by engaging a small group in the same questions, but doing it through a read aloud to provide additional access to the text. These adaptations made in both the planning and enactment of instruction gave students access to complex texts and made it possible for all students in the classroom to be successful readers who talked with each other about the ideas they took from the text. That kind of success builds students' confidence.

In Ms. Racine's class, students shared authority for developing the class's understanding of texts during instruction. Personal questions, those that asked for accessing background knowledge, and text-based comprehension questions all were open-ended, inviting students to state what they knew about the text and how they had come to know it. They worked together to discuss their understanding and surfaced any confusion about ideas they might have had. The whole class conversations centered on students' ideas first, with Ms. Racine working to track those ideas on a chart. She turned ideas back to students to discuss the merit of the thinking and used questioning to help students explain how they came to understand content. Ms. Racine did not let students avoid the heavy lifting. They knew that when they entered Ms. Racine's classroom they couldn't sit back and wait for someone else to do the work because they would be asked to share their thinking and support their classmates. It's this attitude, or mindset, that has influenced how her students interacted with the tasks she provided, and that has led to better student outcomes—not just grades or test scores but in how students showed up. When they came to Ms. Racine's class, they read, they wrote, and they talked. Through preparation and thoughtful instruction that centers students, Ms. Racine demonstrated that she was invested in their success, so students were invested in growing their own knowledge.

The work of Ms. Racine is a beacon of hope for us as we consider how teachers work to support students who come to class with a range of skills and assets. While Spanish was not her first language, Ms. Racine leaned into the idea that her students shouldn't be prevented from learning just because they had different language skills than those that were privileged in BCSD. Instead, she created space for joy to flourish in her classroom. She found joy in teaching by leveraging her collaborative partnerships and professional knowledge to adapt instruction that welcomed her students in. Her students found joy in coming to her classroom because they knew that their contributions mattered and that they would have support from both Ms. Racine and their classmates when they had to work hard to figure ideas out.

Questions for Reflection

1. What one or two big takeaways about adaptation do you have after reading this chapter?
2. Where might you make adaptations to your instruction to better provide access to high-level instruction to every student?
3. For school or district leaders: How might you support content area teachers to adapt instruction to better provide access to high-level instruction to every student?

Notes

1. Interview with Erica Racine by Sara DeMartino, October 2023.
2. R. Gutiérrez, "Framing Equity: Helping Students 'Play the Game' and 'Change the Game,'" *Teaching for Excellence and Equity in Mathematics* 1, no. 1 (2009): 4–8.
3. Benard Odoyo Okal, "Benefits of Multilingualism in Education," *Universal Journal of Educational Research* 2, no. 3 (2014): 223–29.

4 Ofelia García and Tatyana Kleyn, "Translanguaging Theory in Education," in *Translanguaging with Multilingual Students*, eds. Ofelia García and Tatyana Kleyn (New York: Routledge, 2016), 9–33; Ofelia García and Jo Anne Kleifgen, "Translanguaging and Literacies," *Reading Research Quarterly* 55, no. 4 (2020): 553–71.

5 See chapter 8 for more data on student outcomes and an explanation of how schools were matched.

6 R. Gutiérrez, "Framing," 4–8.

7 D. S. Davis and N. Vehabovic, "The Dangers of Test Preparation: What Students Learn (and Don't Learn) About Reading Comprehension from Test-centric Literacy Instruction," *The Reading Teacher* 71, no. 5 (2017): 579–88.

8 James P. Spillane, "External Reform Initiatives and Teachers' Efforts to Reconstruct Their Practice: The Mediating Role of Teachers' Zones of Enactment," *Journal of Curriculum Studies* 31, no. 2 (1999): 143–75, https://doi.org/10.1080/002202799183205.

9 Jennifer Lin Russell, Richard Correnti, Mary Kay Stein, Victoria Bill, Maggie Hannan, Nathaniel Schwartz, Laura Neergaard Booker, Nicole Roberts Pratt, and Chris Matthis, "Learning From Adaptation to Support Instructional Improvement at Scale: Understanding Coach Adaptation in the TN Mathematics Coaching Project," *American Educational Research Journal* 57, no. 1 (2020): 148–87, https://doi.org/10.3102/0002831219854050.

10 EdReports is an independent organization that began evaluating curriculum in 2015. The EdReports website includes reviews for 40+ ELA curriculum materials. Since its inception, the percentage of materials meeting their quality and alignment standards has risen from 40 percent to 52 percent. You can find more information about HQIM at edreports.org.

11 E. Wang, Andrea Prado Tuma, S. Doan, Daniella Henry, R. Lawrence, Ashley Woo, and Julia H. Kaufman, "Teachers' Perceptions of What Makes Instructional Materials Engaging, Appropriately Challenging, and Usable," *RAND Corporation* (2021).

12 Ibid.

13 Mary Kay Stein, Margaret Schwan Smith, Marjorie A. Henningsen, and Edward A. Silver, *Implementing Standards-based Mathematics Instruction: A Casebook for Professional Development* (New York: Teachers College Press, 2009).

14 Cynthia E. Coburn, "Beyond Decoupling: Rethinking the Relationship between the Institutional Environment and the Classroom," *Sociology of Education* 77, no. 3 (2004): 211–44, https://doi.org/10.1177/003804070407700302.

15 Paul Laurence Dunbar, "We Wear the Mask," *Dunbar Music Archive*, no. 169 (1896), https://ecommons.udayton.edu/dunbar/169.

16 Gary Soto, *Buried Onions* (Boston: Houghton Mifflin Harcourt, 2006).

17 Judith A. Langer, "Examining Background Knowledge and Text Comprehension," *Reading Research Quarterly* (1984): 468–81.

18 Soto, *Buried Onions*.

19 Todd M. Pollack, "The Miseducation of a Beginning Teacher: One Educator's Critical Reflections on the Functions and Power of Deficit Narratives," *Multicultural Perspectives* 14, no. 2 (2012): 93–8.
20 Judith A. Langer, "Excellence in English in Middle and High School: How Teachers' Professional Lives Support Student Achievement," *American Educational Research Journal* 37, no. 2 (2000): 397–439.
21 Sarah-Jayne Blakemore, *Inventing Ourselves: The Secret Life of the Teenage Brain* (New York: PublicAffairs, 2018).
22 Interview with Erica Racine by Sara DeMartino, November 2023.
23 Nicole Da Silva, Sara DeMartino, K. Ferrario, and Betsy Gilliland, "NCTE Position Paper on the Role of English Teachers in Educating English Language Learners (ELLs)," National Council of Teachers of English, 2020.
24 Isabel L. Beck, Margaret G. McKeown, and Cheryl A. Sandora, *Robust Comprehension Instruction with Questioning the Author* (New York: Guilford Publications, 2020).
25 Margaret G. McKeown, Isabel L. Beck, and Ronette G. K. Blake, "Rethinking Reading Comprehension Instruction: A Comparison of Instruction for Strategies and Content Approaches," *Reading Research Quarterly* 44, no. 3 (2009): 218–253.
26 Interview with Erica Racine by Sara DeMartino, November 2023.
27 Interview with Erica Racine by Sara DeMartino, October 2023.

7 Two Teachers Adapt the Student-centered Practices to Their Instructional Contexts: Richard Wright Middle School

This chapter focuses on the ways that a principal supported instructional change at Richard Wright Middle School, and how two 8th grade English Language Arts (ELA) teachers adapted the student-centered practices to different contexts, for the benefit of their students. We focus on the leadership of Shay Waters, principal of Wright from 2018 to 2023, and teachers Jackie Pulitzer and Thomas James, who embedded the practices in their instruction. You will learn about:

- how the principal acting as an instructional leader guided change and removed barriers to improvement
- how classrooms became proof points for a district leader skeptical about the uses of the student-centered practices
- how two teachers adapted the student-centered practices to integrate them into changing instructional situations
- how the practices gave students opportunities to think through ideas with their peers and teachers in very different classroom cultures

Instructional Change in Context: Richard Wright Middle School

Richard Wright Middle School is one of Big City School District's older schools. The school, which was part of the NSI from the beginning, underwent one change of principal, in the fifth year of the project. In 2022–23, it served approximately 560 students in grades six through eight. Most of the students at Richard Wright were Black (70 percent) with 27 percent of students identifying as Hispanic. Ninety-seven percent of the students were economically disadvantaged. In 2018, when the NSI began, Wright was classified as a "C" campus, with 21.9 percent of students scoring proficient or above on the ELA state assessment (SA). From the second year of the NSI up through the sixth year, Wright's students performed consistently ahead of peers in thirty-one matched district schools. Wright was one of two NSI schools to be consistently ahead of its matched comparison schools (see Chapter 8 for information about how schools were matched). In both the fourth and fifth years, 33.7 percent of Wright's students scored proficient and above on the ELA SA.

Since 2019–20, the COVID-19 year, Wright has been consistently rated a B school by the state. During that year, Wright's students began to significantly outpace their peers in the matched district schools. That also was a significant year for the 8th grade teachers' uptake of the student-centered practices, with the support of Principal Waters, and for the incorporation of challenging supplementary texts.

First, we discuss Waters' leadership, including a defining moment for both the NSI and for Wright. We then take you into Mr. James' and Ms. Pulitzer's classrooms to see two quite different adaptations of the student-centered practices. You'll read about Mr. James' carefully planned integration of the practices into a lesson designed to prepare his students for the SA. And you'll read about Ms. Pulitzer's unexpected, in-the-moment adaptation of a lesson based on her knowledge of the practices and what she judged would best serve her students.

Principal Leadership

Principal Waters led the school through the implementation of the NSI project, attending Professional Learning Community (PLC) meetings with the

8th grade ELA teachers, and participating on *learning walks* along with the school's assistant principal and the IFL NSI coaches. When the district gave us the green light to add 6th and 7th grades to the NSI's seven middle schools, she took a gradual approach by adding 7th grade first and 6th grade a year later. With a literacy background, she was keenly attuned to literacy practices and the approaches to teaching and learning that made those practices effective for the school's students. She embraced the idea of students working to comprehend texts before taking on analysis and interpretation tasks, as well as the notion that students benefit from having access to complex texts representative of their cultures.

A defining moment for the NSI project and for Waters as a leader occurred in the fall of 2019. We had scheduled a series of school visits with the executive director who was responsible for Wright along with other schools in the Network. Our goal was to observe the level of students' engagement at two of the executive director's schools—one in the morning and the other, Wright, in the afternoon.

Considering that we were in the second year of the project, we saw varying levels of traction in the implementation of the student-centered practices during those observations. At the school we walked prior to Wright, we observed early signs, particularly of student-to-student talk. Teachers followed the district curriculum and students composed quick writes before turning and talking with each other. However, the process we observed seemed mechanical—more like compliance on the part of the teacher and the students than true engagement with the practices. When the teacher asked students to talk, they looked at each other for several seconds before saying a word or two. When the teacher posed a question to the whole class about what the text was about, there was a long silence before the teacher asked a specific student to respond, followed by a few more. In our debrief, we noted that the text was thin, and the students didn't have a task sheet, so they were constantly asking what they were supposed to do. The text, finally, didn't offer students much to talk about, so that left them with very little to say.

The observation at Wright was a significant contrast. We began in the conference room where Principal Waters, the assistant principal, and the instructional school coach provided an overview of the afternoon. We received a schedule and time for each classroom visit. We learned that the teachers had been working on implementing the student-centered practices, selecting complex texts from the curriculum and from supplementary readings, and learning how to ask more open-ended comprehension questions rather than focusing on facts and recall of details. Teachers had taken up the use of task sheets as a tool to help them design focused lessons and make the content and class procedures clear to students.

Principal Waters explained that with the support of the assistant principal, the 8th grade teachers decided to forgo using the district-created unit titled "Freedom." In later conversations with Mr. James and Ms. Pulitzer, they told us that their students read many texts that portrayed Black people as needing to rise up from hardship, a key theme in the "Freedom" unit. Students wanted to read—and teachers wanted to teach—texts that celebrated the richness of Black culture. From that desire, their Harlem Renaissance unit was born. It invited students to explore poetry, prose, visual art, and music created by Black artists during the 1920s and 1930s. The lesson we would see during our observation, we learned, focused on a poem from that newly created unit. However, the executive director had expected to see students engaged with a text from the "Freedom" unit.

The choice of "We Wear the Mask,"[1] by Paul Laurence Dunbar, sparked a visibly tense exchange between Principal Waters and the executive director in the hallway before *The Learning Walk*. The executive director wanted to know why they weren't using a text from the district-approved unit. We could hear her say, "and who gave the teachers permission to use the Dunbar poem?" Without hesitating, Principal Waters said, "I did. I made that decision. Our students need to read more texts by authors like them. They also need to read texts that have enough oomph for them to talk about. We haven't abandoned the district curriculum. We're just enhancing it. When you visit the classrooms, I think you'll see why."

Stepping back now from this exchange, we want to point out that Principal Waters taking responsibility and leading with conviction was an important leadership move. Her advocacy for her teachers and their students to discuss texts with "oomph," as she called it, was for us a key example of instructional leadership. As you'll see, to the executive director's credit also as an instructional leader, she took that moment and her experiences walking those classrooms as a learning opportunity.

We proceeded to visit three 8th grade classrooms, including Mr. James' and Ms. Pulitzer's, where we observed various stages of students' discussion about

"We Wear the Mask." All of the lessons focused on students' comprehension of the big ideas in the text. We saw students in deep, intense discussions about what it means to wear a mask. Mr. James walked around his classroom, where his students were seated in groups of three, listening to their comments and the crosstalk from their groups. He tracked what they were saying and strategically invited additional comments with questions such as: "Who can add to that?" "Can you find that in the text?" "Why do you say that?" and "Why do you disagree?" He was focused and intentional, and his students reflected his manner in their responses. They listened carefully to each other without interrupting and formulated their thinking—often in sidebar conversations with others in their groups—before speaking.

Ms. Pulitzer's class was equally engaging, although her students—like her—were far more animated. They displayed their passion for the text in a discussion bubbling with enthusiasm. They talked about how they felt like *they* were wearing masks, picking up a major theme in Dunbar's poem, when the world didn't see them or only saw them as poor or Black or Brown. At times, Ms. Pulitzer worked hard to restrain herself from jumping into the discussion, as she later told us, because she wanted students to talk and think freely without parroting what she thought.

"In the hallway after the round of observations, we waited in suspense for comments from the executive director. We were all surprised when she began with, 'Wow! Just wow!'"

In the hallway after the round of observations, we waited in suspense for comments from the executive director. We were all surprised when she began with, "Wow! Just wow!" She went on to point to the level of engagement in all the classes and the ways that students were responding to the text and to each other. During the debriefing back in the conference room, she said that she saw the benefits of addressing comprehension first before asking students to analyze or interpret texts and was in complete agreement with Principal Waters' explanation for the text selection. She was keenly aware, she said, of how the student-centered practices can give students structures that enable them to engage and voice their thinking. From that moment on, she became a strong, vocal advocate for the work of the NSI, the practices, and text choice, including telling her stories from the observations at Wright to her peers at their meetings.

Our collective experience of this *Learning Walk* is similar to teachers' experience of their students' successes with texts and tasks that challenge them. Such experiences can change beliefs and expectations in much the same way that the classroom observations from that day became proof points for the executive director, changing her beliefs and expectations.

Mr. James' and Ms. Pulitzer's Students' Discussions

Mr. James' Students Discuss a Ray Bradbury Story

We turn now to an example of student-centered discussion in Mr. James' class that we observed in March of 2023. Before looking at a short transcript of a segment of the discussion, we set the classroom scene and context.

In Mr. James' classroom, students sit in pods of three or four. A Promethean smart board, connected to Mr. James' laptop, rests on a wheeled cart. Based on our observations over the year, we viewed the class as a community. Everyone participates, seems to feel comfortable speaking, and brings a critical lens to the ideas under discussion. In their discussions, students seem accountable to each other, to the task, and to meaning making.

The students had read a supplementary text, "The Pendulum,"[2] by Ray Bradbury. In the story, Layeville has invented a time machine with the help of thirty of the world's most distinguished scientists. It blows up while millions watch, killing the scientists and wounding Layeville. The pendulum machine is turned into a moving prison for Layeville as punishment for killing the scientists. Ages pass. Aliens invade and kill everyone except Layeville. Robots keep the pendulum working. Thousands of years later, visitors from another world show up, turn off the pendulum, and find Layeville's skeleton with his skull seemingly smiling.

Over two days, students completed quick writes on the big ideas that they thought Bradbury was trying to get across to his readers and discussed those with each other in their groups. The transcript picks up as the class is working on an analysis task that asks them to discuss Layeville's main conflict and whether his actions called for the punishment he received. After the discussion that's captured in the transcript, the class continued with a gallery walk of posters that posed generic questions that could prompt responses with just about any text. Those questions mirrored the ones used on the SA for two- or three-sentence constructed responses.

Mr. James integrated the student-centered practices into these lessons to give students an opportunity to use the ideas from their discussions to respond to the SA questions. You'll see those questions and samples of how students used their discussions to frame their responses after the transcript and our recap.

Mr. James had been integrating the student-centered practices regularly into his lessons since the beginning of the year when the texts could hold up their end of the bargain, as he told us, so his students were as comfortable with them as he was. We were interested because it appeared to be a compelling example of how the improvement intervention—the student-centered practices—could be used to give students practice in ways of thinking about a specific text that would prepare them to respond to the SA questions. Mr. James' careful adaptive integration of the practices expanded students' repertoire beyond simple practice answers to the SA prompts while showing them how to use a specific text to respond to generic questions. After observing the sequence of lessons and talking with Mr. James about his planning, we were struck both by the way his familiarity with the practices and continuous improvement gave him tools to imagine the adaptation and by how well it worked for his students. He made believers of us.

During the conversation shown in the transcript, students worked together in groups. Each group was asked to identify a note-taker and a speaker to represent the group's ideas and reasoning. Students 1 to 4 form one group, Students 5 and 6 belong to another group, and Students 7 and 8 belong to a third group. Even though they're sitting in their groups, they're speaking to the class. (There's one more group of four. We don't hear from them because we didn't get their permission to be recorded.)

Mr. James begins by reading the task on the Promethean board out loud. As students talk, he walks from group to group, listening and occasionally asking a question or making a comment.

1	Teacher:	Let me get one person in the group. Let me get the group
2		to designate one person to be the writer. And I want you
3		to think about this question here. What is Layeville's main
4		conflict in the story and did his actions call for this?

5	Student 1:	All right, so, I would say the main conflict wouldn't be killing
6		the thirty scientists. I would say it would be the explosion—
7		no, because you got to think about it. It would be the
8		explosion.
9	Student 2:	It's the same thing.
10	Student 3:	That's how they …
11	Student 2:	That's how they die.
12	Student 4:	I mean, all that could be just put together.
13	Student 2:	Yeah.
14	Student 4:	Yeah, that is his own machine messing up and killing the
15		people and him getting stuck in that machine for all that.
16	Student 2:	So I'm going to write Layeville …
17	Student 1:	I'm focused on this explosion. And that could be useful. And
18		then the reason why I would say that is because they rebuild,
19		they rebuilt his machine, that was destroyed, to trap him in it.
20	Student 4:	They rebuilt his machine?
21	Student 1:	Yes, it was stated. They didn't build it right.
22	Student 2:	They did not rebuild it right though. Yeah, you gotta reread it.
23	Student 1:	It was paragraph five …
24	Student 5:	Remember, that the people believe, uh, Layeville is a
25		murderer, ya know. And that he killed the scientists in cold
26		blood. And the fact that he didn't, I don't think he actually
27		killed anybody. Does anyone have different responses or
28		anything?
29	Student 6:	Well, I'd like to add on to what you said. Um, the people did
30		blame him because, um, the scientists thought his creation
31		was good and perfect enough to test in front of thirty scientists.
32		Which, um, what you said a couple of minutes before were
33		probably his friends, buddies, um, associates and more. Um, like
34		it's the, the main conflict is the people. That's all.
35	Student 7:	Yeah. It's like the people, the people they were feeling
36		mistaken because if you look it says that he was broadcasting
37		this in front of two million people. This is the people that was
38		in the crowds and the people that was at TV. So that's how it'll
39		show that there is going to be no mishap. And the people,
40		they were feeling like, oh, his, this should be perfect if he got
41		thirty of the world's greatest scientists, so nothing should go
42		wrong. But then they blamed him all of a sudden because

43		something got all sudden with the mishap of it blowing up.
44		Then that's how they started blaming him for it. And they say
45		said, kill the murderer of the prisoner of time.
46	Student 1:	Anti-dismemberment because, you know, he departed from
47		that group technically.
48	Student 2:	This says Layeville's main conflict was the explosion, and
49		accidental death and dismemberments of the scientists.
50	Student 4:	So, these scientists are like the smartest in the world.
51	Student 2:	The whole world, yes.
52	Student 1:	I mean I wouldn't really think that, after somebody else
53		rebuilt the machine better.
54	Student 4:	I mean still, you gotta think about it, it was just ...
55	Student 2:	It was probably robots who rebuilt the machine because all
56		the people was dead.
57	Student 1:	That's false.
58	Student 4:	They only killed thirty of the scientists, it probably could, it
59		still could be more scientists out there. And the machine
60		wasn't fully, like, destroyed. Because I'm pretty sure they
61		put ... [begins rereading text to self].
62	Student 2:	So, if his actions caused this ...
63	Teacher:	What do they think? Um, what was the main conflict and did
64		his actions call for this? Um, Morgan would you mind sharing
65		with us, please.
66	Student 8:	So me and my group talked about his main conflict was him
67		being blamed for the death of the scientists, because since
68		he was the one who made it, they thought that he was the
69		reason of the malfunction.
70	Teacher:	Jamal, what were you going to say, sir?
71	Student 3:	Um, to add on to what, uh, Morgan said, uh, I think Layeville's
72		his main conflict was the explosion and accidental death and
73		dismemberment of the scientists. But did his punishment
74		fit his crime? Yes. Uh, yes, his punishment did fit his crime
75		because he killed thirty people from the point of view of the
76		people. He did deserve it.
77	Teacher:	Cool. Keep going.
78	Student 1:	And they also ...
79	Student 2:	I wrote this.
80	Teacher:	What you say, Rami?

81	Student 1:	And it's stated from what they quoted, it says destroy the time
82		machine, they cried. Because that might've been someone's
83		family ya know? And they said destroy the murderer with it.
84	Student 4:	Yeah, cause you got to understand they got to, they probably
85		mad in their feelings cause that's thirty people, that thirty
86		and they scientists. One of the, the smartest scientists in the
87		world and they he just killed them. That's what they seen,
88		and that's just, they don't care about a fair trial. They, all that
89		they see is he killed them thirty scientists.
90	Teacher:	Great minds!
91	Student 2:	But if it was now, like in the times of now, if something
92		like that was to happen now, he will get it fair trial, but he
93		wouldn't win.
94	Teacher:	Hahaha. It's a good shot. He may not, right? I mean …
95	Student 2:	I, I don't think he would. It was thirty people. Accidental. I
96		don't, okay look, I don't feel like it was on purpose, but I do
97		feel like he should be punished for what he did because
98		there were thirty lives. Like, it's not like he killed one person
99		by accident.
100	Student 5:	I'm going to add on to what she was saying and how it,
101		even if the intent was not, even if, sorry, even though he
102		didn't intend on hurting or harming anyone, he still did
103		kill thirty people and the greatest minds at that. You have
104		to understand that these scientists cured possibly, cured
105		diseases like …
106	Teacher:	Right.
107	Student 5:	Found out solutions like world hunger and stuff like that.
108		So you have to understand he killed the world's greatest
109		scientists. So of course he has to have a punishment that fits
110		that type of crime. It's not like they're sending him to like
111		a death sentence or anything. They're still mercying him by
112		letting him live in the pendulum.

There's quite a bit going on in these five minutes. Here's what we pick up on. From lines five to nineteen, students in group one seem to be sorting out the explosion and the death of the thirty scientists as Layeville's conflict. They agree to put those two things together as his conflict. After that, in lines twenty to twenty-three, they sort out the rebuilding of the pendulum, but it wasn't rebuilt "right," meaning it wasn't rebuilt as a time machine. It was rebuilt as a prison for Layeville.

From lines twenty-four to forty-five, Students 5 and 6 appear to be representing their group (two) by focusing on the people who witnessed the explosion and believe that "Layeville is a murderer." Student 5 asks the class if anyone has a different response. Student 6 builds on that by taking the position that "the main conflict is the people," meaning that Layeville's conflict is with the people. That's a different position on the conflict than we see with Students 1 to 4 who think that the killing of the scientists is Layeville's conflict. Student 7 agrees with Students 5 and 6, saying that the conflict is with the people, and adds to the explanation.

In lines forty-six to sixty-two, three of the students in group one seem to be sorting out facts about what happened while sticking to their thinking that the "main conflict was the explosion and accidental death and dismemberment of the scientists." Then at line sixty-three, Mr. James re-presents the task and calls on Student 8 (Morgan) who responds with a slightly different take on Layeville's conflict by saying "his main conflict was him being blamed for the death of the scientists…." Morgan reasons it out by saying Layeville was blamed "because since he was the one who made it, they thought he was the reason of the malfunction." Morgan seems to be thinking along the lines of those students in group two who argue that the conflict is between Layeville and the people.

In line seventy Mr. James calls on Jamal from the first group who doesn't respond to Morgan, although he says he wants to build on what Morgan said. Instead, he reiterates the main argument being made by a number of students that the main conflict was the explosion and accidental death. He also offers a bit of reasoning when he says that the punishment fit the crime "because he killed thirty people from the point of view of the people."

Mr. James moves the discussion along by calling on Student 1, Rami, who has his hand up. Earlier Rami opened the discussion by saying that he thought the conflict was the explosion. He tells the group that the text says the people said, "destroy the time machine … and they said destroy the murderer with it." Maybe he's now thinking that the conflict, then, is with Layeville and the people. Student 4 seems to pick up on this in lines eighty-four to eighty-nine with the argument that the people are mad because of the thirty scientists that were killed, "the smartest scientists in the world," and they, the people, don't care about a fair trial.

Student 2 at line ninety-five opens up another line of thinking by saying, "I don't feel like it was on purpose, but I do feel like he should be punished for what he did because there was thirty lives." Student 5 joins in at line eighty-one and adds that "even though he didn't intend on hurting or harming anyone, he still did kill thirty people...." Then Student 5 adds in lines 107 to 112, that "It's not like they're sending him to like a death sentence or anything. They're still mercying him by letting him live in the pendulum."

Finally, there's no agreement on Layeville's conflict. One group thinks it's with the explosion and the death of thirty scientists and the other two groups take a position that it's with the people and Layeville who they believe is a murderer even if the deaths weren't intentional. A small group of students who have voiced their views think the punishment fits the crime, but all the groups haven't spoken on this.

We were interested in the way students interpreted conflict, especially those who thought Layeville's conflict was the explosion, and in the way Mr. James let students play out their views. It was difficult for us to imagine that an explosion could be a conflict, but after Rami made that claim, other students jumped in and said, "It's the same thing." "That's how they die." "I mean, all that could be just put together." We gather that the meaning here is that the explosion, the unintentional deaths, and the people's reaction come together to put Layeville in conflict with them because of all that happened. The dynamics at work in this discussion seem to push and pull on just what is a conflict, although as a group the class seems to reason its way to Layeville's conflict being with the people.

Adapting and integrating the student-centered practices into exam preparation

Mr. James didn't push the group or individual students to come to a consensus about the conflict. After this discussion, he moved the students on to the charts he had posted around the room. Each had a generic question that has in the past been asked of students on the SA. The SA prompts often ask students for an explanation of a story's conflicts, and they're expected to use a story they've studied in class as an example.

Here are the questions Mr. James posted on the charts. He told students to respond in writing on each chart with sticky notes that he provided.

1. Asking Questions: After reading, what questions do you still have? What made you think of these new wonderings?
2. Making Inferences: What do the character's/person's actions and choices tell you about him or her? Provide support.
3. Making Connections: What connections can be made between this text and the real world?
4. Making Connections: What lesson or "take away" did you learn that you can use in your own life? Explain.

We understand Mr. James' use of the student-centered practices (the quick write followed by small group discussions followed by whole group discussions) as an example of adaptive integration. He could have focused his lesson completely on the questions/SA prompts on the posters without engaging the students in the discussion on Layeville's conflict. Often, to prepare students for the exam questions, teachers simply ask them to pick a story they studied recently and respond to each question in a sentence or two. Instead, Mr. James used the SA questions after the discussion to give students opportunities to use their thinking from the discussion. The gallery walk of the posters, another adaptation of a student-centered practice, gave students the opportunity to read each other's responses to the questions.

In response to question two on the poster, which asked what the character's actions and choices tell you about him or her, a student wrote, "Layeville was considered a monster amongst his peers, but in reality, he was smart and a caring person that went slowly insane in the pendulum." Another wrote, "In paragraph six, it tells us how much remorse he has for the thirty scientists he accidentally killed." In response to question four on the lessons or take aways, one student wrote, "From the real world, you should always have a back-up plan to make sure a test goes smoothly." Another jotted, "There are always consequences, good or bad."

These responses are in keeping with the kinds of answers expected of them on the exam but with a bit more explanation and text citations. "In paragraph six," as one student wrote, would be good enough to count for an unelaborated citation.

Ms. Pulitzer's Students Discuss Frankenstein

Ms. Pulitzer's classroom was organized into pods of three desks like Mr. James' class. The pods were arranged in a semi-circle for a class discussion of excerpts from *Frankenstein*,[3] by Mary Shelley, that students had read. Students were expected to talk amongst themselves in their pods and have representatives speak for them. Ms. Pulitzer sat at a student's desk next to a group of students. The Promethean board showed the question for the discussion. There was a lot of energy in the room. When a student spoke, for instance, others raised and waved their hands, often turning around or lifting themselves up.

The question on the board—"Is Frankenstein's monster human?"—came from the curriculum. Teachers were instructed to have students turn and talk to a partner in preparation for writing an essay on the question. Each student had already completed a quick write to get their thinking down. During the turn and talk, Ms. Pulitzer walked around the room to listen in. She heard so many ideas from students that she decided on the spot to have a whole class discussion.

This transcript is taken from the first five minutes of the discussion, which continued for most of the period. Afterward, Ms. Pulitzer gave students directions for writing their essays.

You'll notice that except for couple of moments in the discussion where students responded to each other, the pattern is student talk followed by a comment from Ms. Pulitzer. She revoices students' responses, manages the discussion, confirms responses, and comments on what they have to say. She elevates students' responses with statements such as, "All right. Cool…." and "I like that." She calls on students with their hands raised by name, and when multiple students have their hands raised, she names the order in which they can speak. When students begin talking amongst themselves, she asks, "Are we listening?" to gather everyone's attention.

Unlike Mr. James' adaptation of the student-centered practices to support test preparation, Ms. Pulitzer's adaptation is to the curriculum. She told us that she values students' whole group discussions, along with the turn and talk usually suggested in the curriculum, because students get to hear each other's ideas in their own words and respond to their classmates' explanations and reasoning with their own explanations and reasoning. She likes to be involved in the discussions, because she thinks it's important for her to question some ideas and emphasize others, or just to say what she likes in what she heard. She sees this type of guidance on her part as a form of modeling. When her interjections work together with student talk, as they seem to do in this discussion, everyone gets to hear what Ms. Pulitzer thinks about their thinking and language. That type of participation sets expectations that her students want to live up to, she said, because they know she's listening carefully to them and will respond to their ideas and thinking.

As you read the transcript, it won't be possible to tell where students are sitting. The talk jumps around from group to group. Six students, representing their groups, carry the discussion. Group members often talk quietly amongst themselves in response to what was said by others. Notice how Ms. Pulitzer's management of the discussion influences the ways students' ideas and arguments evolve.

```
1  Student 1:  You know, I want to say you was arguing that he is human,
2              right? So, y'all know how like, you know, that saying, what
3              have you like? Oh, that that like that animal was a human or
4              something. I think that backs up with what he said.
5  Teacher:    Something like when you see people when they post their
6              animals doing stuff and it was like, oh, this got to be a human?
7  Student 1:  Right.
8  Teacher:    Chase, what do you want to add to that?
9  Student 2:  I want to say just because he's showing feelings of a human
10             in expressing how humans are doing, punishing that doesn't
11             make him automatically human. Just because, as he said his
12             own self, he's his own different type of being. And on number
13             five it says, "why the pain, he must be the same species." He's
14             his own species. He's not a part of mankind.
15 Teacher:    So you feel like if he's using the word species, he's trying to
16             say that I'm not of this species? Agree or disagree? You want
17             to add something? Maya, anybody? Wanna add something?
18             All right, Francine? Okay, I'm sorry. Okay, Francine then Maya.
19 Student 3:  I say I agree with Chase because the creature when
20             Frankenstein was making him he had to use like powers and
21             stuff and witchcraft to make him, but he didn't come out like
22             naturally like everybody, like all the other humans do and he
23             didn't grow up like a actual human like he didn't develop
```

24		and grow. And also, when Chase said, when he said that he
25		needed a companion, I agree because he needs to make a
26		whole another, a whole another type like the same type of
27		species as him because nobody else accepts him because
28		he's not the same as all the other humans.
29	Teacher:	All right. Cool. Maya?
30	Student 4:	So yeah, basically I was going to say the same thing. But I
31		only I disagree because no matter how much he acts like a
32		human, I mean, I would like I agree on some parts because
33		he can have sympathy but all the while again, you will always
34		be like detested by humanity. Because he was different, so
35		he could not fit into modern society, even as like hard as he
36		tried.
37	Teacher:	Love her word choice. Um, so, I'll wait. Scott?
38	Student 5:	Francine said that um, the creature did not like grow up and
39		did not develop. But just like Ayana said, the creature did
40		learn how to read and write doesn't that mean he developed
41		more [inaudible].
42	Teacher:	I like that.
43	Student 1:	Okay, so basically, you're saying he didn't grow physically, but
44		mentally he did?
45	Student 6:	And because babies got to do that too. Babies … you can't
46		just come out of the womb and know everything. You have
47		to like watch from human from like older people to actually
48		get on to it. And Francine said that he was like, he had to be
49		witchcraft to be … [cross-talking going on here].
50	Teacher:	Are we listening?
51	Student 6:	And like by electric, like electricity and stuff but he was also
52		built by human body parts, so even though he was like, he
53		had to do all that, he still is human because he still has the
54		human body parts. Yeah, he still deformed and everything,
55		but he still has a heart, a brain, everything that a human has.
56	Teacher:	Okay. Let me ask this question. Right quick. Could you argue
57		both sides?
58	Students:	Yeah. Yeah.
59	Teacher:	That's where you want to go with that? Okay, Chase?
60	Student 2:	I disagree because even though he was made from human
61		body parts, they are decomposed body parts, they come

62		from a graveyard from dead people. And since they're
63		decomposing, they're not able to contain life because the
64		blood cells get no supplies of oxygen and blood no more
65		meaning you can't have life. Like there's no way he can get
66		life plus he doesn't have any internal organs.
67	Student 6:	He can still walk and talk.
68	Student 2:	Cause he was made of bones, and he was created from dark
69		magic. That's what brung him to life.

As the discussion evolves, we hear two basic points of view—Frankenstein's creation is not human or is human, and at least mentally, he behaves like a human because he can walk and talk like one. Student 1 begins by referencing animals doing human things, but Chase, Student 2, is waving his hand in the air. He makes a point that just because the monster shows feelings, that "doesn't make him automatically human.... He's his own species. He's not a part of mankind."

In the next turn, Ms. Pulitzer revoices Chase's claim about the creation being "not of the species" and asks if others agree or disagree. Many waving hands go up. In line eighteen, Ms. Pulitzer indicates the order in which those students can speak. First Student 3 agrees with Chase that the monster isn't human but is "another type ... not the same as all the other humans." The reasoning that he's not like other humans gives Student 4 in lines thirty to thirty-six the opportunity to say that even though the monster expresses sympathy, he'll "always be like detested by humanity" because he's different and will never fit in no matter how hard he tries. Student 5 responds (lines thirty-eight to forty-one) that the monster didn't grow up and develop but he did learn how to read and write, "so doesn't that mean he developed more...." Ms. Pulitzer likes that.

Student 1 comes back in line forty-three and sums up the argument—the monster didn't grow physically but he did grow mentally. Student 6 then says he didn't grow the way babies do and agrees that it had to be witchcraft. In response to this statement, students begin talking loudly in their groups amongst themselves. Ms. Pulitzer asks just as loudly, "Are we listening?" From there the argument evolves into the logic of one position that claims the monster has everything human beings have even though he's deformed. Another position claims the body parts are incapable of carrying life, so he's not human. In the midst of this divergent argument, Ms. Pulitzer asks, "Could you argue both sides?" The whole class responds, "Yeah. Yeah." That agreement on being able to argue both sides seems to be where Ms. Pulitzer has been going with her management of the discussion. It seems to us that she intended students to see that multiple arguments could be made and supported.

What We Learned from Mr. James's and Ms. Pulitzer's Classes

As we have described, both teachers adapted the student-centered practices to their goals and contexts. Adaptive integrations of the practices like these taught us the importance of understanding teachers' variations of the tests of change—the student-centered practices—for the ways they shaped or influenced their uptake with teachers and students while keeping to the larger vision of student-centered instruction.

Thinking about these classes together, we're struck by the ease with which the students in both classes engaged with each other and their ideas. These are late winter classes, so the students have had a fairly steady experience with the student-centered practices in various forms. The students also had experienced the practices in 7th grade, and some may have had those opportunities in 6th grade. And even though the classes proceed in different ways, they both show us spaces in which students feel safe engaging with their peers and their teachers, staying close to the texts, and challenging each other's ideas. The videos of these classes give the impression that both work as communities in which a culture of talk and critical exchange is the norm. We know, though, that such cultures don't simply happen. They take time to cultivate. In the ease and enthusiasm of the exchanges, we see the outlines of the work that had to precede these moments. In general, students are accustomed to teachers talking most of the time; they see their own roles as responding to teacher questions with the answers that teachers seem to be fishing for. These 8th graders, on the other hand, learned that their voices mattered, and that their talk with their peers was accountable to the task at hand and to their classmates,[4] not just to their teachers.

> "In such discussions, students' ideas evolve and take on lives of their own, permutating into variations, and solidifying even over a brief time as they convince themselves and others to champion particular lines of thinking."

Both teachers show themselves to be close listeners by the ways they respond to and manage the discussions. Their students also show themselves to be close listeners who track their peers' comments and questions and respond to them, often referencing what others have said. In five minutes of discussion, we learned how students (1) explained their ideas in response to big questions about a text, (2) explained their thinking and made connections to their peers' thinking—whether in agreement, amplification, or disagreement—and (3) worked together along with their teachers as class communities supporting and challenging ideas and reasoning. In such discussions, students' ideas evolve and take on lives of their own, permutating into variations, and solidifying even over a brief time as they convince themselves and others to champion particular lines of thinking.

We're struck too, as we've said a number of times, by the way the practices can be adapted for different purposes. Mr. James used them at the front of a small set of lessons designed to prepare students for specific types of assessment tasks. Ms. Pulitzer made the decision to segue into a whole class discussion after hearing a range of students' ideas in response to a turn and talk that was indicated in the curriculum. They made these adaptations with ease because they were deeply familiar with the student-centered practices and what they could offer students. Mr. James' students benefited from the quick write on Layeville's conflict in the story and their small and whole group discussions of the ideas that they surfaced in their quick writes. Their engagement through those activities gave them a familiarity with the story that they could use to respond to generic assessment prompts. Ms. Pulitzer's students benefited from hearing a variety of their peers' ideas in response to the question about the monster's humanity. They learned that multiple arguments could be developed and supported. The depth of their discussion helped prepare them to write an essay about the topic. It also helped teach them the benefits of talking through ideas with a group—the benefits, that is, of socializing intelligence.[5]

Questions for Reflection

1 How would you explain adaptive integration of the tests of the change—the student-centered practices—to someone who hasn't read this chapter?

2 If you were to coach Mr. James and Ms. Pulitzer on the next steps to develop student-centered teaching and learning based on what you've read here, what would you offer them?

3 How would you scale the notions and examples of adaptive integration of the tests of change to other schools new to continuous improvement and the student-centered practices?

Notes

1 Paul Laurence Dunbar, "We Wear the Mask," Poetry Foundation, accessed November 6, 2024, https://www.poetryfoundation.org/poems/44203/we-wear-the-mask.
2 Ray Bradbury, "The Pendulum," *Futuria Fantasia* 1 no. 2 (Fall 1939).
3 Mary Shelley, *Frankenstein* (London: Penguin Classics, 2012).
4 Lauren B. Resnick, Christa S.C. Asterhan, and Sherice N. Clarke, "Accountable Talk: Instructional Dialogue that Builds the Mind," *Educational Practices* Series 29, UNESCO International Bureau of Education, 2018.
5 Lauren B. Resnick and Sandra Nelson-Le Gall, "Socializing Intelligence," in *Piaget, Vygotsky, and Beyond*, ed. Leslie Smith, Julie Dockrell, and Peter Tomlinson (London: Routledge, 1997), 145–58.

8 How We Assessed the NSI Instructional Changes and Their Implementation

Anna E. Premo and Christian D. Schunn

Assessment is a part of any conversation about educational change. Assessment in the form of standardized test scores is considered the gold standard for understanding student growth by some, a necessary evil by others, and a relic of the past by a growing contingent. However, it is generally agreed that it is important to understand how educational changes impact student learning. In the case of our NSI, it was particularly important to understand the impact of the instructional practices teachers were implementing.

Our NSI had a five- (turned six-) year time horizon, so knowing early on if these practices were promoting student learning was essential. The NSI involved working with teachers in fourteen schools and with a diverse population of students, so we needed to understand not only if these practices were having a general positive impact, but also whether that impact was felt by all students in all schools.

> *"Answers to our data questions helped us correct our course along the way, gain the necessary leadership support, and provide evidence that empowering teachers as decision-makers in their own classrooms fosters student learning."*

For the Network analytics team, assessment of the NSI wasn't just about how these students performed on state tests (did the NSI schools' scores go up?). Rather, we wanted to assess the impact of the instructional changes on individual student growth (did students in NSI classrooms where teachers regularly used our instructional practices learn more?) and school growth (did NSI schools improve more than similar non-NSI schools?). To do so, we used many data sources that will be described throughout this chapter.

Answering these questions is, of course, key to being able to call the NSI a "success." More importantly, however, these answers helped us correct our course along the way, gain the necessary leadership support, and provide evidence that empowering teachers as decision-makers in their own classrooms fosters student learning.

Are These Instructional Practices Impacting Student Learning?

As a Network Hub, our key goal was to know if our work was impacting student learning. Practically speaking, that meant we were constantly asking questions and trying to use data to answer them. Some of these questions had to do with exploring how the Network-supported practices were being used by teachers: *To what extent are these instructional practices being implemented?* Others were concerned with investigating the relationship between these practices and student outcomes: *Is more frequent implementation of the practices related to student learning?* Still others focused on understanding differential impact: *Which student groups are benefiting from these practices?*

As you may have realized by now, the NSI approach is a little different from other approaches to educational change. Notably, while other approaches tend to emphasize teaching with fidelity to a specific model, the NSI emphasized teacher-led *adaptation*. Teacher-led adaptation allows teachers (and their local support teams) to find ways to make it possible to implement the practices at all, as well as potentially improving embedded supports for specific students.

However, we understand that teachers with relatively little experience with student-centered pedagogy might impose teacher-centered adaptations that would greatly reduce the effectiveness of the pedagogical approach (e.g., taking away learning opportunities by providing too much support).

Also, these practices may not be sufficient to address students' foundational needs, especially given the broad set of barriers to success identified in the root cause analysis work. We kept these possibilities in mind as we created questions and looked at data.

> *"Over the six years, two main sources helped us understand how instructional practices were impacting student learning: teacher surveys and student test data."*

How We Gathered Data

To answer our questions, we needed data. Importantly, we needed data that were easy to obtain and analyze so the results could be used to inform practice. Over the six years, two main sources helped us understand how instructional practices were impacting student learning: teacher surveys and student test data.

Teacher surveys are valuable tools for understanding what's happening in classrooms in teachers' own voices, especially when there are large numbers of teachers distributed across many schools. Surveys are also easy to implement, a priority in educational contexts where nearly everyone involved is already at or over capacity.

In the design and administration of the surveys, we used a number of strategies to encourage participation and honest reporting (see Figure 8.1), and to avoid producing misleadingly positive views of implementation and effects. First, we guaranteed teachers' anonymity. We also explicitly told them their responses would not be used for accountability or any other purpose beyond understanding and improving the Network. To that end, in our capacity as an intermediary, we administered the surveys. We did need to know teacher identities to link the responses to student growth. Still, we promised that individual responses or even building-specific patterns would never be shared with building and district leaders.

Second, we designed the surveys such that no response was framed as "correct" or "ideal." Consistent with the improvement science approach, we asked about which practices were used and how often. When we asked

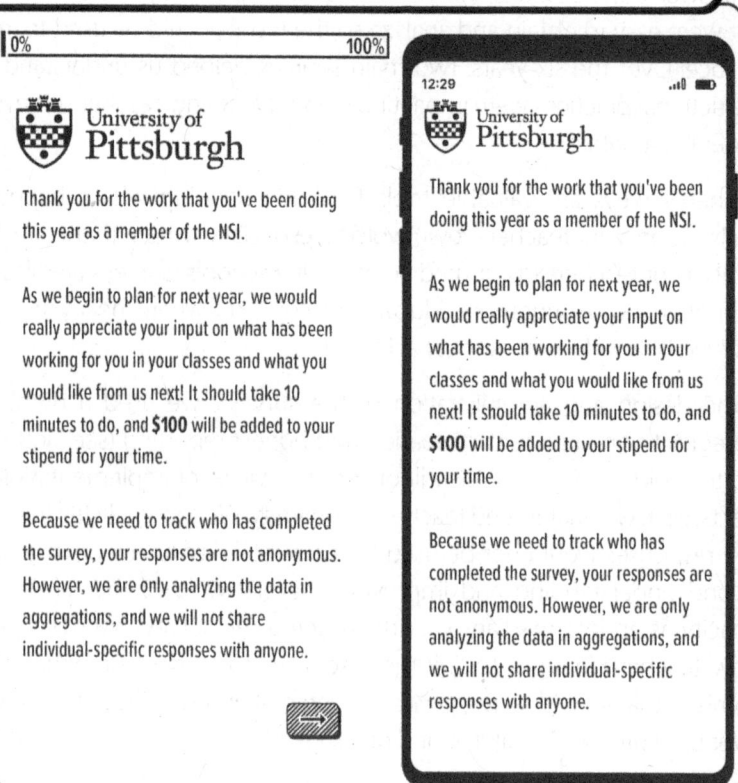

Figure 8.1 Examples of communications to teachers in 2022. Top: The email message sent from the Network Hub asking for survey responses. Bottom: An excerpt from the implementation survey that emphasizes teacher anonymity.

about barriers to implementation, we framed the responses as reasonable (see Figure 8.2). Anonymity here was particularly important. If inconsistent leader messages or priorities were the cause of non-implementation, teachers would feel safe to say so.

The surveys also asked teachers about their self-efficacy (e.g., "At this point in your professional learning, could you successfully implement each of these practices in your classes using materials given to you?") and willingness to engage with them (e.g., "If you had encouragement from your principal/AP and lead teacher, how likely would you be to regularly include these practices in your teaching next year [i.e., implement three or more times in a nine-week period]?"). Information on self-efficacy and willingness can provide important insights into whether implementation is likely to continue. This

---

In having students work with a complex text, I taught **text-based comprehension work before engaging in other text-based tasks**.
- Never
- Once
- 2-3 times
- More than 3 times

Please tell us more about your thoughts on using text comprehension work before engaging in other text-based tasks. (select all that apply)

☐ I don't know what this involves
☐ I need more support to implement those steps
☐ I am not sure I am allowed to implement it
☐ I would like a NSI Network meeting on this approach
☐ I would like my school PLC to focus on this approach
☐ I don't think this approach will be appropriate for most of my students
☐ I do not have time to teach a comprehension task

Figure 8.2 Sample questions from the survey administered to teachers in 2021. The second question appeared for teachers who indicated they had experienced barriers.

also helped us to be sure the survey data gave insights into implementation levels, not just a general endorsement of the approach.

In terms of measuring student learning, specific tests are, of course, only one source. For all their limitations, tests already in use in a district are a pragmatic data source. In the case of our work, we were fortunate to have access to results from multiple assessments. In particular, students took one test at multiple time points throughout the year: the Northwest Evaluation Association's Measures of Academic Progress (MAP), as mentioned in Chapter 1. This test provided us with a unique opportunity to understand individual student growth over the course of a semester (or year) within a specific teacher's classroom. Moreover, MAP uses high-quality performance measures emphasizing more advanced forms of thinking compared to other administered assessments.

What We Did with Data

Once we had the survey and test data (which were linked using district-provided data about which students were associated with which ELA teachers), we had to decide what to do with them. We first looked at our data about implementation. From the surveys, we learned that the majority of the teachers were implementing most of the practices on a regular basis. The surveys also showed some barriers to implementation (e.g., in Year 3, teachers did not know how to integrate quick writes into the curriculum). To address these issues, the NSI Hub Team discussed them first with leaders and then in Network meetings with teachers. In later years, as a result of these data-informed interventions, surveys reflected large improvements in areas where barriers had been reported. We also saw that variation in self-reported implementation rates roughly corresponded with our observations of teacher implementation from school visits.

Next, we turned to connecting the implementation data to the student learning data. Understanding the relationship between teacher implementation and student performance isn't as easy as it sounds. We decided to examine whether higher vs. lower implementation of the practices (as two categories) was related to greater student learning. This higher vs. lower implementation approach had multiple advantages. First, it made the reporting easier to understand. Second, it made the desired goal seem more obtainable. But what even counts as "higher implementation"? Here, we asked the Network leaders who worked closely with the teachers how many times we could reasonably expect teachers to implement each of the instructional practices over a nine-week period. Their answer was three or more times. Using this definition, we classified each teacher as a higher implementer or a lower implementer.

We then had to decide how to define student growth. MAP is administered at the beginning, middle, and end of the school year. That means we needed to choose between looking at growth across the fall semester, spring semester, or full year. As is often the case, the answer was based on our specific context. For NSI schools, the spring semester came with a strong emphasis on state assessment test preparation activities—and correspondingly, a de-emphasis on NSI activities. Tactically, that meant the fall would likely provide a clearer picture of the relationship between implementation and student learning.

Our analysis of MAP scores suggested that students in classrooms where teachers more frequently implemented student-centered practices saw growth equal to 2.5 months of additional learning over that same time period. These results held true for both years analyzed (the Network's third and fourth years). For researcher and methodologist audiences, we also used a wide variety of statistical techniques to establish for the field that this simple approach produces trustworthy results.[1]

We knew from survey responses that many teachers felt they were able to implement the practices successfully and would be willing to do so the following year. Importantly, we found that whether or not they *actually* implemented the practices frequently was associated with student growth.

The NSI Hub Team was happy with the results. However, just because there were positive results overall does not mean that all students saw the same benefit. Using demographic data, we also investigated if student groups who often receive less effective instruction (e.g., female students, Black students, Hispanic students, emergent multilingual students, students with special needs, and students from low SES households) differentially benefited. While there was variation in the degree of impact, all student groups with enough data for analysis experienced at least some benefit from more frequent implementation. Benefits for emergent multilingual students and female students were particularly strong across both years with impacts close to an extra four months of learning. The Hub Team and district leaders used this information to guide planning for future professional learning sessions and other Network activities.

How we shared the results was also a key design decision. While detailed descriptions of our methods and results could easily take up pages upon pages, such lengthy forms are not practical when the intent is to inform decision-making and practice. Instead, we regularly produced one- to two-page analytic memos that we could circulate to share our learnings (see Figure 8.3). These memos also evolved with our shifting focus. For example, some emphasized the variation in benefits for different student groups (see Figure 8.3a) while others emphasized the variation in benefits seen across different assessments (see Figure 8.3b).

... But Will State Test Scores Go Up?

And so we return to the issue of state test scores. Regardless of how we envision the ideal educational system of the future, state tests are a foundational part of the current culture and reward system. Big City School District (BCSD) is no exception, and test performance therefore influences many decisions. In particular, district leaders make a myriad of decisions about what initiatives to participate in. They decide where to have teachers and students spend their valuable time. Having a quantifiable, standardized, recognized measure of the positive impact of an initiative is essential, particularly if that initiative spans multiple years—years in which district leaders are presented with opportunities to transition to other initiatives.

While our NSI's instructional practices were competing with teaching methods that emphasize practice with test materials and formats, we nevertheless predicted that student scores would improve. Students can be taught rote memorization that may serve them well on individual tests, but research suggests such an approach tends not to yield long-term improvements in student skills.[2] Our NSI's instructional practices promoted learning designed to increase student capacity, meaning that we expected our students to grow in what they could do year-over-year, rather than restarting at zero each year. But our prediction was just that, and we needed data to know if the promise of our approach held true even on assessments that did not place such high value on advanced thinking.

TEMPLATE
**Quantitative Evaluation of Impact on Students
in the IFL/BCSD Network for School Improvement (NSI)**
[Report Date]

Impact on MAP growth in Year # of the NSI
(include this section in all reports to orient reader)

We focus on what percentage of students in each teacher's class show more than 4 points of growth on the MAP Reading score. At the overall system level, 4 points on the MAP reading scores is the expected amount of growth from Fall to Winter in the national norms; it is also the amount of growth in a child that is clearly not just measurement noise.

Based upon surveys that teachers completed, we divided teachers into 1) those implementing many of the practices that were recommended/supported in the NSI and 2) those implementing few of those practices.

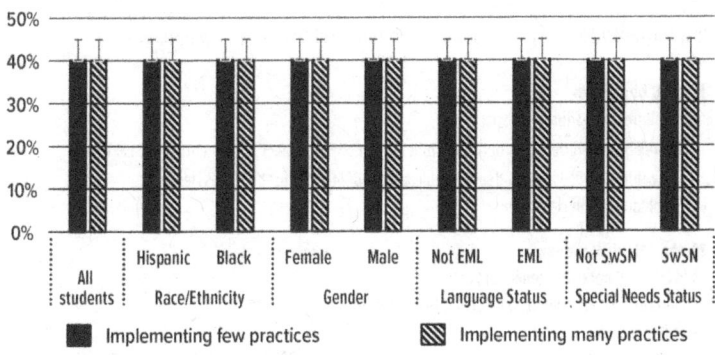

Figure 1. (Use this template to generate and insert a chart) Percentage of students showing ≥4 points MAP growth (with SE bars) for teachers implementing many or few practices

Finding highlights
Add bulleted notes for items such as:
- overall growth/differences between students in higher vs. lower implementation classrooms
- growth/differences within demographic groups of interest for higher vs. lower implementation classrooms

Methodological notes
Add bulleted notes for items such as:
- variation across buildings, teachers, test dates, etc.
- missing data
- patterns across data

Figure 8.3a Template for analytic memo exploring relationships between implementation and student outcomes in different student groups

TEMPLATE
IFL/BCSD Network for School Improvement (NSI) Analytic Memo
Overall Student Outcomes in Year #
[Report Date]

Relationship of Implementation to Changes in Assessment Scores

Using YYYY-YY MAP, DCA, and SA data, we examined the relationship between teachers who implemented the student-centered practices three or more times per 9-week marking period and their students' reading outcomes (see table below). We used data from # middle schools and # high schools (# schools excluded due to insufficient implementation data).

Pre-Test Data	MAP Reading Beginning of Year (BOY)
Post-Test Data	MAP Reading Middle of Year (MOY)
	MAP Reading End of Year (EOY)
	Fall ELA DCA
	State Assessment
Implementation Data	Teacher implementation survey responses

Finding highlights
Add bulleted notes for items such as:
- overall growth/differences between students in higher vs. lower implementation classrooms
- growth/differences within demographic groups of interest for higher vs. lower implementation classrooms

Methodological notes
Add bulleted notes for items such as:
- variation across buildings, teachers, test dates, etc.
- missing data
- patterns across data

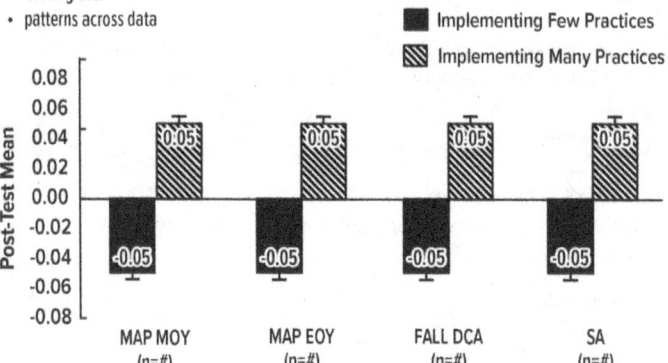

Figure 1. Post-test means and standard errors for students in low- versus high-implementation classrooms across YY-YY Reading/ELA assessments: MAP MOY, MAP EOY, DCA, and SA exams (using z-scores for standardization). Z scores (convert to mean of 0 and st dev of 1) are used for each measure to allow for easy comparison across tests.

Figure 8.3b Template for analytic memo exploring relationships between implementation and student outcomes across different assessments.

How We Gathered Data

To answer this question, we used publicly available state test data. That decision aligned with our prioritization of data that were easy to collect and analyze. We could then also compare data across years and across initiatives.

Student state test outcome data from the state education agency's website provided an important measure of the NSI's impact. We used school-level data (e.g., the percentage of students who scored proficient and above) for each of the fourteen NSI schools. While this test performance metric is by no means the only measure of impact, it is especially key for leadership support.

We also collected data that would help us understand the individual contexts of our NSI schools, as well as BCSD overall. We used school demographic data (e.g., the percentage of Black students, the percentage of Hispanic students), school performance data (e.g., annual school rating), and district data (e.g., district type), again from the state education agency's website.

Lastly, we used supplementary data from the NSI to help us understand variation from school to school within the initiative. These data included teacher attendance at Network events and our observation-based ratings of teacher expertise, both averaged for each school and year. We expected that schools with teachers who participated more frequently and demonstrated a higher level of expertise had stronger performance.

What We Did with Data

We decided to answer this question by comparing each NSI school to very similar non-NSI schools, an approach known as "matching." A school that had a state accountability rating of A, for instance, would be very different from our NSI schools, which were all rated C or D at the start of our initiative. These accountability ratings have far-ranging impacts, including access to funds and the imposition of stringent requirements from the state. For this reason, we matched our NSI schools to schools that had similar ratings, student populations, and prior student achievement on the state test. In total, we were able to match twelve of our NSI schools to ninety-five similar schools outside of the initiative.[3]

This approach provided us with another way of understanding the performance of our NSI schools. Comparing matched schools allowed us to take into account possible shifts in performance due to external factors affecting overall test performance in all schools, such as COVID-19, or changes in testing methods or standards. We were also able to dig into meaningful subsets of the data, such as middle schools versus high schools.

Although they started at similar performance levels in the first year of the NSI, the Network schools showed noticeably better performance by Year 5 compared to the matched schools, which showed little growth on average. We also saw that middle schools seemed to have particularly strong growth—especially relative to their matches (see Figure 8.4).

Even within middle schools, however, there was still variation (see Figure 8.5). While some middle schools showed strong, consistent outperformance of their matches, others only sometimes outperformed their matches. One middle school's performance was comparable to its matches across all initiative years.

Understanding why such variation occurred across schools was also important to the Hub Team. What drove this variation? What could be improved upon in future years or initiatives? To answer these questions, we turned to our NSI's own collected data about teacher attendance and teacher expertise. As we had predicted, those schools with stronger performance relative to their matches had higher attendance rates at NSI events

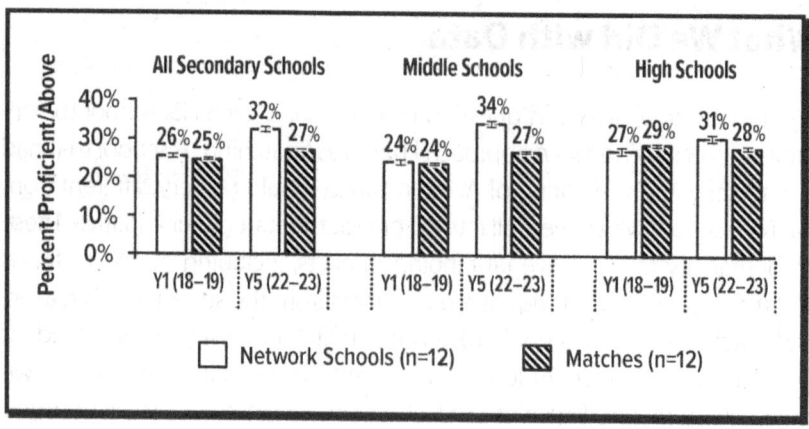

Figure 8.4 Performance of NSI schools vs. matches overall and by middle school/high school.

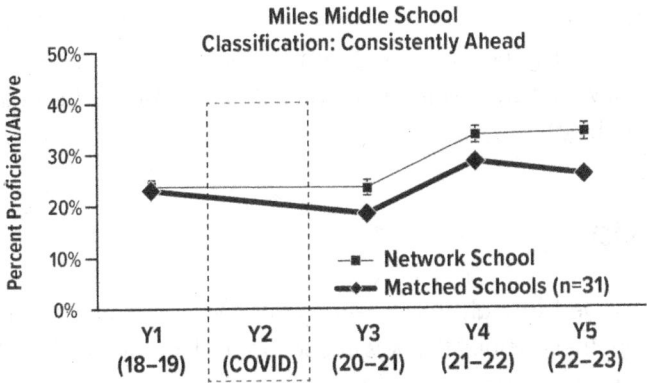

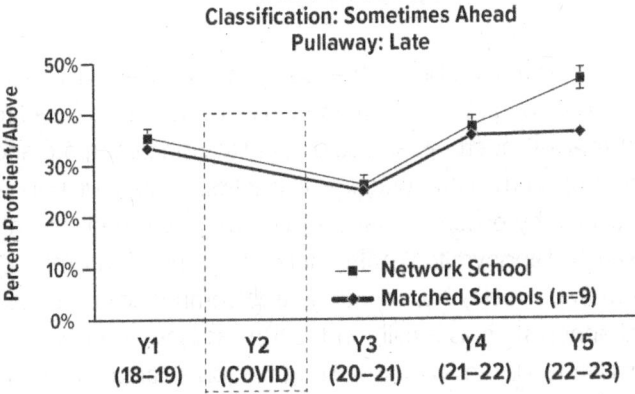

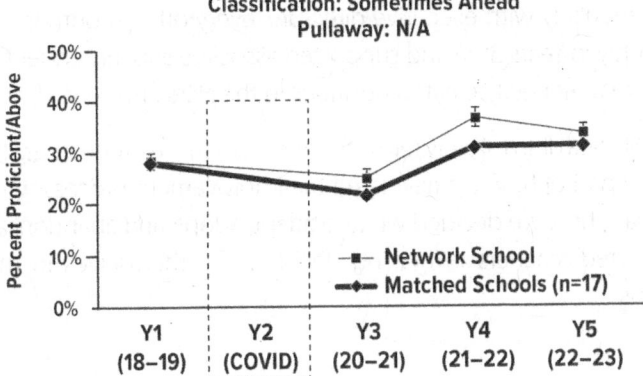

Figure 8.5 Performance of three exemplar middle schools showing one that consistently outperformed its matches, one that was sometimes ahead of its matches, and one that was on par with its matches.

(58 percent in schools that were consistently ahead versus 34 percent in schools that were generally behind) and higher expert ratings (83 percent in schools that were consistently ahead versus 25 percent in schools that were generally behind).

Wrap Up

Our NSI believed strongly in the value of data. We used data to understand not only whether our initiative was impacting student learning but also what was driving that impact and how it varied across students and schools. Data, however, are not inherently valuable, but rather gain value through how they are used.

To create a culture that embraces the use of data requires trust: trust that the data will be used for good rather than for harm. Data can be used to inform, excite, and improve, but they can also be used to judge, compare, and punish. We did not support the latter practices in our NSI. Instead, we built trust with the NSI teachers by ensuring that the data they provided would be used without breach of anonymity. We also met with teachers in monthly meetings, joined them in bi-weekly PLC meetings, and communicated through more informal channels such as emails and text messages. In turn, we built trust with district leaders by showing them that we appreciated the pressures they were under and would help them understand the impact of the NSI in ways that aligned with the constraints and responsibilities of their positions. We also met regularly with executive directors (every other month in Years 1–2 and monthly in Years 3–5) and supported associate superintendents as they moved into their newly created positions in the NSI's fifth year.

For our NSI, data didn't simply tell us that we were successful. Rather, they were an integral part of how we navigated the improvement process throughout our six years, how we decided what to adapt, adopt, and abandon, and how we supported teachers in making decisions for themselves in their own classrooms.

Notes

1   Anna E. Premo, "Exploring Practitioner Data Use to Support Improvement Work in Education" (doctoral dissertation, University of Pittsburgh, 2024) and Anna E.

Premo and Christian Schunn, "A Networked Improvement Community Focused Upon Student-Centered Reading Practices in 13 Schools in the US: Effects of Higher Implementation Frequency on Reading Outcomes," *School Effectiveness and School Improvement* (2025). https://doi.org/10.1080/09243453.2025.2574592

2. Wayne Au, "High-Stakes Testing and Curricular Control: A Qualitative Metasynthesis," *Educational Researcher* 36, no. 5 (2007): 258; David Blazar and Cynthia Pollard, "Does Test Preparation Mean Low-Quality Instruction?," *Educational Researcher* 46, no. 8 (November 2017): 420–33, https://doi.org/10.3102/0013189X17725525.

3. Anna E. Premo and Christian Schunn, "Network, School, and Student Demographic Level Effects of a Networked Improvement Community on Student Reading Outcomes," *Studies in Educational Evaluation* 85 (2025): 101451.

9 A Theory of Improvement for Instructionally Focused Change

In Chapter 1 we shared both our driver diagram and our vision of collaborative work. The driver diagram (Figure 1.1, page 10) is pretty standard fare for improvement. The diagram our Network created carried our theory of action, which states that if teachers rooted their instruction in complex and relevant texts, utilized student-centered practices to center students' knowledge, organized instruction using student-facing task sheets, and valued their students as individuals, then the number of students deemed on-track in literacy by the end of 9th grade would increase. The success or failure of this theory depended upon the people in the Network. Specifically, it depended on how teachers, school and district leaders, and the NSI Hub members understood their roles in enacting and supporting each of the drivers. We created the Vision of Collaborative Work document (Table 1.2, page 14) to help them understand what was expected of them as members of the Network and see how different members of our Network community should work together to support each other.

From these two documents we've created a Theory of Improvement (ToI) organized to support alignment and coherence, the guiding principle of our theory. We see four key components that, when present in a network, contribute to the success of aligned and coherent instructional improvement. The key components are:

1 Shared Problem of Practice
2 Focused Set of Change Ideas
3 Structured Support for Implementation and Adaptive Integration
4 Networked Collaboration

You saw these components emerge in the stories we shared across the chapters in this book. Mr. Drew, Ms. Racine, Ms. Pulitzer, and Mr. James used what they learned in collaboration with their Network peers to support collaborative planning, enacting, and studying instructional change. They were invested in understanding the learning experiences of their students, making instructional decisions based on evidence of students' knowledge building, and making adjustments when the instruction they tried didn't lead to the intended outcome. You can also see the ToI emerge in the leadership work of Principal Turner and Principal Coates. Through engaging in instructional inquiry, teachers identified the aspects of high-level literacy instruction that their students needed to build content knowledge and skills, and Principal Turner and Principal Coates created structures to support them. When they walked into classrooms, they used the student-centered practices as lenses. Rather than evaluating the instruction as compliant or not compliant with district mandates, they talked with teachers about what they noticed about student-to-student interaction and students' discussions about content. They collaborated with teachers and building coaches to spread promising practice and solved problems when practice wasn't working so well. They removed barriers that prevented teachers from collaborating and opened up space in PLCs for teachers to talk about the teaching and learning happening in their classrooms.

In the section that follows, we begin with a brief discussion about our work to align improvement across role groups, curriculum, and important district initiatives, and to communicate that alignment and coherence to teachers and leaders. We then discuss how each component of our ToI surfaces in key aspects of the NSI and the work presented across the chapters of the book. Finally, we share some implications for practice that should be considered by anyone looking to start or improve an instructionally focused network.

Theory of Improvement

Alignment and Coherence

We learned early that alignment and coherence were the linchpins that supported improvement and would hold the Network together. We had to work to make sure that Network role groups were aligned in understanding the problem of practice and that they would work collaboratively to build and support an instructional model around the tests of change to improve students' literacy proficiency. Coherence around the vision of student-centered teaching and learning began with the understandings about BCSD's baseline instruction we developed with teachers, coaches, and principals during the root cause analysis. The various types of data we studied together to understand the problem of practice and research-based approaches to addressing it coalesced around a collaborative agreement on the support students would need to build their literacy proficiency and the understanding that teachers would need to provide it.

> "With each cycle of improvement, teacher beliefs about the abilities of their students increased, along with the challenge of the literacy instruction teachers were providing."

Coherence around the vision of high-quality student-centered teaching and learning evolved over the years. Opportunities for teachers and leaders to collaborate on developing student-centered lessons, testing them, and sharing the artifacts along with success stories affected their beliefs—and district leaders' beliefs—about what students could do, and helped calibrate expectations for student engagement. With each cycle of improvement, teacher beliefs about the abilities of their students increased, along with the challenge of the literacy instruction teachers were providing. Working together to implement a shared vision of student-centered teaching and learning in a networked community of practice was a critical driver of instructional coherence.

Over time, we better understood the fourteen NSI schools as a system within the system, which helped us understand the various role groups in the vertical system of support for teachers. That led us to develop a coherent vision for implementing strategies to support teachers. We identified role groups in the system that teachers depended on, including the IFL NSI coaches, and named the way each group supported those they touched and the types of support we could give each one. The Vision of Collaborative Work document describes the ways that each role group would engage in (1) planning and doing, (2) reflecting and adapting, and (3) learning and sharing to support the vision of high-quality student-centered teaching and learning. Although the chart became an important representation of all the roles, we often thought of it as a nested system with students and teachers at the center surrounded by outwardly expanding rings of school coaches, principals, executive directors, instructional district coaches, and central office leaders.

This approach of focusing the driver diagram on teachers' engagements with students and then mapping out the system's role groups could have been a next step after we developed the driver diagram in the first year. That would have given us a clearer way to understand the system and, consequently, how we could align the NSI professional learning by engaging with and supporting its vertically aligned role groups. We did eventually get there in the third year.

> *"Sharing the problem of practice across role groups meant that we were all thinking about one clear intervention—the student-centered practices—that built out to an instructional model and a vision for teaching and learning."*

Shared Problem of Practice

Throughout this book, we lay out how the NSI schools worked as their own network focused on one problem of practice: reimagining instruction to build the literacy proficiency students needed to be college and career ready by the end of 9th grade. Sharing this problem of practice across role groups meant that we were all thinking about one clear intervention—the student-centered practices—that built out to an instructional model and a vision for teaching and learning. In Chapter 5, for example, Principal Turner and Principal Coates demonstrate how sharing in the problem of practice facilitated their support of teachers using the tests of change. The shared problem of practice across role groups influenced how leaders approached classroom visits and contributed to leaders being better able to identify and remove barriers to implementation. Students benefited from leaders working alongside teachers because teachers felt comfortable taking on improvement when they knew leaders understood the reasoning behind instructional changes. The shared understanding created more space for teachers to engage in instructional inquiry with additional minds on the problem. The coherence from these shared understandings allowed teachers to imagine the tests of change as a part of their ongoing instruction rather than feeling like they were something additional.

To take a specific example, having one shared problem of practice allowed the NSI teachers to develop a vision of teaching and learning that embraced beginning text-based instruction with comprehension tasks. Our research-based view of "comprehension first" stands in contrast to the low-level recall and identification tasks frequently used as stand-ins for comprehension and often aligned to state testing.[1] When students begin text-based instruction by writing about and discussing a high-level, open-ended comprehension question, like the ones the Network teachers shared in this book, students then have a foundation from which to build as they analyze and interpret ideas in a text, and grow text-based knowledge and literacy skills.

Focused Set of Change Ideas

The literature on networked improvement locates change ideas as being rooted in the theory of action, grounded in the local context, and coming out of shared learning.[2] The root cause analysis work that teachers and leaders took on during the first year clearly identified the need for students to have more opportunities to engage in high-level instruction around complex and relevant texts. As a hub for the Network and experts in the field of literacy, the IFL NSI coaches had a set of change ideas grounded in the student-centered practices that we knew from research[3] and experience would create changes in the learning opportunities offered to students in the classrooms of Network teachers. We knew that if we sharply focused the changes teachers could try out as they engaged in instructional inquiry, it would contribute to coherence, and it would offer teachers quick instructional wins. Those successes, more than anything else, led to changes in beliefs about what students could do and changes in expectations up the chain of vertical role groups.

Keeping to a focused set of change ideas initially felt limiting to both teachers and the Hub team but proved to be an asset to improvement. The change ideas didn't require a lot of foundational professional learning each year. This meant that new teachers could come into the project and learn about them fairly quickly, engage in some planning work, and try one with their students. You saw evidence of this in Chapter 6 with Ms. Racine. Ms. Racine was new to the Network when she first tried out a task sheet using a poem she had heard about from other Network teachers, "We Wear the Mask,"[4] by Paul Laurence Dunbar. The coherence that having a focused set of change ideas created allowed her to try out a change quickly at the beginning of the third year, and feel comfortable enough to come to a Network meeting for feedback on her early attempts at a task sheet. The teachers in the meeting shared a body of work that supported working toward change. Their feedback about the task sheet was coherent because they spoke from a shared vision of instruction and knowledge of the change ideas.

In addition, a focused set of change ideas helped leaders maintain an understanding of the vision of teaching and learning across time. Chapter 5 describes principals' collaborative work during an early Network meeting to understand how the change ideas (i.e., the various student-centered practices) played out when used together as a sequence outlined in a student-facing task sheet. We revisited the change ideas with them periodically to help maintain their thinking about what they should see and hear in the classrooms of Network teachers. However, we didn't need to revisit the vision for literacy teaching and learning, even when the new superintendent released her priorities for instruction, because the change ideas were rooted in best practice, were stable, and provided stability to our vision of teaching and learning.

Structured Support for Implementation and Adaptive Integration

Just as teachers' improvement was guided by student data, we made decisions about our continued support of the Network through the data we collected from teachers and students. As we report in Chapter 2, we developed a measurement system to gauge teacher implementation of the student-centered practices and to relate the degree of implementation to students' performances on the assessments that mattered to district colleagues: MAP reading comprehension and the state ELA/Reading assessments. Being able to demonstrate that high and regular implementation of the student-centered practices led to significant growth and achievement in students' performances on those measures contributed to the NSI's legitimacy and sustainability with all district role groups. We shared that data back to teachers and leaders as part of our support. It helped teachers see that their instructional changes made a difference to students' performances on assessments and helped teachers build the case for instructional improvement with their peers. It helped building leaders make the case for improvement with new district leaders, and it helped the Hub to continue to broker conversations with district offices not involved with the NSI.

Having strong data to show the positive outcomes of instructional improvement kept district doors open to us. Whether intended or unintended, the tools a district uses or develops carry theory. Building relationships with key role groups outside of the Network helped us to better understand (and sometimes influence) the theory that district tools carried. For example, we developed relationships with the staff in the office of teaching and learning. They were responsible for rolling out curriculum across the district. In response to conversations we had with them, they began including suggestions in their guidance documents about where student-centered practices might benefit students. This eased some of the cognitive lift for Network teachers in later years when new tools, such as coaching protocols, reflected the Network's influence. Our influence over some of the theory carried by district tools also bolstered the support IFL NSI coaches were able to provide teachers and leaders.

Because of the churn of tools, we learned that it was necessary to begin each year by taking stock of district priorities and discussing how continuing instructional inquiry worked to support those priorities, a process you see in its early stages in Chapter 5. We invited district leaders responsible for implementing new initiatives to speak with Network teachers, learn about instructional inquiry, and discuss teachers' and leaders' concerns about implementation of the initiatives and why it was so important to teachers and leaders to continue using the practices. These conversations often played an integral role in building alignment and coherence. They helped teachers and leaders make connections across the change ideas and various initiatives. They also helped district leaders not involved in the Network to integrate Network practices into the district-wide tools they were creating.

Our monthly convenings followed a predictable pattern of sharing, sense making, and reflecting. Professional learning in these meetings formed a large part of the support structure for the Network. We knew it wouldn't be enough to hand teams change ideas and hope for the best. To help teachers and leaders make sense of the change ideas, we regularly engaged them in the student-centered practices. This often meant that we engaged teams in adapted instructional tasks from the curriculum in real time, during regularly scheduled Network meetings. This type of professional learning—experiences that provide access to content expertise and pedagogy—coupled with teachers' use of the work with their students, has been shown to increase teachers' feelings of efficacy with implementation.[5] And in turn, in Chapter 2, our data show that students benefited when teachers took what they learned back to their classrooms.

We saw evidence of teacher uptake of the professional learning in the sharing opportunities that became a central structure in our Network convenings. Sharing artifacts of instruction provided teachers and leaders with opportunities to see how others in the Network were thinking about and using the change ideas, ask questions to get clarity on what was being shared, and make notes of promising practice they wanted to test out themselves. We saw examples, for instance, of teachers adapting scripted curriculum lessons to embed selected student-centered practices when they seemed useful. In discussions about the tasks being shared, we heard teachers questioning whether the practices needed to be used as a set or in the sequence in which we presented them, and they debated amongst themselves about the advantages of different patterning of practices drawing from what they had learned about varying the practices with their students. As we report in Chapter 7, we also learned that teachers were using selected practices in their instruction to prepare students for the state assessments. By the second year of the project, the language of adaptation and adaptive integration entered the vocabulary of Network teachers and principals and brought another type of alignment—alignment, that is, to teachers' goals for and uses of the practices—to the project. Opening space for sharing and discussion in the regularly scheduled Network meetings, and when possible in school PLCs, provided teachers with the needed agency to take ownership of instructional improvement.

Consequently, we found uptake of instructional inquiry to be more pervasive among teachers and leaders who engaged in reflective discussions of how the practices, coupled with some of the more complex texts in the curriculum, could help students develop knowledge and skills that could be used flexibly in the classroom, outside of the classroom, and for assessments. We often asked leaders to think about how they could support teachers in instructional inquiry. For Principals Coates and Turner, reflections became action items for the work back at their schools. Mr. Turner worked to build teacher capacity for instructional planning with the practices through being an active participant in PLCs, while Ms. Coates supported teachers through collaborative conversations both before and after *learning walks*.

Networked Collaboration

Collaboration in the Network was a marriage of the teaching expertise of the Network teachers and the content expertise of the IFL NSI coaches. Given the identified drivers and the problem of practice, we knew from research and experience what would help teachers improve their instruction while maintaining coherence with the district's curriculum. Our job, then, was to provide support for teachers to use their expertise to adapt and implement those ideas in ways that both meshed with district initiatives and brought student-centered teaching and learning to classrooms. Chapter 7 provides a strong example of the expertise teachers brought to adapting the change ideas. The team at Richard Wright Middle School had developed flexibility with the change ideas as they became part of teachers' repertoires. Early on in the NSI, teachers at Wright had spent time using, studying, and refining those ideas. Keeping that focus allowed Ms. Pulitzer to draw from her instructional toolkit in the moment, adjusting instruction to center students' ideas through a whole group discussion of *Frankenstein*[6] when it was warranted. A revolving door of change ideas across the years would have created a list of "engagement strategies," but would not have provided the opportunity to build schema around student-centered instruction in the way that having a small, focused set of change ideas did.

Collaboration features heavily in our ToI. It took place at schools with teams of teachers, as you saw in Chapter 4 with the team at Arlington, at cross-school Network meetings, and across role groups with teachers and leaders working together. It made sense that collaboration became an important component as we worked on our shared problem. If our problem could have been solved with a standardized solution, like a new curriculum that could have just been rolled out to teachers, then we wouldn't have truly been working toward improvement. Our problem required a shared understanding of the causes and continued study to understand its evolution as change ideas were tried and new students arrived in classrooms each year. Mr. Drew demonstrated dedication to understanding how change ideas needed continuous revisiting to learn from past enactment and to adapt for a new group of students. You saw how he worked with teachers during the initial planning for the tasks on "Curanderismo,"[7] but you also saw how the inquiry work with the comprehension task did not end the year it was planned. The PLC conversation that Mr. Drew led two years later around comprehension of the poem shows how the Arlington team continued to collaborate, drawing from past student data and their own teaching expertise, to make decisions about improvements that would benefit their current group of students. This episode also demonstrates that cycles of inquiry on instruction take more time than traditional PDSA cycles. It can be a semester or an academic year before teachers return to a specific text to make adaptations using information learned from previous classes.

In addition to the collaborations at schools, teachers and leaders came to Network meetings with artifacts of their own teaching and leadership to share the ways they took up change ideas in their contexts and to talk about how contextual shifts made an impact on student learning. It was the collaborative conversations around those artifacts, both when they demonstrated a successful change and when they demonstrated a challenge, that helped teachers and leaders make forward progress in increasing students' literacy proficiency. Those conversations also worked to create a community that was no longer teaching in silos, but was dependent upon feedback from critical friends across schools that would help each other get better at their craft.

> *"Through our six years of work in BCSD learning about continuous improvement for instruction and getting to know the students, teachers, leaders, and communities of the fourteen Network schools, we learned that for improvement to really take hold, a system needs to identify as a continuous improvement organization, a place where improvement is championed and supported at all levels."*

Implications for Practice

In this section, we offer guidance and the benefit of our experience to anyone who wants to create, support, or improve an instructionally focused network.

Through our six years of work in BCSD learning about continuous improvement for instruction and getting to know the students, teachers, leaders, and communities of the fourteen Network schools, we learned that for improvement to really take hold, a system needs to identify as a continuous improvement organization, a place where improvement is championed and supported at all levels. The schools in the BCSD/IFL Network for School Improvement ultimately formed their own continuous improvement organization within the district and worked to support each other up and down the organizational spine as they learned what it meant to take on and adapt instructional inquiry to meet the needs of their students and mesh with the non-negotiable policies and practices of BCSD. As we have suggested, we see alignment and coherence as central to the success of improvement networks. To reach that alignment and coherence, we had to understand the system, be prepared to use its structures, and put new ones in place (i.e., regularly scheduled cross-school meetings). We had to prepare the participants in the NSI to be ready to study, adapt, and share practice.

See the System as a Whole

At the start of our collaborative project we knew that we were going into a large and complex system. What we didn't realize was that the system itself wasn't set up for the kinds of cross-school communication and collaboration the Network required. District leaders had differing levels of understanding of how principals were expected to support the Network, principals had received differing messages about how they were supposed to engage with and support the Network, and teachers were unsure of how principals and district leaders had been primed to see the change ideas play out in Network classrooms. We had to deal with the uncertainty, for example, that teachers felt early on in the project about using the tests of change by meeting as needed with principals and executive directors to gain their support. Once we developed the Vision of Collaborative Work chart, we were able to use that as a tool to engage in conversations across role groups about how each group functioned in relationship to the problem of practice. The clarity that chart brought to understanding how the system was aligned to support the work of Network teachers finally eased concerns all around.

We would advise anyone looking to start a network to begin with seeing the system. Know who the important players are and the nuances of the adult relationships within the system. Power dynamics can create barriers to successful communication and collaboration within and across schools. We were fortunate that no one person or office within the BCSD system proved to be an insurmountable barrier. However, we did learn that there were priority initiatives, such as Reaching New Heights and preparations for the state assessments, that could have become significant barriers if we had not taken the time to understand the initiative's intended goals and help the system see how the student-centered change ideas worked to directly support those goals. We also made sure to create space for the champions of various initiatives to engage teachers in conversation about their inquiry work and the impact it was having on students. While these champions were not members of Network teams, they became a part of the community dedicated to creating meaningful instructional change.

Taking a wide lens to a system also helps to gauge teachers' and leaders' willingness and ability to collaborate. We learned quickly that the evaluation model used by the district caused teachers to close their doors and avoid sharing their work. Before the Network, if teachers found practices that improved outcomes for students, they often kept them to themselves. If their students showed larger gains than students from other classrooms or other schools, their own pay increased. Conversely, teachers also feared too many evaluative eyes drawing attention to their classroom. A negative evaluation meant the loss of agency to make instructional decisions. As we stated earlier, developing a shared vision for teaching and learning aided in aligning the evaluation process to the work of Network teachers. The Vision for Collaborative Work helped teachers see how their principals and district leaders were engaged in aligned work focused on supporting instruction.

While the data we studied for our root cause analysis were helpful for understanding the day-to-day realities of the instruction students were receiving, the Network would have benefited from a careful study of the tools, such as the district's teacher evaluation protocols, that came from outside of the classroom but directly impacted teachers' instruction. An early analysis of those tools could have highlighted the messaging they sent about teaching and learning. Empathy interviews could have helped us to understand how teachers used those tools in developing their instruction. Understanding how teachers receive implicit messaging about their instruction could help with early conversations with leaders about their work in supporting a network and aligning for coherence. A network whose members are able to see the impact of its component parts early on will run into fewer barriers to implementation at the beginning.

Additionally, we strongly suggest a periodic revisiting of system conditions throughout the life of a network to continue to understand shifts in barriers, beliefs, and opportunities for change. The BCSD reorganization, for instance, changed the system organization and conditions by establishing new leadership positions and bringing in newly appointed leaders to existing positions. We had to quickly establish relationships with the new leaders and educate them about the NSI, especially what they should expect to see in NSI teachers' classrooms.

Change Begets Change

Root cause analysis work is meant to identify the larger factors that contribute to a problem of practice. The analysis doesn't always surface factors that may be unique in certain contexts, or causes that we don't yet understand ourselves. For these reasons, an annual check on system conditions at the school and network levels can normalize understanding that a theory of action needs adjustment based on what teams continue to learn about the system as they engage in inquiry work. At the school level, this might be the need to understand how logistics contribute to teachers' ability to collaborate. Intrinsic motivation and seeing the benefits of collaboration around instruction are strong foundations that lead toward collaborative planning. However, bell schedules and location may prevent that from happening in any meaningful way. These factors may not have arisen in the initial root cause analysis. This might mean that during the annual check-in, teachers indicate that they don't have the necessary time to collaboratively work on inquiry despite having dedicated PLC time. Teachers' planning periods often don't line up. They get asked to cover classes. They may have to travel from one end of the school to the other to meet and plan. Or it may be impossible for them to travel across the district for network meetings. In organizations committed to continuous improvement, these logistical issues may signal that master schedules need to shift, classrooms have to move, and meetings need to be planned to accommodate everyone's travel time. In Chapter 4, for example, we describe how teachers' time for the collaborative work expanded when Principal Ruiz changed the master schedule to have all grade-level content area teachers share a planning period and moved classrooms to have teachers be in close proximity. This allowed teachers more time to work together to plan, as well as opportunities to collaborate on the enactment of instructional change.

Have a Unifying Focus

In our conversations with network leaders from across the country, we often find that the instructional networks that struggle to get off the ground and maintain improvement are the ones that take on several distinct problems of practice. This multi-focus might mean, for example, that the principal works on teacher retention while teachers focus on increasing 8th graders' access to algebra. While the problems could be parallel, because teachers having agency to work on math instruction might contribute to job satisfaction and retention, the problems of practice are distinct. Both require a good deal of focused inquiry, and teachers and leaders may not often come together to explore either problem collaboratively. This leads to gaps in understanding the purpose of the work undertaken by both groups. For improvement to take hold, sustain, and flourish over time, the work of improving on a problem of practice needs to be shared across all role groups.

Having a unified focus contributes to coherence and alignment across network role groups and across the context in which the network exists. A shared problem of practice creates the opportunity for all role groups in the network to contribute to understanding the causes of the problem as well as the theory of action supporting the network's aim. As you start to identify a problem that is worthy of networked improvement, you'll want to make sure that you are identifying a complex and challenging issue with variation that is resistant to an easy solution and requires iterative and adaptive approaches to facilitating change.[8] These so-called "wicked problems"[9] need the eyes and thinking of multiple role groups to understand and improve. If you find yourself thinking that your identified problem doesn't need, for example, leadership support to improve or only requires a change at the leadership level, it might be that the problem you've identified is too narrow or not complex enough to warrant the development of a network. That's not to say that different role groups can't be working on different facets of the problem at the same time. It is necessary, though, that everyone understand how the work they are engaged in supports and builds on the work being undertaken by other groups in the network and how all work coheres toward supporting the network aim.

This unifying focus brings power to the network and creates a reciprocal space for teachers and leaders to share ownership of teaching and learning rather than receiving decisions about instruction that are handed down. It was

Ms. Newbaugh's work, described in Chapter 5, that helped leaders envision student-centered teaching and learning, and collaborative conversations between Principal Coates and the teachers at Zora Neale Hurston Middle School that refined what student-centered instruction looked like at the school after COVID-19. Without that unifying focus, the professional learning for leaders may have looked different and created a chasm between what teachers understood as the driving factors leading toward change and what leadership saw as a priority.

Lean on Experts

Expertise takes many forms. Experts can be found both inside and outside of schools and districts. As the Hub for our Network, the IFL NSI coaches were certainly not the experts on the BCSD community. Veteran teachers and school and district leaders knew their school communities best, as well as the politics and protocols of teaching and learning within those communities. They had the social capital within the system to influence other Network members and teachers at their schools. They also had a wealth of instructional knowledge that they used to make sense of the change ideas and how they could best be adapted to meet their students' needs. These teachers were our early adopters, the people who were the first to bring back change ideas to the classroom and were vocal about the impact of instructional inquiry at early Network meetings.

Those veteran teachers and leaders became the champions of the BCSD/IFL NSI. As you launch your own network, you'll want to identify those champions early on. You'll want to create opportunities for them to first share their work and then work with them to build capacity to design and lead network meetings. This takes some attention and effort to organize. We found that teachers who haven't previously been empowered to lead, even those who are eager to share during network meetings, can be reluctant to facilitate a group of their peers. However, when groups of early adopters and champions come together as a team, it provides the opportunity for all teachers to contribute to the collective planning and developing of materials while those few early adopters and champions take the lead in facilitation.

Design teams are a way to leverage teacher expertise while allowing for different levels of participation. A network design team can discuss what they see in classrooms related to the network's improvement efforts and what they see as needed next steps for network teachers. As we mention in Chapter 1, when we had to figure out what our work looked like during the early months of COVID-19, the design team came together and noted that Network teachers were struggling with how to make sense of the student-centered practices in digital spaces. They organized and facilitated convenings to demonstrate how various online tools promoted student-to-student interaction and then facilitated the sharing of teachers' uptake of those tools in the following months.

Teachers as experts took on new meaning both for us and for district leaders in our fifth and sixth years. The just-in-time implementation of the new middle school curriculum meant that there was very little time to prepare and make sense of the texts and materials prior to teachers having to engage students in instruction. Centering teacher experience and questions about the curriculum allowed us to leverage a different group of early adopters: the teachers who had been able to make sense of the new materials and had been supported by school coaches and leadership to begin adapting for the student-centered change ideas early in their use of the new materials. While we didn't formally call this group a design team, we relied on these teachers to lead Network discussions about the curriculum.

Leaning on teachers and instructional leaders works to build internal capacity for improvement. However, we also recommend bringing in partners as content experts when necessary. This doesn't mean that you have to bring in an outside group to facilitate all aspects of a network, but we'd recommend engaging with experts to develop and build knowledge around change ideas that support improvement toward your shared goals. Teachers already operate with a time deficit. There's not enough time for planning, there's not enough time for instruction. Asking teachers to try to create time in order to reinvent change ideas creates additional stress and can make instructional improvement feel like a daunting task. Given the identified drivers, experts can bring research-backed practices to the table and provide guidance on implementation and adaptation. When deciding on outside partners, you'll want to consider their philosophy of adult learning. A "sit and get model" of professional learning is ineffective for instructional change. We've found, and teachers have confirmed, that when experts use practices central to the change ideas in professional learning, it helps teachers create a framework for implementation and creates a contrast to the instruction already happening in their classrooms.

Experts also bring a range of tools for measurement keyed specifically to implementation of the research-backed practices. From our own experiences, we know that developing a measurement system for implementation of instructional change can feel overwhelming, especially when systems have traditionally looked at outcome data as a sole measure of progress. In BCSD, this frequently looked like students responding to a weekly demonstration of learning keyed to a specific state standard. To understand and measure improvement, the types of data and how those data are reported back to the network need to be thought of a little differently. Rather than understanding teaching and learning only through the lens of state standards, improvement benefits from considering students' perceived experiences through their responses to tightly focused questions on exit tickets, teachers' self-reported use of change ideas through surveys, observational data taken both by leaders and coaches, and some quantitative outcome data. These data can be collected periodically, some more frequently than others, reported back in visual representations, and discussed in meetings to bring clarity to the impact that change is having on students.

In our early work on measurement, we provided raw data from practical measures—such as student exit tickets—directly back to teachers. Students completed exit tickets and we sent the teachers the raw numbers of responses for each question for each of their classrooms with the assumption that teachers would read and make sense of the numbers themselves. We found that teachers needed support in processing that information to understand what it was telling them about students' learning experiences, as well as support in thinking through changes or next steps based on those data. Data experts should be able to provide both measurement and processing support, providing timely, accessible reports that help mark improvement progress and highlight potential areas for growth.

In Conclusion

In the current climate of uncertainty in education, we see the potential of networks to bring communities of educators together to serve the needs of their students. It's not an easy process. Our early attempts were not always right and often incomplete, but we learned a thing or two about improvement, networks, and ourselves along the way. We learned that collaborations in networks that meet regularly with clearly understood goals and procedures have the power to engage and inspire teachers. And with that, we will end with the words of a teacher from BCSD:

> I completely feel this has rejuvenated my teaching. After 22 years, it is easy to fall into complacency when the curriculum is lacking, the other teachers have little buy in and all of the pieces seem to encourage you to do the practices you are given without going farther, without pushing yourself. This work was so grounded in a professional atmosphere of collaboration and resource sharing that it was deeply inspirational every month. The changes [for students] will be seen over a lifetime, because the earlier we capture learners' hearts, more time can be spent in our academic centers steering them toward greater success.

Notes

1. Philip Capin et al., "Reading Comprehension Instruction: Evaluating Our Progress Since Durkin's Seminal Study," *Scientific Studies of Reading* 29, no. 1 (2025): 85–114.
2. Anthony S. Bryk, Louis M. Gomez, Alicia Grunow, and Paul G. LeMahieu, *Learning to Improve: How America's Schools Can Get Better at Getting Better* (Cambridge, MA: Harvard Education Press, 2015).
3. The Introduction provides an extensive list of research on the student-centered practices.
4. Paul Laurence Dunbar, "We Wear the Mask," *Dunbar Music Archive* no. 169 (1896), https://ecommons.udayton.edu/dunbar/169.
5. Thomas R. Guskey, "The Past and Future of Teacher Efficacy," *Educational Leadership* 79, no. 3 (2021): 20.
6. Mary Shelley, *Frankenstein* (London: Penguin Classics, 2012).
7. Ariana Brown, "Curanderismo," in *Sana Sana* (Boston: Game Over Books, 2020).
8. A. S. Bryk, L. M. Gomez, and A. Grunow, "Getting Ideas into Action: Building Networked Improvement Communities in Education," in *Frontiers in Sociology of Education* (Dordrecht: Springer Netherlands, 2011), 127–62.
9. Horst W. J. Rittel and Melvin M. Webber, "Dilemmas in a General Theory of Planning," *Policy Sciences* 4, no. 2 (1973): 155–69.

Appendix A

TASK
Comprehension

Purpose:
Today you will read "Curanderismo" by Arianna Brown.

This is the first of several readings you'll do of "Curanderismo." The purpose of this first reading is for you to get the gist of the poem and to take a first pass at expressing what you understand about Brown's central idea. This will provide you with a foundation for later tasks that ask you to examine how Brown uses language to communicate her ideas.

As part of this first reading, you'll also identify moments in the text that you find difficult or confusing; this will alert you to places to focus your attention during later readings.

Task:
Step 1:
Please read "Curanderismo." As you read, mark the following:

- Highlight moments that seem important to what Brown is saying.
- In the margin, explain why you highlighted each moment.
- Underline moments that you find confusing or difficult to understand. You'll talk with your partner about these moments.

Step 2:
When you're finished reading, look over your marked moments and compose two quick writes discussing the following questions:

- What do you think Brown is saying in this poem? In other words, how would you explain Brown's central idea to someone who has not read this poem? Draw on evidence from across the poem to support your response.
- Discuss a new understanding that came from your initial read of this text.

Step 3:
Take 5 minutes to share your quick writes with a partner. As you share, notice where you agree and where you disagree with each other.

Once you and your partner have both shared, work together to create a chart that captures what you think Brown is saying. Be sure to note where you and your partner agree and where you disagree on Brown's ideas.

Step 4:
Once everyone has posted their charts, please participate in a gallery walk. As you walk around and look at each poster, please note where you agree with your peers, where you disagree with your peers, and any places where you see ideas that you find particularly interesting.

Step 5:
After the gallery walk, we will meet for a whole group discussion. After the whole group discussion, please compose a quick write in response to the following:

- How was your thinking about "Curanderismo" confirmed or changed after completing the gallery walk and whole group discussion? What did you hear or see from your classmates that confirmed or changed your thinking?

Step 6: Metacognitive Reflection
Finally, please create a list of what you did as a reader to understand the big idea when you read the poem. This list will make visible what you did as a reader to understand the big ideas and it will help your peers see how others work to understand the big ideas in a poem.

Figure A.1 Task sheet developed by teachers at Arlington High School.

Appendix B

Prepare Before PLC

Prepare

One member of the PLC should
- collect a total of 8-10 samples of student writing from several teachers from a shared comprehension task:
    - The writing should represent a range of student abilities.
    - The writing should be a paragraph or longer and capture what students comprehend about the text under study after reading, initial writing, talk, and getting a chance to revise their thinking.
- number each sample to allow for easy reference when discussing the writing; and
- prepare copies of each sample for each member of the PLC.
- Each member of the PLC should have completed the comprehension task during the Planning Forward phase. If not, PLC members should read the text students read and complete the comprehension task. This will help PLC members determine if student writing demonstrates comprehension of the text.

Setting Expectations

Set the Context and Focus

- Share the student writing samples with the members of the PLC.
- If necessary, provide PLC members with the task sheet students used to produce the writing to help members remember the work students did to complete the task.
- Set the expectation that the PLC will be studying the student work samples to describe what students comprehended and how they explained their thinking as a result of participating in the comprehension task. The group will use the **Studying Student Work Protocol** to guide the process.

Study Writing

Individual: Describe Student Learning

- Each member of the PLC works with a packet of student work to describe how each piece of writing demonstrates what students comprehend about the text under study and the ways students support their thinking with text-based evidence.
- Focus on understanding the features of students' academic explanations of the text.

Figure B.1a Arlington High School Debrief Protocol.

Discuss

Whole Group: Describe Student Learning

- Discuss each paper as a group, describing how each piece of writing demonstrates students' explanations of the text.
- Sort each piece of writing into a stack numbered 1, 2, 3, or 4 based on how well it demonstrates understanding of the text and how well it uses text-based evidence to support ideas. Papers numbered with a 4 should be the most proficient.
- Work to describe the patterns that arise in each collection of writing (1s, 2s, 3s, and 4s) and what the patterns say about students' comprehension and students' learning to develop explanations in writing.

Planning Forward

Instructional Next Steps

- Working from what you've learned about students' progress towards comprehending the text and students' use of text-based evidence to support their ideas, plan instructional next steps. As you plan, consider the following questions:
    - How might you pose questions differently to allow for a range of text-based responses?
    - How might you structure the routine students use to respond to a task to facilitate socializing of understanding before students are asked to write?
    - What scaffolds might you provide to less proficient students to better help them comprehend the text without doing too much heavy lifting for them?
- Work with your PLC team to develop a small set (2 or 3) of tasks that will move students' learning forward from what they demonstrated in the comprehension task. Work with your team to sequence the practices students will experience to facilitate socializing student understanding and that allows students opportunities to revise their writing based on conversation. Write out the tasks to be student-facing using the **Student-centered Practices** document and the **Comprehension Task Sheet Exemplar** as resources.
- Additionally, work with your team to anticipate the responses that students might give to the tasks. Working from the anticipated responses, both those that provide text-based explanations and those that aren't well explained, plan how you might scaffold the tasks based on where students are in their comprehension. Consider the following questions to guide your thinking:
    - How can you pair students to help each other?
    - How can you use a variety of well-reasoned student responses to model different ways that text-based ideas and reasoning can be stated?

Figure B.1b The debrief protocol *continued*.

Bibliography

Applebee, Arthur N., and Judith A. Langer. "A Snapshot of Writing Instruction in Middle Schools and High Schools." *English Journal* 100, no. 6 (2011): 14–27.

Au, Wayne. "High-Stakes Testing and Curricular Control: A Qualitative Metasynthesis." *Educational Researcher* 36, no. 5 (2007): 258.

Barth, Roland S. "Improving Relationships Within the Schoolhouse." *Educational Leadership* 63, no. 6 (2006): 8.

Beck, Isabel L., Margaret G. McKeown, and Cheryl A. Sandora. *Robust Comprehension Instruction with Questioning the Author*. New York: Guilford Publications, 2020.

Bichell, Rae Ellen. "Scientists Start To Tease Out The Subtler Ways Racism Hurts Health." *National Public Radio*, November 11, 2017. https://www.npr.org/sections/health-shots/2017/11/11/562623815/scientists-start-to-tease-out-the-subtler-ways-racism-hurts-health.

Bill & Melinda Gates Foundation. "Teachers Know Best: Teachers' Views on Professional Development." December 2014. https://eric.ed.gov/?id=ED576976.

Blakemore, Sarah-Jayne. *Inventing Ourselves: The Secret Life of the Teenage Brain*. New York: PublicAffairs, 2018.

Blazar, David, and Cynthia Pollard. "Does Test Preparation Mean Low-Quality Instruction?" *Educational Researcher* 46, no. 8 (November 2017): 420–33. https://doi.org/10.3102/0013189X17725525.

Bradbury, Ray. "The Pendulum." *Futuria Fantasia* 1, no. 2 (Fall 1939).

Branch, G. F., E. A. Hanushek, and S. G. Rivkin. "School Leaders Matter: Measuring the Impact of Effective Principals." *Education Next* 13, no. 1 (Winter 2013): 62–9. https://educationnext.org/school-leaders-matter/.

Bredeson, Paul V., and Jay Paredes Scribner. "Statewide Professional Development Conference." *Education Policy Analysis Archives* 8 (2000): 13.

Brown, Ariana. "Curanderismo." In *Sana Sana*. Boston: Game Over Books, 2020.

Brown, John Seely, Alan Collins, and Paul Duguid. "Situated Cognition and the Culture of Learning." In *Subject Learning in the Primary Curriculum: Issues in English, Science, and Mathematics*, edited by Jeni Riley and Roy Prentice, 301–19. London: Routledge, 1995.

Bryk, Anthony S., and Louis M. Gomez. "Networked Improvement Communities: The Power of Improvement Science in Education." *Educational Leadership* 74, no. 2 (2016): 36–40.

Bryk, Anthony S., Louis M. Gomez, and Alicia Grunow. "Getting Ideas into Action: Building Networked Improvement Communities in Education." In *Frontiers in Sociology of Education*, edited by Maureen Hallinan. New York: Springer Publishing, 2011.

Bryk, Anthony S., Louis M. Gomez, Alicia Grunow, and Paul G. LeMahieu. *Learning to Improve: How America's Schools Can Get Better at Getting Better*. Cambridge, MA: Harvard Education Press, 2015.

Bryk, Anthony S., Penny Bender Sebring, Elaine Allensworth, Stuart Luppescue, and John Q. Easton. *Organizing Schools for Improvement: Lessons from Chicago*. Chicago: University of Chicago Press, 2020.

Capin, Philip, Kristen Dahl-Leonard, Caitlin Hall, Nayoung Yoon, Eunsoo Cho, Eleni Chatzoglou, Sarah Reiley, Michelle Walker, Emily Shanahan, Tara Andress, and Sharon Vaughn. "Reading Comprehension Instruction: Evaluating Our Progress since Durkin's Seminal Study." *Scientific Studies of Reading* 29, no. 1 (2025): 85–114. https://doi.org/10.1080/10888438.2024.2418582.

Coates, Ta-Nehisi. *Between the World and Me*. New York: Spiegel & Grau, 2015.

Coburn, Cynthia E. "Beyond Decoupling: Rethinking the Relationship between the Institutional Environment and the Classroom." *Sociology of Education* 77, no. 3 (2004): 211–44. https://doi.org/10.1177/003804070407700302.

Cornelius-White, Jeffrey. "Learner-Centered Teacher-Student Relationships are Effective: A Meta-Analysis." *Review of Educational Research* 77, no. 1 (2007): 113–43.

Cottingham, B. W., H. J. Hough, and J. Myung. *What Does It Take to Accelerate the Learning of Every Child? Early Insights from a CCEE School-Improvement Pilot*. Policy Analysis for California Education, December 2023. https://edpolicyinca.org/publications/what-does-it-take-accelerate-learning-every-child.

CRLT at University of Michigan. "Equity-Focused Teaching Framework." Center for Research on Learning and Teaching, University of Michigan. Accessed October 14, 2024. https://crlt.umich.edu/equity-focused-teaching.

Darling-Hammond, Linda. "Teacher Quality and Student Achievement." *Education Policy Analysis Archives* 8 (January 2000): 1. https://doi.org/10.14507/epaa.v8n1.2000.

Darling-Hammond, Linda, Maria E. Hyler, and Madelyn Gardner. *Effective Teacher Professional Development*. Report, Learning Policy Institute, June 5, 2017. https://learningpolicyinstitute.org/product/effective-teacher-professional-development-report.

Da Silva, Nicole, Sara DeMartino, K. Ferrario, and Betsy Gilliland. "NCTE Position Paper on the Role of English Teachers in Educating English Language Learners (ELLs)." National Council of Teachers of English, 2020.

Davis, D. S., and N. Vehabovic. "The Dangers of Test Preparation: What Students Learn (and Don't Learn) About Reading Comprehension from Test-centric Literacy Instruction." *The Reading Teacher* 71, no. 5 (2017): 579–88.

Davis, Linda. "Toward a Lifetime of Literacy: The Effects of Student-Centered and Skills-Based Reading Instruction on the Experiences of Children." *Literacy Teaching and Learning* 15 (2020): 53–79.

DeMartino, Sara, Glenn Nolly, and Anthony Petrosky. "Teacher Leaders Help Change Ideas Stick." *The Learning Professional* 44, no. 2 (2023): 46–50.

Doan, Sy, Joshua Eagan, David Grant, and Julia H. Kaufman. *American Instructional Resources Surveys: 2024 Technical Documentation and Survey Results*. Santa Monica, CA: RAND Corporation, 2024. https://www.rand.org/pubs/research_reports/RRA134-24.html.

Doyle, Brian. "Joyas Voladoras." *Now I'm Just a Shot in the Dark* (blog), February 7, 2008. http://nowimjustashotinthedark.blogspot.com/2008/02/joyas-voladoras-by-brian-doyle.html.

DuFour, Richard, Rebecca DuFour, Robert Eaker, M. A. Mattos, Anthony Muhammad, and ProQuest. *Revisiting Professional Learning Communities at Work: Proven Insights for Sustained, Substantive School Improvement*. 2nd edition. Bloomington, IN: Solution Tree Press, 2021.

DuFour, Rick, and Douglas Reeves. "The Futility of PLC Lite." *Phi Delta Kappan* 97, no. 6 (2016): 69–71.

Dunbar, Paul Laurence. "We Wear the Mask." Poetry Foundation. Accessed November 6, 2024. https://www.poetryfoundation.org/poems/44203/we-wear-the-mask.

Filderman, Michael J., Christina R. Austin, Alexis N. Boucher, Kelly O'Donnell, and Elizabeth A. Swanson. "A Meta-Analysis of the Effects of Reading Comprehension Interventions on the Reading Comprehension Outcomes of Struggling Readers in Third Through 12th Grades." *Exceptional Children* 88, no. 2 (2022): 163–84.

García, Ofelia, and Jo Anne Kleifgen. "Translanguaging and Literacies." *Reading Research Quarterly* 55, no. 4 (2020): 553–71.

García, Ofelia, and Tatyana Kleyn. "Translanguaging Theory in Education." In *Translanguaging with Multilingual Students*, edited by Ofelia García and Tatyana Kleyn, 9–33. New York: Routledge, 2016.

Graham, Steve, and Michael Hebert. "Writing to Read: A Meta-Analysis of the Impact of Writing and Writing Instruction on Reading." *Harvard Educational Review* 81, no. 4 (2011): 7107–144.

Graham, Steve, Xinghua Liu, Brendan Bartlett, Clarence Ng, Karen R. Harris, Angelique Aitken, Ashley Barkel, Courtney Kavanaugh, and Javed Talukdar. "Reading for Writing: A Meta-Analysis of the Impact of Reading Interventions on Writing." *Review of Educational Research* 88, no. 2 (2018): 243–84.

Grissom, Jason A., A. J. Egalite, and Charles A. Lindsay. *How Principals Affect Students and Schools: A Systematic Synthesis of Two Decades of Research*. New York: The Wallace Foundation, 2021.

Grunow, Alicia, Sandra Park, and Brandon Bennett. *Journey to Improvement: A Team Guide to Systems Change in Education, Health Care, and Social Welfare*. Lanham, MD: Rowman & Littlefield, 2024.

Guskey, Thomas R. "Does It Make a Difference? Evaluating Professional Development." *Educational Leadership* 59, no. 6 (March 2022): 45–51. https://tguskey.com/wp-content/uploads/Professional-Learning-4-Evaluating-Professional-Development.pdf.

Guskey, Thomas R. "The Past and Future of Teacher Efficacy." *Educational Leadership* 79, no. 3 (2021): 20.

Gutiérrez, R. "Framing Equity: Helping Students 'Play the Game' and 'Change the Game.'" *Teaching for Excellence and Equity in Mathematics* 1, no. 1 (2009): 4–8.

Hammond, Zaretta L. *Culturally Responsive Teaching and the Brain: Promoting Authentic Engagement and Rigor Among Culturally and Linguistically Diverse Students*. Thousand Oaks, CA: Corwin Press, 2015.

Ladson-Billings, Gloria. "Culturally Relevant Pedagogy 2.0: Aka the Remix." *Harvard Educational Review* 84, no. 1 (2014): 74–84.

Ladson-Billings, Gloria. *The Dreamkeepers: Successful Teachers of African American Children*. San Francisco: Jossey-Bass Publishers, 1994.

Langer, Judith A. "Examining Background Knowledge and Text Comprehension." *Reading Research Quarterly* (1984): 468–81.

Langer, Judith A. "Excellence in English in Middle and High School: How Teachers' Professional Lives Support Student Achievement." *American Educational Research Journal* 37, no. 2 (2000): 397–439.

Leithwood, K., K. S. Louis, S. Anderson, and K. Wahlstrom. *Review of Research: How Leadership Influences Student Learning*. 2004. Accessed December 2024. http://www.wallacefoundation.org/knowledge-center/school-leadership/key-research/documents/how-leadership-influences-student-learning.pdf.

LeMahieu, Paul G., Alicia Grunow, Laura Baker, Lee E. Nordstrum, and Louis M. Gomez. "Networked Improvement Communities: The Discipline of Improvement Science Meets the Power of Networks." *Quality Assurance in Education* 25, no. 1 (2017): 5–25.

McKeown, Margaret G., Isabel L. Beck, and Ronette G. K. Blake. "Rethinking Reading Comprehension Instruction: A Comparison of Instruction for Strategies and Content Approaches." *Reading Research Quarterly* 44, no. 3 (2009): 218–53.

McKeown, Margaret G., Isabel L. Beck, and M. Jo Worthy. "Grappling with Text Ideas: Questioning the Author." *The Reading Teacher* 46, no. 7 (1993): 560–66.

Mann, L. "My Ceremony for Taking." In *My Ceremony for Taking*. Champaign: University of Illinois at Urbana-Champaign, 2009.

Marshall, Tanji Reed, and William H. Rodick. "The Search for More Complex Racial and Ethnic Representation in Grade School Books." *The Education Trust*, 2023.

Marshall, Tanji Reed, and William H. Rodick. "Guess What? There's Already Under-Representation in School Curricula." *The Education Trust*. Accessed

January 8, 2025. https://edtrust.org/blog/guess-what-theres-already-under-representation-in-school-curricula/.

Martínez, R. A. "Beyond the English Learner Label: Recognizing the Richness of Bi/Multilingual Students' Linguistic Repertoires." *The Reading Teacher* 71, no. 5 (2018): 515–22.

Matsumura, Lindsay C., Cheryl Sandora, Sara DeMartino, and Diana Zook-Howell. "Student-Centered Routines for Analytic Writing Online and In Person." *The Reading Teacher* 75, no. 4 (2022): 513–19.

Matthews, J. L., and Gary M. Crow. *The Principalship: New Roles in a Professional Learning Community*. New York: Allyn and Bacon, 2010.

Michaels, Sarah, Catherine O'Connor, and Lauren B. Resnick. "Deliberative Discourse Idealized and Realized: Accountable Talk in the Classroom and in Civic Life." *Studies in Philosophy and Education* 27 (2008): 283–97.

Muhammad, Gholdy. *Cultivating Genius: An Equity Framework for Culturally and Historically Responsive Literacy*. New York: Scholastic, 2020.

National Institute of Child Health and Human Development, NIH, DHHS. "Report of the National Reading Panel: Teaching Children to Read: Reports of the Subgroups." Washington, DC: U.S. Government Printing Office, 2000.

Noguera, Pedro A. "The Trouble with Black Boys: The Role and Influence of Environmental and Cultural Factors on the Academic Performance of African American Males." *Urban Education* 38, no. 4 (2003): 431–59.

Novotny, Kathryn Grace Rowe. "Reading Comprehension in the Secondary Classroom." Masters paper, Minnesota State University, Mankato, 2011. Cornerstone: A Collection of Scholarly and Creative Works for Minnesota State University, Mankato. https://cornerstone.lib.mnsu.edu/etds/102/.

Office of Elementary and Secondary Education. "Root Cause Analysis in Action." U.S. Department of Education. Accessed February 27, 2025. https://www.ed.gov/teaching-and-administration/lead-and-manage-my-school/state-support-Network/ssn-resources/root-cause-analysis-in-action.

Okal, Benard Odoyo. "Benefits of Multilingualism in Education." *Universal Journal of Educational Research* 2, no. 3 (2014): 223–29.

Owen, Susanne. "Professional Learning Communities: Building Skills, Reinvigorating the Passion, and Nurturing Teacher Wellbeing and 'Flourishing' within Significantly Innovative Schooling Contexts." *Educational Review* 68, no. 4 (2016): 403–19.

Pollack, Todd M. "The Miseducation of a Beginning Teacher: One Educator's Critical Reflections on the Functions and Power of Deficit Narratives." *Multicultural Perspectives* 14, no. 2 (2012): 93–8.

Premo, Anna E. "Exploring Practitioner Data Use to Support Improvement Work in Education." Doctoral dissertation, University of Pittsburgh, 2024.

Anna E. Premo and Christian Schunn, "A Networked Improvement Community Focused Upon Student-Centered Reading Practices in 13 Schools in the US: Effects of Higher Implementation Frequency on Reading Outcomes," *School Effectiveness and School Improvement* (2025). https://doi.org/10.1080/09243453.2025.2574592

Premo, Anna E., and Christian Schunn. "Network, School, and Student Demographic Level Effects of a Networked Improvement Community on Student Reading Outcomes." *Studies in Educational Evaluation* 85 (2025): 101451.

Research Partnership for Professional Learning. "RPPL Insights Hub." Accessed March 5, 2025. https://rpplpartnership.org/insights-hub/.

Resnick, Lauren B., Christa S.C. Asterhan, and Sherice N. Clarke. "Accountable Talk: Instructional Dialogue that Builds the Mind." *Educational Practices* Series 29, UNESCO International Bureau of Education, 2018.

Resnick, Lauren B., and Sandra Nelson-Le Gall. "Socializing Intelligence." In *Piaget, Vygotsky, and Beyond*, edited by Leslie Smith, Julie Dockrell, and Peter Tomlinson, 145–58. London: Routledge, 1997.

Rittel, Horst W. J., and Melvin M. Webber. "Dilemmas in a General Theory of Planning." *Policy Sciences* 4, no. 2 (1973): 155–69.

Roth, K. J., C. D. Wilson, J. A. Taylor, M. A. M. Stuhlsatz, and C. Hvidsten. "Comparing the Effects of Analysis-of-Practice and Content-Based Professional Development on Teacher and Student Outcomes in Science." *American Educational Research Journal* 56, no. 4 (2019): 1217–253.

Rothkopf, Ernest Zindel. "Reflections on the Field: Aspirations of Learning Science and the Practical Logic of Instructional Enterprises." *Educational Psychology Review* 20, no. 3 (2008): 351–68.

Russell, J. L., A. S. Bryk, D. Peurach, D. Sherer, E. Khachatryan, P. G. LeMahieu, J.Z. Sherer, and M. Hannan. "The Social Structure of Networked Improvement Communities: Cultivating the Emergence of a Scientific-professional Learning Community." *American Educational Research Association Annual Meeting*, Toronto, ON, April 2019.

Russell, Jennifer Lin, Anthony S. Bryk, Jonathan R. Dolle, Louis M. Gomez, Paul G. LeMahieu, and Alicia Grunow. "A Framework for the Initiation of Networked Improvement Communities." *Teachers College Record* 119, no. 5 (2017): 1–36.

Russell, Jennifer Lin, Richard Correnti, Mary Kay Stein, Victoria Bill, Maggie Hannan, Nathaniel Schwartz, Laura Neergaard Booker, Nicole Roberts Pratt, and Chris Matthis. "Learning From Adaptation to Support Instructional Improvement at Scale: Understanding Coach Adaptation in the TN Mathematics Coaching Project." *American Educational Research Journal* 57, no. 1 (2020): 148–87. https://doi.org/10.3102/0002831219854050.

Scott, K., G. Dawson, and J. Quach, "How Are We Measuring Domains That Influence Teacher Readiness for Change? A Scoping Review of Existing Instruments in Non-Tertiary Settings," *Journal of Educational Change* (2024): 1–38.

Sebring, Penny Bender, Elaine Allensworth, Anthony S. Bryk, John Q. Easton, and Stuart Luppescu. "The Essential Supports for School Improvement. Research Report." *Consortium on Chicago School Research*, 2006.

Shelley, Mary. *Frankenstein*. London: Penguin Classics, 2012.

Sherer, David, and Paul Cobb. "A Framework for the Initiation of Networked Improvement Communities." *Phi Delta Kappan* 100, no. 5 (2019): 23–7.

Sims, Sam, Harry Fletcher-Wood, Alison O'Mara-Eves, Sarah Cottingham, Claire Stansfield, Josh Goodrich, Jo Van Herwegen, and Jake Anders. "Effective Teacher Professional Development: New Theory and a Meta-Analytic Test." *Review of Educational Research* 93, no. 6 (December 2023): 1048–092. https://doi.org/10.3102/00346543231217480.

Soto, Gary. *Buried Onions*. Boston: Houghton Mifflin Harcourt, 2006.

Spillane, James P. "External Reform Initiatives and Teachers' Efforts to Reconstruct Their Practice: The Mediating Role of Teachers' Zones of Enactment." *Journal of Curriculum Studies* 31, no. 2 (1999): 143–75. https://doi.org/10.1080/002202799183205.

Stein, Mary Kay, Margaret Schwan Smith, Marjorie A. Henningsen, and Edward A. Silver. *Implementing Standards-based Mathematics Instruction: A Casebook for Professional Development*. New York: Teachers College Press, 2009.

TNTP. "The Mirage: Confronting the Hard Truth about Our Quest for Teacher Development." August 4, 2015. https://eric.ed.gov/?id=ED558206.

Truth, Sojourner. "Ain't I A Woman?" Speech, Women's Rights Convention, Akron, Ohio, 1851.

Wang, E., Andrea Prado Tuma, S. Doan, Daniella Henry, R. Lawrence, Ashley Woo, and Julia H. Kaufman. "Teachers' Perceptions of What Makes Instructional Materials Engaging, Appropriately Challenging, and Usable." RAND Corporation, 2021.

Weiner, Bryan J. "A Theory of Organizational Readiness for Change." In *Handbook on Implementation Science*, 215–32. Northampton: Edward Elgar Publishing, 2020.

Wenger, Etienne. *Communities of Practice: Learning, Meaning, and Identity*. Cambridge: Cambridge University Press, 1998.

Wenger-Trayner, Etienne, Beverly Wenger-Trayner, Phil Reid, and Claude Bruderlein. *Communities of Practice Within and Across Organizations*. Sesimbra : Social Learning Lab, 2023.

Williams, Ray, Ken Brien, Crista Sprague, and Gerald Sullivan. "Professional Learning Communities: Developing a School-Level Readiness Instrument." *Canadian Journal of Educational Administration and Policy* 74 (2008): 1–17.

Woodland, Rebecca H. "Evaluating PK–12 Professional Learning Communities: An Improvement Science Perspective." *American Journal of Evaluation* 37, no. 4 (2016): 505–21.

Index

access, high-level instruction 188–9
actions for change, prioritization 9, 11–12
adaptation 9, 11–12, 13, 172–4
    mutual adaptation 194–5
    planning tools 117–23
    theories of improvement 240–2
"Ain't I A Woman?" (Truth) 35, 109
alignment and coherence (theories of improvement) 236–8
Arlington High School 113–40

beginning of the year (BOY) MAP reading comprehension 55–6, 57, 58–9, 67–8, 84–5
Bennett, Brandon 118
"Beyond the *English Learner* Label: Recognizing the Richness of Bi/Multilingual Students' Linguistic Repertoires" (Martínez) 109
Bichell, Rae Ellen 109, 148–9
Big City School District (BCSD) 1–51, 63, 81–2, 84–6, 200, 226, 229
    brief year-by-year overview 2–8
    district teams 2, 3
    key initiatives year by year 8–9
        year 1 (2018–19) 9–12
        year 2 (2019–20) 13–25
        year 3 (2020–21) 26–30
        year 4 (2021–22) 30–9
        year 5 (2022–23) 39–48
        year 6 (2023–24) 48–50
    Miles Middle School case study 169–98
    network health surveys, engagement and 63
    PLCs and instructional inquiry 114–15
    reorganization 39, 43–6
    theories of improvement 244–51
    Vision of Collaborative Work 13, 38–9, 235, 237–8, 245–6
    Zora Neale Hurston Middle School/Rose-Wood High School case studies 141–67
Black culture 202
    see also race, racial aspects
Blakemore, Sarah-Jayne 184–8
boxplots 72–4
BOY (beginning of the year MAP reading comprehension) 55–6, 57, 58–9, 67–8, 84–5
Bradbury, Ray 204–10
Brown, Arianna 109, 123–30, 134–5, 243–4
Bryk, Tony 92–4, 101, 107
Buried Onions (Soto) 175–9

capacity-building 44, 45, 48–50, 113–40
Center for Urban Education (CUE) vii
centering students' assets 195
change *see* adaptation
"change begets change" mindsets 247
Chief Academic Officers 8
climate, environment and productivity 150–1
coherence (theories of improvement) 236–8
collaborative time 194
collaborative work 13, 14–15, 30, 38–9, 153–8, 182–3
    theories of improvement 243–4
    see also communities of practice; support(s); Vision of Collaborative Work
communities of practice (COPs) 91–112
    benefits, instructional improvement 96–7

community building 92–6
    NSIs data on 94–6
    evolution into a community 100–4
    hallmarks of the teachers' community 104–5
    middle school pilot testing and New Curricula 105–8
    NSIs early meetings (2018–20) 98–100
    professional learning 97–8
community building 92–6
"comprehension first" support 62
content knowledge 133–5
context, contextual approaches 131–3, 143–4, 170–2, 200
    Contexts for Improvement 63
    PLCs and instructional inquiry 114–15, 131–3
    see also student-centered practices
Continuous Improvement 14, 36, 55, 63, 74–6, 158, 205, 244–5, 247
COVID-19 pandemic 1, 4, 24, 26, 91, 159, 161–2, 230, 249–50
    COPs and hybrid instruction 102
    exit tickets 21, 24
    on-track 8th and 9th grade indicators 63–4
    PLCs and instructional inquiry 113–40
    qualitative and quantitative outcomes 54–5, 77
    Richard Wright Middle School 200
    Zora Neale Hurston Middle School/ Rose-Wood High School cases 141–67
CUE (Center for Urban Education) vii
culture, Harlem Renaissance 202
culture, whole school cultures of improvement 136–8
"Curanderismo" (Brown) 109, 123–30, 134–5, 243–4

data 221–33
    community building 92–6
    see also qualitative and quantitative outcomes
Data and Analytics 7–8
    see also Hub Teams
data, delivery and use 30, 36–8
debriefings 126–8
deep work 41, 131–5

deficit thinking 181–2
Demonstration of Learning (DOL) 156, 157, 251
demonstration teachers 48–50
Design Teams 21, 23, 103, 104, 249–50
district coaches/leaders 1, 48–50, 225–6
    see also leaders, leadership
District Course Assessment (DCA) 6, 17, 55, 57, 63–4, 67–8, 78–80
district teams 2, 3
district-friendly approaches 13, 14
Doyle, Brian 137
driver diagrams 9, 10, 13
drivers for change 172–4
drivers of instructional inquiry 115–23
DuFour model 115–16, 122
Dunbar, Paul Laurence 175–9, 202–3

economically disadvantaged students 36–7, 200, 225–6
    see also Emergent Multilingual students; race, racial aspects
Emergent Multilingual (EML) students 4–5, 11, 36–7, 68–71, 82–3, 125, 159–60, 186, 189, 191
    deficit thinking 181–2
empathy interviews 60–2, 74–7, 246
end-of-year (EOY) MAP reading comprehension 55, 79–80
English achievement
    for NSI middle schools 67–8
    see also reading assessments/ comprehension
English Language Arts (ELA) 1, 2, 6–12, 16, 18, 151–2, 161–4
    District Course Assessment 6, 17, 55, 57, 63, 67–8, 78–80
    empathy interviews 60, 74–5
    and IDCs, capacity-building 48–9
    New Curriculum 6–7, 39–42, 48–9, 91, 96–7, 105–8
    PLCs and instructional inquiry 113
    Richard Wright Middle School case study 199–218
    theories of improvement 240
    see also State Assessment
equitable instruction 7–8, 30, 34–6
    see also Hub Teams
ethnicity see race, racial aspects

evidence-based feedback 158–9
exam preparation *see* test performances
Executive Directors 103–4
   see also leaders, leadership
exit tickets 13, 19–24
   see also task sheets
expertise
   leaning on 249–50
   see also leaders, leadership

Flipgrid 27
focused set of change ideas (theories of improvement) 239–40
Frankenstein (Shelley) 212–16, 243

gender 59–60, 98–9, 225–6
Grunow, Alicia 118
Guskey, Thomas R. 98

Harlem Renaissance 202
health survey measures 72–4
high-level instruction, access to 188–9
high-quality instructional materials (HQIM) 173–4, 193–4
Hub Leadership 63
Hub Teams 1, 7–8, 225–6
hybrid instruction 26–9, 57–8, 65, 102, 103

IFL (Institute for Learning)
   assessment, instructional change and its implementation 219–33
   communities of practice 91–112
   Hub Teams 7–8
   qualitative and quantitative outcomes 53–90
   Vision of Collaborative Work 13, 38–9, 235, 237–8, 245–6
   see also Big City School District
improvement science vii, xi, 9, 11, 19, 34, 54, 64, 93, 221–2
in-person instruction 5–6, 26–7, 30–3, 60, 65, 102
inquiry cycle 116, 141, 145–6, 151–3, 162
inquiry stance 195
inquiry-based improvements of teaching and learning 135–6
instructional district coaches (IDCs) 1, 48–50
   see also district coaches/leaders

instructional inquiry 113–40, 195
   see also inquiry cycle
Instructional Planning Calendar (IPC) 44, 46
instructional school coaches (ISCs) 1, 2
integration 240–2
   see also adaptation
internalization 41
Inventing Ourselves: The Secret Life of the Teenage Brain (Blakemore) 184–8

"Joyas Voladoras" (Doyle) 137
just-in-time implementation 40, 184, 250

K–12 schools 39, 116

leaders, leadership 200–1
   BCSD reorganization 43–6
   district teams 2, 3
   empathy interviews 74–7
   Hub Leadership 63
   for instructional change 141–67
   network health surveys, engagement and 63, 72
   PLCs and instructional inquiry 131–6
   see also network meetings
Learning Research and Development Center (LRDC) vii, x 269
The Learning Walk, learning walks 4–8, 15, 30, 56, 67–8, 109, 148, 158–62, 200–3, 242
levels of implementation 57–8, 65–6, 79–80
"Look Forward" initiatives 118–19

Management and Communications 7–8
   see also Hub Teams
Mann, Lara 124, 134–5
Martínez, R.A. 109
Measures of Academic Progress (MAP) 5–6, 29–30, 39, 224, 225
   BOY 55–6, 57, 58–9, 67–8, 84–5
   capacity-building 49
   data, delivery and use 36
   EOY 55, 79–80
   MOY 49, 55–6, 57, 58–9, 67–8, 79–80, 84–5
   qualitative and quantitative outcomes 54–60, 63–4, 67–77, 78, 84–90
   student growth relative to teachers 58–60, 68–77

student-centered practices, test performances 29–30
theories of improvement 240
see also beginning of the year; middle of year
middle of the year (MOY) MAP reading comprehension 49, 55–6, 57, 58–9, 67–8, 79–80, 84–5
Miles Middle School 169–98
    adaptation and change 172–4
    beginning with collaborative planning 182–3
    beginnings of instructional work/change 174–82
    case story 182–92
    instructional change in context 170–2
    mutual adaptation 194–6
    student-facing task sheets 192–4
monthly meetings 99–100
    see also network meetings
mutual adaptation 172–3
"My Ceremony for Taking" (Mann) 124, 134–5

National Council of Teachers of English (NCTE) 92
National Council of Teachers of Mathematics (NCTM) 92
Nearpod 24
Network Connections 63
network health surveys, engagement and 63, 72
network meetings 13, 18–19, 21–2, 31–2, 58, 242
    online teaching 26–7, 28–9
    principals and their efficiency 145–6
    see also communities of practice
Network Roles & Engagement 63
networked collaboration 243–4
networked improvement communities (NICs) 92–8, 104–5
New Curriculum (of the ELA) 6–7, 39–42, 48–9, 91, 96–7, 105–8
Northwest Evaluation Association 5
    see also Measures of Academic Progress
NPR broadcasts 109, 148–9
NSI (Network for School Improvement)
    communities of practice 94–100
    Equity-Focused Webinar Series 35

Hub Equity Team 35
see also IFL (Institute for Learning)

online instruction 60
    exit ticket reports 21, 22
    hybrid teaching and its effects 26–7
    in-school, mitigation of 30–3
    shifting to 13, 24–5
    see also hybrid instruction
on-track 8th and 9th grade indicators 63–4

Padlet 24, 27, 32
paper & pencil exit ticket summary reports 20, 21
Park, Sandra 118
passing rates 79–81
PDSA (Plan, Do, Study, Act) 11, 56–7, 115–17, 124–5, 243–4
Pear Deck 24, 27, 105
peer-to-peer interactions 6, 27, 32–3, 117
"The Pendulum" (Bradbury) 204–10
pilot programs 39–42, 105–8
    see also New Curriculum
planning tools 117–23
    see also task sheets
Pollack, Todd M. 181
"power standards" 17
principals 145–6, 200–1
    network meetings 107–9
    see also leaders, leadership
professional learning 97–8, 99–100
Professional Learning Community (PLCs) 4–5, 12, 16, 23–7, 56, 67–8, 107, 141, 149–52, 156–8, 162–6, 200–1
    deficit thinking 181–2
    exit tickets 19–20
    middle school New Curriculum pilot tests 41
    Planning Protocol 123–30
    and support for instructional inquiry 113–40
    case story 123–30
    characteristics of effective teacher leadership 131–6
    in context, Arlington High School 114–15
    as drivers of instructional inquiry 115–23

whole school cultures of
improvement 136–8
theories of improvement 236, 242, 247

qualitative and quantitative outcomes
53–90
key fifth-year outcomes 77–83
key first- and second-year outcomes
56–7
key fourth-year outcomes 62–6
key sixth-year outcomes 83–4
key takeaways and outcomes 86–90
key third-year outcomes 57–62
summary of gathered data, by year 54–6
year 6 interim evaluation, May 2024
84–6
qualities of effective network principals
145–6
Questioning the Author (QtA) 187–8

race, racial aspects 5, 59–63, 68–70, 98–9,
132, 200, 202–3, 225–6
Harlem Renaissance 202
Rae Ellen Bichell 109, 148–9
see also economically disadvantaged
students
Racine, Erica 169–98
Reaching New Heights (RNH) 67–8, 146,
245–6
readiness for change 164–5
reading assessments/comprehension
67–8, 240
see also Measures of Academic Progress
reasonable pacing 42
relationships-building 226–8
adaptation 174
see also collaborative work
Research 7–8
see also Hub Teams
Richard Wright Middle School 199–218
instructional change in context 200
principal leadership 200–1
students' discussions 204–10
root cause analysis 9–12
Rose-Wood High School (RWHS) 141–3
instruction, focus on 155–62
principals and their qualities 145–6
and readiness for change 164–5
school contexts 143

student outcomes 144–5
student-centered practices 162–4
support networks 146–55
Rose-Wood Independent School District
(RWISD) 143

scaffolds, scaffolding 120–2, 133, 142, 162,
169–72, 175, 178–95
school context see context, contextual
approaches
School and District Leadership Support 7–8
see also Hub Teams
"Scientists Start To Tease Out The Subtler
Ways Racism Hurts Health" 109,
148–9
self-adaptation 194
shared problem(s) of practice (theories of
improvement) 238–9
shared visions of teaching and learning
147–8
Vision of Collaborative Work 13, 38–9,
235, 237–8, 245–6
see also collaborative work
Shelley, Mary 212–16, 243
"shifts in focus" thinking 99–100, 155–62,
239–40, 248–9
silos 135, 244
"sit and get" models 98, 250
Soto, Gary 175–9
State Assessment (SA) 6, 54–7, 62–4,
68–81, 86–90, 200, 210–11
state scores 226–7
see also test performances
state urban schools 81–3
see also urban districts
Steering Committee 7–8
see also Hub Teams
structured support for implementation
and adaptive integration 240–2
student-centered practices xix, xxiv, xxviii,
26, 29–30, 101, 162–4, 199–218
see also qualitative and quantitative
outcomes
student-facing paper & pencil exit ticket
surveys 20
student-facing task sheets 192–4
students
MAP reading comprehension (growth)
67–8

Index 267

relative to teachers 58–60, 68–77
see also Emergent Multilingual (EML) students
Students with Special Needs (SwSN) 36–7, 59–63, 68–71, 98–9, 159–60, 225–6
support(s)
  "comprehension first" support 62
  Miles Middle School case study 169–98
  PLCs and instructional inquiry 113–40
  principals, teaching and learning 146–55
  for teachers' successes 46–8
  theories of improvement 240–2

task sheets xxviii, xxxi, 2–4, 119–23, 156–8, 174–82, 192–5, 201–2
  actions for change, prioritization 11–12
  communities of practice 101, 105, 109
  district teams 2, 3
  district-friendly approaches 13, 14
  empathy interviews 61–2, 74–5
  exit tickets 20, 21
  mitigating online in-school instruction 31
  qualitative and quantitative outcomes 56, 58, 66, 84
  student-centered practices 79
  student-facing 192–4
  theories of improvement 235, 239–40
teachers
  COPs 103, 104–5
  district teams 2, 3
  empathy interviews 60–2, 74–7
  hybrid online teaching 26–7
  levels of implementation 57–8, 65–6
  MAP reading comprehension (growth) relative to students 58–60, 68–77
  network health surveys, engagement and 63, 72
  networks, communities of practice 91–112
  turnover 30, 33–4
  see also Design Teams; *individual schools*, leaders, leadership
'technical core of schooling' 146
test performances 210–11, 226–7
preparation as instruction, adapting to 13–18
see also Measures of Academic Progress
tests of change (ToC) 159, 160
theories of improvement 235–52
  alignment and coherence 236–8
  focused set of change ideas 239–40
  implications for practice 244–5
  shared problem(s) of practice 238–9
  structured support for implementation and adaptive integration 240–2
translanguaging 170–1
  see also Emergent Multilingual students
Truth, Sojourner 35, 109

unifying focus 248–9
urban districts 39, 67–8, 81–3

virtual instruction problems 101–2
  see also online instruction
Vision of Collaborative Work 13, 38–9, 235, 237–8, 245–6
Vision for Instructional Change 164–5
visualization, key features 72

Waters, Shay 199–218
"We Wear the Mask" (Dunbar) 175–9, 202–3
Wenger, Etienne 92
"what do you think?", power of 138
whole school cultures of improvement 136–8
whole systems thinking 245–6
WWAM (What, Weird, Attitude, and Message) 178–9

Zora Neale Hurston Middle School (ZNHMS) 141–3
  instruction, focus on 155–62
  principals and their qualities 145–6
  and readiness for change 164–5
  school contexts 144
  student outcomes 144–5
  student-centered practices 162–4
  support networks 146–55

About the Authors

Sara DeMartino began her career in education as a high school English language arts teacher in Hillsborough County, Florida. She now works with both pre-service and in-service English language arts teachers as a fellow at the Institute for Learning (IFL). In her work at IFL, Sara provides collaborative content support for school-based PLCs and works collaboratively with educators in various school districts on research, curriculum development, and professional development. She has been a teaching fellow at the University of Pittsburgh's graduate School of Education where she taught graduate level methods courses and has worked with researchers from the Learning Research and Development Center (LRDC) to study secondary students' writing development and their use of peer review. Sara holds a bachelor's degree in English, a master's in English education, and a Ph.D. in language, literacy, and culture. Sara is the proud mother of two amazing children who have grown up alongside the NSI. In her spare time, Sara enjoys reading, running, and spoiling her dogs (who do not run).

Anthony Petrosky directs the Institute for Learning (IFL) at the Learning Research & Development Center (LRDC) at the University of Pittsburgh. He is a research scientist at LRDC and a professor in the School of Education. He has worked with professional learning and curriculum development in English and literacy for IFL with teachers and district leaders in the public schools across the country. He began his career as an 9th grade English teacher.

Along with David Bartholomae, Petrosky is the co-author and co-editor of five books: *Facts, Artifacts, and Counterfacts: Theory and Method for a Reading and Writing Course*; *The Teaching of Writing*; *Ways of Reading*; *Ways of Reading Words and Images*; and *History and Ethnography: Reading and Writing About Others*. With Stephanie McConachie, he co-authored and co-edited *Content Matters: A Disciplinary Literacy Approach to Improving Student Learning*.

Petrosky's first collection of poetry, *Jurgis Petraskas* received the Walt Whitman Award from the Academy of American Poets and a Notable Book Award from the American Library Association. He has published two other collections of poetry, *Red and Yellow Boat* and *Crazy Love*.

Glenn Nolly has worked in public education for over thirty-five years advocating for students who have been marginalized. He started his career teaching 7th and 8th grade English. After teaching for ten years he embarked on the journey of administration where he held the positions of assistant principal, high school principal, area superintendent, director of professional learning, and associate superintendent of high schools. A highlight of his career as a high school principal was building an Advanced Placement program with an enrollment that mirrored the population of his diverse student body. As associate superintendent of high schools, he built community among a group of fourteen principals, and oversaw the implementation of teacher-led Professional Learning Communities within each high school.

Currently, Nolly is an assistant professor of practice at the University of Texas at Austin and a fellow at the Institute for Learning located in the Learning, Research & Development Center at the University of Pittsburgh. Nolly is co-author of *Equity Audits: A Practical Leadership Tool for Developing Equitable and Excellent Schools*.